FOURTEEN BATTLE STARS

USS Hughes DD-410

The WWII Destroyer That Survived The Pacific, A Kamikaze Attack and Two Atomic Bombs

Christopher Hurst

Kilimanjaro Kutembea Publishing
Wind River Associates, Inc.
62504 Indian Summer Way E
Enumclaw, WA 98022 USA

Print Book ISBN: 9798322310778

Printed in the United States of America & Worldwide
on Kindle Direct Publishing

First Edition, April 30, 2024

This book is dedicated to the memory of the sailors of the Greatest Generation who fought in WWII on the USS Hughes DD-410 throughout the war in the Atlantic and Pacific to free the world from radical nationalism. It is also dedicated to their family members, who still carry the burden of those sacrifices. Many thanks to those family members who supplied documents, pictures, journals, letters, and personal stories to help this book come to life.

On April 2, 2024, Walter Resh passed away at 103. He was the second-to-last living member of the USS Hughes crew in WWII. As of the publication date of this book, Oliver Jones, who lives in Arizona, is now the sole living member of her crew.

Oliver - Thanks so much for your help on this story. I hope you enjoy the book!

USS HUGHES DD-410 WAR RECORD

14 Battle Stars

- February 1, 1942 - Pacific Raids – Marshall & Gilbert Islands
- June 3 – 6, 1942 - Midway Island Battle
- September 8 – 9, 1942 – Capture and Defense of Guadalcanal
- October 5, 1942 – Buin, Faisi & Tonolai Raids
- October 26, 1942 – Santa Cruz Islands
- November 12 – 15, 1942 – Guadalcanal – Third Savo
- January 29 – 30, 1943 – Rennel Island
- May 11 – June 2, 1943 – Aleutian Operations – Attu Occupation
- November 20 – December 7, 1943 – Gilbert Islands Operation
- January 31 – February 24, 1943 – Marshall Islands – Kwajalein & Eniwetok
- March 30 – April 1, 1944 – Palau, Yap, Ulithi, Woleai Raids
- April 21 – September 15, 1944 – Western New Guinea Raids
- October 17 – November 18, 1944 – Leyte Gulf & Ormoc Bay Landings
- June 25 – August 11, 1945 – Kurile Islands & Occupation of Japan

Additional Battle Awards

- Philippines Liberation Ribbon with Two Stars
- American Area Ribbon

- Atlantic Ribbon with "A"
- Navy Occupation Service Medal, Asia, for September 2 – October 30, 1945

Other Awards

- Forty Purple Hearts were awarded to members of the USS Hughes.
- Three Silver Stars were awarded posthumously for outstanding performance on December 10, 1944, at Leyte Gulf battle and the attack by a Japanese Kamikaze aircraft:
  - Lieutenant Frank McClelland
  - Seaman Harold Schmidt
  - Seaman James Smith

Members of the USS Hughes won one Navy Cross, Five Silver Stars, Five Bronze Stars, Five Commendation Ribbon Bars, and numerous commendations.

ARTWORK AND PHOTO CREDITS

The remarkable cover painting of the USS Hughes on December 10, 1944, is by Ed Karasek, who served in the U.S. Army Air Force in WWII. It is used with the gracious permission of his son, Gary Karasek, and his daughter, Carolyn Karasek-Needles, both artists carrying on the family tradition.

The back cover photo credits are listed below for images 10B, 12, 81, and 88.

Photo credits by image number:

Images 8A, 8B, 9, 10A, 10B, 11A, 11B, 24, 29, 40, and 64.
These photographs are in the public domain in Japan because their copyrights have expired according to Article 23 of the 1899 Copyright Act of Japan and Article 2 of Supplemental Provisions of the Copyright Act of 1970. They were published before January 1, 1957, and photographed before January 1, 1947. They are also in the public domain in the United States because the copyrights expired in Japan by 1970 and were not restored by the Uruguay Round Agreements Act.

Images 1, 2A, 2B, 7, 12, 14, 15, 19, 22, 25, 27, 28, 31, 33A, 33B, 34, 35, 36, 37, 42, 43, 44, 46, 53, 55, 56, 57, 60, 62, 65, 67, 68, 72, 73, 75, 76, 77, 78, 79, 80, 81, 85, 87, 88, 89, and 90.
These images are the work of a sailor, soldier, Signal Corps, U.S. Naval Intelligence Service, Army, Atomic Energy Commission, or an employee of the U.S. Navy or U.S. Government, taken or made as part of that person's official duties. As a work of the U.S. federal government, they are in the public domain in the United States.

Images 4, 5, 47, and 74.
These images are licensed under the Creative Commons Attribution-Share Alike 3.0 Germany (Bundesarchiv) provisions and have not been altered in any way except for cropping to fit the format of this book. No changes were made that would alter the initial depictions.

Images 13, 26,
Files licensed under the Creative Commons Attribution-Share Alike 4.0 International license. No changes were made to the files.
Location: https://creativecommons.org/licenses/by-sa/4.0/deed.en

Image 3.
The United Kingdom Government created this work, and it is in the public domain because it was taken prior to June 1, 1957, and it was published prior to 1974. HMSO has declared that the expiry of Crown Copyrights applies worldwide: https://www.nationalarchives.gov.uk/information-management/re-using-public-sector-information/uk-government-licensing-framework/crown-copyright/

Image 30.
The license was purchased through Alamy.

All other image use and printing rights were obtained from the family members of those who took the photos before, during, and after WWII.

A note on footnotes and endnotes:

Ninety-five percent of this book is told through the stories of the sailors who served on the USS Hughes throughout WWII in the Atlantic and Pacific. Adding 100 pages of footnotes or endnotes would be a waste of paper and a significant and unnecessary extra cost to the book. Their words and stories are what they saw and experienced at the time. Some differ from each other. That is the "fog of war." This is not a technical or forensic examination of WWII. It is the story of a ship and the men who sailed on her in battle. The general references and quotes from notable or elected officials are well documented and have been published and republished thousands of times. They are easily searchable if someone wants to look them up online. Some statistics are in question as numerous things, like casualties from a specific battle, have been reported in different numbers in various sources, and the U.S. routinely underreported deaths and injuries during the war. Every attempt has been made to use generally accepted numbers, but some, like the death toll from atomic bombs in Japan, will never be known for sure. Whenever possible, the stories were checked against the official USS Hughes Deck Logs obtained from the U.S. Navy in the National Archives, and some notations and corrections have been made to the stories based on information contained in those documents. This book accurately shows the ship and her crew's experiences as they saw the events unfold in the war against Germany and the Empire of Japan.

CONTENTS

INTRODUCTION

Bath Iron Works Christening Day preparations,
17 June 1939. Chester Bradley collection. U.S. Navy photo.

The history of the destroyer USS *Hughes* at war is deeply inter-twined with the strategy of the kamikaze attacks by Japan, intended to extend WWII to a more favorable conclusion, and the fallout from the discovery of the atomic bomb and its use during and after the war. The USS *Hughes* defined the period, participating in almost every sea battle between the Empire of Japan and the United States. She earned an astonishing 14 battle stars along the way and played an integral part in developing American policy for the use of atomic weapons after 1945. This haunting episode and the impact on her sailors and the world remain untold until now.

The story of the USS *Hughes* in battle begins long before America entered WWII in Europe and the Pacific. The USS *Hughes* became an instrument of American policy in combat in the North Atlantic before any other American destroyer. After the war ended, the USS *Hughes* was sent on another secret mission, shuttling Japanese officials back and forth for the confidential negotiations finalizing the surrender and occupation documents. No other American ship served longer in combat than the USS *Hughes*.

As the war dragged on, it became apparent that Japan could not defeat America, a belief many Japanese naval officers suspected even before the attack on Pearl Harbor. One of those Japanese officers was Admiral Takijiro Onishi, a pilot and flight instructor earlier in his career. He would become the architect of a new way to keep America from defeating Japan and forcing an unconditional surrender. The goal was to prolong the war to the extent that Americans could no longer accept the loss of lives of their countrymen and would sue for peace with terms favorable to Japan. This shocking tactic, one he called immoral earlier in his career, began in earnest on October 25, 1944, and continued during 274 days of terror for American sailors. It was the "Divine Wind" or kamikaze attacks on American warships.

The ambitions of the nationalist government of Japan intersected with the destiny of the USS *Hughes* in the kamikaze attacks near Leyte Gulf in the Philippine Islands in December 1944. After six weeks of attacks and seeing other destroyers sunk near her, the USS *Hughes* would be hit and almost sunk by a kamikaze airplane. A young volunteer Japanese pilot maneuvered his plane at the ship and penetrated her deck, with the aircraft and bomb exploding deep in her engine and fire control rooms on a warm, sunny afternoon. The deep blue waters of Leyte Gulf ran red with the sailors' blood and became covered with oil from the ship and plane.

The USS *Hughes* had been fighting in the Pacific since December 7, 1941, to clear the Japanese from the islands in the Pacific. This was being done so large, land-based American bombers could attack and bomb Japanese cities into submission. A secret almost no one knew at the time was that this was also being done so America could drop atomic bombs on Japanese cities. Among the islands they helped clear was Tinian. From there, the B-29 *Enola Gay* would take off on August 6, 1945, to drop America's second atomic bomb on Hiroshima. Nagasaki was bombed with America's third nuclear bomb on August 9, 1945. The two bombings killed roughly 200,000 people in an instant and possibly hundreds of thousands more in the following years. This remains the only use of atomic weapons against an enemy in combat, but it was nowhere near the end of American use of nuclear bombs, as the sailors of the USS *Hughes* would find out in 1946.

Who were the leaders who brought Japan, America, the USS *Hughes*, and the rest of the world to this intersection where humans willingly volunteered to sacrifice themselves by crashing airplanes into ships for their country and created weapons so powerful that they could destroy all human life on Earth? What did a young pilot in Japan and a young man growing up on a ranch in Montana have in common in the 1930s? How would they someday meet at sea off the Philippines, one from the air and one aboard a Navy ship? How would a professor of physics at Berkeley, California, create a deliverable atomic bomb to defeat the flight instructor from Japan who went on to create the kamikaze fighting force? How did ordinary American sailors pave the way for these contests?

Near the war's end, America placed its hopes and fears to quickly end the war on the efforts of a small group of scientists led by physicist

Robert Oppenheimer at Los Alamos, New Mexico. This was the race between Oppenheimer and Admiral Takijiro Onishi of the Japanese Empire. The story of the USS *Hughes* is intricately interwoven into this tale, and her sailors saw it all firsthand.

This is also the tale of two samurai swords, one used to take the life of the leader of the kamikaze forces, which now rests in a museum in Japan, and one given to a lieutenant from the USS *Hughes*, a painful reminder of the war. The latter one now rests inside the wall of a house somewhere in Seattle after being placed there many years ago, all but lost to time and memory.

This book is about the recollections of the sailors who served on the USS *Hughes*, not an exhaustive or forensic document of the war. Stories were checked against official records wherever possible, and many corrections were made, but the accounts from various sailors sometimes differed on a single event. That is the nature of the "fog" of war. This book is a window into the thoughts, experiences, and opinions of the sailors on the USS *Hughes* during WWII. Some minor dates or facts might be slightly out of order or incorrect. It is now 78 years since WWII ended. Their stories are true, but as with all accounts, memories are subject to the human frailty that comes over time or to the trauma from when the events occurred.

The bones of the USS *Hughes* do not rest peacefully at the bottom of the Pacific Ocean off the coast of California. The stories of her sailors, some who retired to civilian life after the war, some lost in combat at sea, and others who died slowly of radiation poisoning, remain with her to this day. Their stories are unfinished.

People often do not understand their place in history when significant events unfold around them. Many never think that what they experienced will be remembered. Fortunately, in the case of the USS *Hughes*, several of her sailors kept remarkable records of their time at war as it unfolded in the Pacific. Seamen Tony Skic and Ollie Stine kept remarkably detailed diaries while on the USS

Hughes. Personal record keeping on a ship at war was unlawful at the time due to the fear of such documents falling into enemy hands if the ship were sunk, but a few sailors created them nonetheless. Sailors from the USS *Hughes* brought them home from the war, and their daughters eventually typed up these handwritten documents and provided these remarkable stories for use in this book. They will help to tell the story of the USS *Hughes*. Other sailors created papers about their time on the USS *Hughes* shortly after the war, and their families have also submitted these records for this book. Other documents from seamen on the USS *Hughes* did not survive.

Worth Ishmuel Capps joined the USS *Hughes* on March 21, 1943, as the chief pharmacist mate. Famous among the crew for his medical care, including the administration of dreaded vaccines, he treated many wounded and dying shipmates, along with more routine ailments like personal infections contracted while on shore leave in friendly ports. He also completed an astonishing six volumes of notebooks while on the ship. These documents did not survive. His daughter, Jane Capps Craddock, explained, "Here is an excerpt from a letter my father wrote to my sister and me during the summer of 1959. We received it when we were vacationing with relatives. The six notebooks he completed during the war on the USS *Hughes* were written to our mother. She destroyed the notebooks after she read them at my father's request. This was the only time my father mentioned his experiences serving on the USS *Hughes*, DD-410, in this letter to us."

The letter from Worth Ishmuel Capps to his young daughters reads:

> During the war, I filled about six notebook diaries just talking
> to her [his wife] in writing. I wrote about all my loneliness, fear,
> and terror in the war and everything that came into my mind.
> I brought them home to her and spent the next three years

begging her to destroy them before you got old enough to read. I guess I didn't want anyone else in the world to read all about my naked emotions and my fears during that terrible time. It did help me an awful lot to sit down and write some of the tension out of my system. I used to get so afraid that my stomach would draw up into a knot of pain, and I would break out in a stinking sweat that would almost make me heave. I would stand by the rail of the ship and pray over and over the same prayers. It sure helped me write all those things in my diary. Maybe I shouldn't have brought them home, though. According to custom, it is bad if a man lets his woman know his fears and weaknesses. Well, everyone has them. I don't see any reason to be ashamed if one faces the facts.

Although Worth Ishmuel Capps never talked about the war after his return, except on this one occasion, he moved on with his life and had a remarkable career as a research technician in medical virological research. He worked at the National Institute of Allergy and Infectious Diseases and the National Institutes for Health, Bethesda, Maryland. He co-authored 13 scientific publications on studies about the role of viruses in cancer. Known to his shipmates as "Hank," he came from a tobacco farm in Guilford County, North Carolina, the oldest of six siblings. Like others from the heartland, he joined the Navy to serve his country and was in the Atlantic on convoy protection duty until the Japanese bombed Pearl Harbor. His record of the war is now long gone. With the burning of his notebooks, he took these stories with him to his grave. But his pain and terror from his time on the USS *Hughes* survive with this single letter to his young daughters in 1959. His daughters believe he was proud of his time on the USS *Hughes*. They kept a letter of commendation from the United States Navy that reads in part, "To CAPPS, Worth

I., CPhM, USN. I take pleasure in forwarding a commendation and ribbon bar awarded to you by the Commander Seventh Fleet for distinguishing yourself by excellent service when a bomb struck the USS HUGHES on 10 December 1944.—R. J. HARDY, Commander, USN." The letter to his daughters is the sole contribution by Worth Ishmuel Capps to this story, but it is a part of the collective soul of the USS *Hughes* that remains.

Many of the storied ships of significant battles in WWII lie at the bottom of the sea, but many more were scrapped when the war was over. Some were used as target practice to get rid of them. No one wanted to remember much about the battles of WWII after the war ended. The "Greatest Generation" members were expected to remain silent about their participation in the war and begin their lives anew as if nothing had ever happened. There was too much darkness for Americans, and the country wanted to move along to brighter days and thoughts. Soldiers, sailors, and airmen were expected to keep their experiences to themselves and move on. Nevertheless, the wounds that many of them carried were deep and painful.

We now see the error in this thinking. Preserving those stories was necessary. Talking about them and bringing them to light was also part of a healing process for those who lived them. In many cases, the lives of the survivors were severely impacted by being unable to talk to others. We know that now. These lessons are also necessary to avoid repeating the mistakes of the past. Defeating nationalism in WWII was not enough. Fascism is a rising threat today, partly because the populace wanted to move on and ignore it, thinking it could never happen again. Only in telling and re-telling these stories can the lessons of WWII and radical nationalism keep us from repeating past errors.

The USS *Hughes* was a ship in remarkable times. Her sailors did not, at the time, fully understand their place in history as it unfolded.

"THE HAND THAT HELD THE DAGGER HAS STRUCK IT INTO THE BACK OF ITS NEIGHBOR"

USS Hughes - Official U.S. Navy Photo August 1, 1942, #4353-42.

On September 15, 1937, the keel was laid for the USS *Hughes* at the Bath Iron Works on the Kennebec River in Maine. A *Sims*-class destroyer, she would be launched on June 17, 1939, and was fully commissioned for combat operations on September 21, 1939.

She was 348 feet long and just over 36 feet wide. With high-pressure super-heated boilers, geared turbines, and twin screws with 50,000 horsepower, she could initially reach over 35 knots and cruise

3,660 nautical miles at 20 knots. She would have 192 crewmembers, fully staffed for combat, including ten officers and 182 enlisted men. Her main armaments included five five-inch guns in single mounts, four .50 caliber machine guns, eight 21-inch torpedo tubes, and two depth charge racks.

Not all American-built destroyers were the same. There were many design changes over the years, each trying to improve on the last. Even though the U.S. was not at war with Japan in 1937, its *Sims*-class destroyer model was specifically engineered for use against Japanese ships. American designers were already aware of the risk of long-range torpedoes that Japan was developing, which could travel 40,000 yards without being detected. This placed large American warships at risk in a war against Japan. The *Sims*-class destroyers were designed to counter this threat with enhanced submarine detection and more depth-charge countermeasures.

Some *Sims*-class destroyers also had the new Mark 37 computer to control the weapons systems. This was a primitive but highly effective early computer for determining where to fire their weapons at other ships and submarines.

For a war against Japan, the U.S. Navy General Board set new requirements for the new *Sims*-class destroyers: "Special emphasis is to be placed upon ruggedness and dependability." These modifications would become critical in a war against Japan. The board demanded high speed and quick acceleration from the ships. These requirements became crucial in evading kamikaze attacks, something no one in the world had envisioned.

The early fate of the USS *Hughes* intersected with the opening days of WWII when Germany was attacking Europe. England was desperate for America to come to her aid. The Germans had been sinking British ships since 1939 to isolate the island nation from supplies arriving from the United States.

German U-boats would not sink the first American destroyer until October 31, 1941, when the USS *Ruben James* (DD 245) went down, losing 115 Americans. This was only weeks away from the Japanese attack on Pearl Harbor. The *Ruben James* was doing escort duty from America to England, pioneered by the USS *Hughes*, long before America entered the war. But how could an American warship escort a British convoy into a battle zone before America formally entered the war? The answer comes from the relationship and ongoing diplomacy between President Franklin D. Roosevelt and English Prime Minister Winston Churchill in the late 1930s.

Americans suffered greatly during WWI and were not interested in entering foreign entanglements again anytime soon. Isolationist feelings were spreading across America. WWI was heralded as the "war to end all wars," and America took that at face value. Yet the end of WWI left Germany reeling under reparations debt it could never repay to the world for the damages it had inflicted. Germans were left to cobble their old country together without addressing the foundational illness of unchallenged nationalism. Humiliated, defeated, and starving, ordinary Germans looked for a leader, any leader, who could define a future worth living for.

Hitler told the German people they were not at fault for their difficulties. He told them ethnic and religious minorities and foreigners were to blame. He said he could make Germany great again. He promised to build an empire that would last a thousand years. The lies and simple-minded slogans of Hitler and the Nazi party offered no real solutions or answers to complex social or political questions, but they felt good to those hearing them. The promise of a return to glory made sense to the suffering German masses.

Winston Churchill watched and listened closely while English Prime Minister Chamberlin attempted to appease Hitler by giving him the Sudetenland, territory he had no right to offer, in exchange

Prime Minister Winston Churchill and President Roosevelt seated in the garden of the villa in Casablanca, Morocco. Public domain photo UK.

for English safety. Chamberlin called it "Peace with honor. Peace for our time." But there was no peace, and there would never be peace while Hitler and the Nazi leadership were left alive in Germany. Many were willing to give up much, if not all, of the rest of Europe to Hitler for the sake of peace. Churchill was unalterably opposed to any negotiations or talk of peace with Hitler. He stood firmly opposed to any deal with Nazi Germany. Churchill soon became prime minister and led England in a different direction.

As an island nation, England was particularly susceptible to any blockade of materials or food they could not acquire or grow independently. Hitler knew this and sent U-boats to stop the flow of materials and supplies from America and other countries. The incremental strangling of England was meant to soften it up for an invasion once Hitler's demands of surrender to Germany and the Nazi goal of world domination did not work politically. Hitler offered England a Nazi-style "peace," but Churchill rejected that offer.

Hitler was right that England was in a hopeless situation. It could not long survive on its own. If France and much of Europe fell, England's salvation would entirely depend on America. Churchill privately pressed America to enter this war against Hitler.

American President Roosevelt was facing issues of his own. On June 10, 1940, Roosevelt gave a speech on a rainy day in Charlottesville at the University of Virginia Law School. In this speech, he tested public opinion and their will to see how far he could push Americans. "On this 10th day of June 1940, the hand that held the dagger has struck it into the back of its neighbor." He went on to suggest a new line of thinking for Americans: "In our American unity, we will pursue two obvious and simultaneous courses: we will extend to the opponents of force the material resources of this nation; and, at the same time, we will harness and speed up the use of those resources so that we in the Americas may have equipment and training equal to the task of any emergency and every defense."

This sounded like a commitment to provide significant resources right away. Churchill, who listened to the speech with keen interest, immediately told Roosevelt, "We all listened to you last night and were fortified by the grand scope of your declaration." He added, "I send you my heartfelt thanks and those of my colleagues for all you are doing and seeking to do for what we may now call the Common Cause." But his optimism for imminent support of England was still a distant dream in America.

In late June, Roosevelt received a recommendation from the War and Navy Departments that suggested an opposite course. General George C. Marshall wrote to Roosevelt, "Further release of war material now in the hands of our armed forces will seriously weaken our present defense." The report stated, "One could argue that we would increase our defensive strength by giving more aid to Britain and Canada. That might be true, but it is not provable, and if Britain were defeated, the Army and Administration could never justify to the American people the risk they had taken." American public opinion wasn't much better. America was not on Roosevelt's side at that time.

Things were falling apart for Churchill. France was about to collapse to Nazi Germany, and England faced a horrible defeat at Dunkirk. Churchill desperately needed weapons to fight against the U-boats that were sinking critical supply ships. Roosevelt knew that America would face war with Germany and probably Japan soon. However, the American public still needed to be in his corner, and the armed forces were struggling to build a force that could defend America's shores, let alone fight anywhere else in the world. The December 7, 1941, attack by Japan that would thrust America into war against Japan and Germany was still a year and a half away. Roosevelt and Churchill had talked about sending a fleet of older destroyers to England to shore up their defenses until America entered the war, but this was a complex political question.

At this same time, long before America entered the war, the USS *Hughes* sailed into the U-boat-infested waters of the North Atlantic to escort British convoys to England.

"BUT WHO IN HIS SENSES WOULD TRUST THE WORD OF HITLER?"

Hitler & Albert Speer- Bundesarchiv Bild 183-V00555-3
Obersalzberg German Archives.

After her completion in 1939, the USS *Hughes* set sail for the Gulf of Mexico for a shakedown cruise. Early summer, before the hurricane season, was a pleasant and warm time in the sunny and calm waters of the Gulf of Mexico. Pelicans drifted in the gentle breezes across the face of the sea as the sun sank low in the western sky, and the colors seemed to warm the souls of the crewmen. The sailors enjoyed these tranquil waters during the hectic training and vessel-testing period. The winds were often calm. The news of German submarines sinking ships headed to England had intensified, but this was of little consequence to the sailors of the USS *Hughes*, for whom the storm clouds of war in the North Atlantic seemed a world away.

On June 1, 1940, the USS *Hughes* reported to Newport, Rhode Island, where she participated in torpedo test runs. The sailors knew that the warm Caribbean water's calm days were probably ending.

On May 10, 1940, France surrendered to Germany. An armistice between Germany and France was put into effect on June 25. Terms stated that the French fleet would be under German control. The leading portion of the French naval forces were in French North Africa. The German government had "solemnly declared" that it had no intention of using the French vessels, but Churchill knew that Hitler and the Nazis could not be trusted. "But who in his senses would trust the word of Hitler after his shameful record and the facts of the hour?" said Churchill. "There was, in fact, no security for us at all," he said. "At all costs, at all risks, in one way or another, we must make sure that the Navy of France did not fall into the wrong hands and then perhaps bring us and others to ruin."

Churchill, once a naval cabinet minister, made one of the most painful decisions of his life. He ordered the execution of Operation Catapult. Over two hundred French vessels were seized by the British. On July 3, 1940, Force H was sent by Churchill to Mers el Kebir, where portions of the French fleet were at anchor. British Admiral Somerville attempted negotiations with French Admiral Marcel Gensoul, commander of the French squadron. These French sailors would not meet with Somerville's emissary, so the British tried to communicate the terms of their surrender in writing.

The French Naval forces were to "(1) put to sea and join forces with the Royal Navy; (2) to sail with reduced crews to British ports, where the vessels would be impounded and their complements repatriated; (3) to sail with reduced crews to the base at Dakar, where the ships would be immobilized; or (4) to scuttle his ships within six hours."

The British admiral was ordered to sink the French fleet if they failed to meet these demands.

The French fleet began preparations to leave the harbor, and the British opened fire, something they called "a highly disagreeable task." After a 10-minute bombardment, British Force H damaged many of Gensoul's ships, and many sailors died or were injured. A cease-fire was announced to allow the French sailors to abandon their remaining ships. About 1,250 French seamen were dead. In the ensuing days, the main battle fleet of the French was either in British hands or lying on the bottom of the ocean.

In October of 1940, the USS *Hughes* was based at Santa Lucia in the Caribbean to watch over the remnants of the French fleet, and in December of 1940, the USS *Hughes* returned to Philadelphia for a brief rest.

In January of 1941, the USS *Hughes* went to Norfolk, Virginia, to re-fit for combat patrol. With a top speed of nearly 40 knots, she was now one of the fastest U.S. Navy destroyers ever built. She participated in what was called the Neutrality Patrols under the command of Admiral R. C. Griffin. These extended almost halfway across the Atlantic. But then a very different order came down to the USS

Hughes. She was sent to Hvalfjord, Iceland, in the summer of 1941, many months before America officially entered WWII.

On August 31, 1941, a British convoy came under heavy attack by German submarines, and the USS *Hughes* was nearby. The USS *Hughes* was ordered to aid the stricken convoy and attack the German wolf-pack submarines. No German U-boats were officially listed as sunk by the USS *Hughes,* but after joining the battle to save the convoy, she screened ahead until the ships reached England.

The USS *Hughes* was the first American ship to escort a British convoy to English ports. It was done at enormous risk to the vessel and crew of a country not at war with Germany. The Germans would not have known the ship's identity during this encounter. Germany sank over three thousand merchant and naval vessels in the waters of the North Atlantic. The USS *Hughes* could have easily been the first American ship to sink. Looking back, no one can say if the USS *Hughes* being sunk would have brought America into the war months before Pearl Harbor, but it could have. The sinking of an armed U.S. Navy destroyer off the waters of Iceland could have provided just such a reason.

Shortly after the August 31, 1941, incident, a report came into Hvalfjord that the German pocket battleship *Bismarck* was nearby. The USS *Hughes* was sent out to intercept her. In June of 1941, Commander Alan Evans of the U.S. Navy recalled, "The report came into Hvalfjord that the German pocket-battleship *Bismarck* was on the loose. The threat to convoys, if she should raid them, was severe, and the USS *Hughes* was sent out to intercept her. Although the search carried across the Arctic Circle and up the Straights of Denmark, no sign of the raider could be found. It was not until some months later that she broke loose and was sunk."

Pressure from the USS *Hughes* kept *Bismarck* pinned in the northern water for most of her short eight months of existence, and she never joined the battle against British convoys. In direct combat,

Pocket Battleship Bismarck- Bundesarchiv Bild 193-04-1-26,
Schlachtschiff German Archives.

it is unlikely that the USS *Hughes* would have survived, again, possibly thrusting America into war with Germany.

On August 22, 1941, the USS *Hughes* was steaming through the icy North Atlantic waters when she was accidentally rammed by the British ship SS *Chulmleigh*. At 5:12 PM, the deck log notes, "Sounded General Alarm. We passed the word to clear living compartments aft. Collision starboard, frame 160. S.S. *Chulmleigh* rammed *Hughes* at frame 163. Outboard strake sheared from the main deck to the water line. Fuel oil tank C-11-F punctured, causing oil leak into the damaged compartments."

Five hours later, the hole in the ship was repaired. A board of investigation was initiated at one o'clock in the morning. A general court-martial was then convened, and Seaman Joseph Mersereau was found guilty of neglect of duty. He was sentenced to perform ten days of extra police duty and fined $18.00 monthly for four months. Even though $72.00 was a relatively large sum for a sailor back then, the process and sentence were mostly symbolic. There would be accountability for errors when the ship was at sea in combat conditions.

In November, the USS *Hughes* returned to the Boston Navy Yard. She was painted in zebra combat colors, and on December 7, 1941, the day of the Japanese attack on Pearl Harbor, she was docked in Portland, Maine.

The United States was now at war, and America was finally on Roosevelt's side. On December 11, in a rambling, unsteady, and troubled speech, Hitler officially declared war against America.

CHAPTER THREE

"WHAT IN THE HELL IS THE MATTER WITH YOU?"

Oliver Jones from Montana in 1943 and 2023 at his home in Arizona.
Markey Dubose photo.

Oliver Jones grew up in Montana's cattle ranching land. As soon as he was old enough, his parents got him a pony, and even then, it had to lie down so he could get on it. As he grew up, he fell in love with the Montana of his youth. The vast rolling hills and mountains stretched as far as he could see. In the fall, the family rode throughout the mountains, gathered the cattle, and brought them back to the ranch for the harsh, cold winters.

Nothing in Jones's youth could have ever prepared him to fight on a ship in the South Pacific in WWII. Jones said, "After we got all the Japs out of Hollandia, New Guinea, we were stationed there. New Guinea was nothing like the mountains of Montana." Montana was as far as you could get from the Pacific Ocean. One of his lasting memories that he still recalls from his home in Mesa, Arizona, at 97 years old, is just how big the Pacific Ocean seemed to him.

> I was originally from rural Montana. We had a ranch in Fergus County when I was young. I went to school in Montana, in Billings and Grass Range. I quit high school when I was 16 and joined the Navy. This was after Pearl Harbor. It was 1942 when I signed up, and in 1943, I went in.
>
> I'd tried to join the Army. My brother was three years older, and he was in the Army. I wanted to go with him and tried signing up, but no one wanted me. Finally, the Navy said they would take me the next month, that was November. I was 16 when they agreed to take me, but I had to wait until the day I turned 17.

When asked how his parents felt about him joining the Navy, he said:

> Oh, I talked them into signing it. I said, please, please, please, I want to serve like Robert. That was my brother. They didn't say too much. They disagreed that I should go but told me they

would sign. My brother was fighting in Europe at the time. It was a long time before he got loose and got to come home, but we both made it back to Montana one day after the war was over.

They sent me to Farragut, Idaho, for training. It was in the fall of the year. I was in training for six months. The training was pretty tough. We had to climb hand over hand up a very long rope from the floor to a very high ceiling. Fortunately, I was in pretty good shape from horse and rodeo riding, and I was a boxer. I was pretty tough coming from the ranch in Montana.

There were five of us from my part of Montana who tried to get into the Navy, but I was the only one who made it to a ship. The others didn't pass the tests after joining. We were good buddies, and I was surprised the others didn't make it. They got kicked out and went home from training.

Then came Jones's assignment to a ship, but it wasn't the USS *Hughes*. His first ship, the USS *Hoel,* was also a Navy destroyer.

I had just learned what type of ship I would be on after my graduation. I was sent to California, where they picked out the USS *Hoel* as my ship. I felt something was wrong when I walked aboard. On a shake-down cruise, we went up to Washington. As soon as we got underway, I put in for a transfer. We got up to Washington, and I put in for another transfer. We started back, and I put in for another transfer. Just as we returned to Cali-fornia, the Executive Officer called me into his office and said, "What in the hell is the matter with you? I've got four transfers that you want off the ship." I said, "Well, sir, I felt something was wrong when I came aboard the ship. Something I didn't like. That drove me to put in for the transfers." He said, "I'll tell you what. You're God damn sure on your way out because I just transferred you." I was on that ship for about 12 days. I could feel danger. There was something wrong with that ship. I'll finish my story and tell you why I did that. When we got to battle in the Philippines, the USS *Hughes* and the USS *Hoel* were both in battle over there, and I was on the USS *Hughes*. The USS *Hoel* steamed right into the bay, and there was a Japanese battleship and a cruiser, and they started firing. The USS *Hoel* was hit and sunk, and most of the crew went down with her. I said, "Thank you, Lord, thank you." It was then that I realized why I wanted off that ship. Both a Japanese battleship and a cruiser knocked her down. She got sunk. I didn't work on the USS *Hoel* all that long, so I didn't get to know those guys well, but I feel bad for them. I lived to tell that story, and I've lived it ever since.

When they transferred me off the USS *Hoel* in California, I wasn't there very long, and the USS *Hughes* was moored there. We left for the South Pacific when I boarded the USS *Hughes*.

When Jones told the commanders of the USS *Hoel* his fears, it concerned them, and for good reason, as this was bold talk for a newly minted seaman from Montana. Two things were clear to them. The first was that Jones was entirely convinced of this belief that the ship was doomed. The second was that Seaman Jones would likely repeat this fear, time and again, to other sailors on board the USS *Hoel*. The captain faced not only a new sailor who was possibly crazy but also the prospect of Jones spreading this fear to other crew members while they were at sea and sailing toward combat with the Japanese.

Superstitions among sailors go far back in history. These beliefs are not necessarily unfounded. Some come from legends, myths, folklore, and traditional stories, but some are from the vast, unknown ocean. When ships and sailors are lost at sea, often nothing remains to explain their fate, and a person's mind can wander. Historically, the risks of sailing or crossing the world's oceans, along with the concept of good and bad luck, can be overwhelming. Omens fill the void

USS Hoel (DD-533) underway in San Francisco Bay,
California, August 1943. U.S. Navy photo.

in people's minds when they do not have concrete facts to explain events. Having a person on board at these times, claiming that all hands are sailing on a doomed ship, is the last thing any captain wants on board a long or difficult voyage.

Some crew members' activities, beliefs, and behaviors on a ship can be addressed with discipline or even just time at sea. But this was not one of those occasions for the captain of the USS *Hoel*. He just wanted Seaman Oliver Jones to get the hell off his ship. So, Jones left the USS *Hoel* on October 31, 1943, and stepped onto the USS *Hughes*, where he would spend the rest of his naval combat career. Both ships would head to the Pacific and fight in major battles against the Empire of Japan. The USS *Hoel* would never return. A kamikaze aircraft attack would almost sink the USS *Hughes*, but she would survive and return to combat. Seaman Oliver Jones was right about the fate of the USS *Hoel*.

Both destroyers were assigned to protect the fleet responsible for landing the invasion force to re-take portions of the Philippines in 1944. The USS *Hoel* took a position between the U.S. escort carrier group Task Group 77.4 and the Imperial Japanese fleet sailing from the North to attack it. The Japanese planned to kill the American soldiers on their transport ships before they could land. Without adequate cover from aircraft and naval vessels, the Americans were an easy target for the Japanese. The USS *Hoel* was attached to Taffy 3, the northern carrier group guarding part of the invasion force near Leyte Gulf.

On October 25, 1944, the USS *Hoel* steamed northeast of Samar Island, off the Philippines. Everyone thought Admiral Halsey's Third Fleet was covering the Japanese fleet to the north. But Halsey had sailed his ships far from these waters, chasing reports of Japanese aircraft carriers further out in the Pacific. False information, designed by the Japanese, lured Halsey's Third Fleet away from the Japanese striking force. The USS *Hoel* and two other American destroyers were attacked by four Japanese battleships, six heavy cruisers, two light cruisers, and 11 destroyers. They were hopelessly outmatched, and retreat seemed the only logical option for the three small American destroyers. They could hope that additional help would come from the south, but they faced certain destruction without it.

A small number of aircraft flew north to assist the three American destroyers. Still, it would be nowhere near enough to stop the steaming Japanese fleet intent on killing American soldiers on the transport ships. This carnage was unthinkable to the U.S. skippers on the USS *Hoel, Johnston,* and *Heermann.* They attempted to put down a smokescreen to block the view of the advancing Japanese fleet. The weather changed, bringing rain to assist this effort, but it was not enough. Admiral Clifton Sprague ordered the USS *Hoel, Johnston,* and *Heermann* to attack the Japanese fleet, a last-ditch suicide mission, hoping they could at least slow the advancing Japanese. The captain told his crew they would turn and attack the Japanese fleet and would likely not survive.

The USS *Hoel* attacked the closest Japanese vessel, the battleship *Kongo*, a ship 17 times her size. She opened fire with her guns and torpedoes. This caused the *Kongo* to change course away from the American transports. The Japanese ships continued firing on the three American destroyers, and repeated hits severely damaged the USS *Hoel*. She lost three of her guns, one of her engines, and the steering controls from her bridge, but she and her crew kept up the attack. Over 40 shells hit her, severely damaging her along the waterline, but she was still in the fight.

A Japanese commander knew a damaged destroyer could still inflict a fatal blow to any Japanese vessel. The addition of a smoke screen further imperiled the Japanese ships. The USS *Johnston* launched ten torpedoes from ten thousand yards, one of which hit the Japanese heavy cruiser *Kumano,* the flagship of one of the two Japanese cruiser divisions. In return, she was hit by three 14-inch shells, severely damaging her and knocking out her rear guns. Her speed dropped to 17 knots, but a rainstorm hid her long enough to make simple repairs. Her radar-ranging system still worked; she could continue directing her guns to fire on the *Kongo*. The USS *Hoel* fired six torpedoes at the *Kumano*. Although none hit, she had to break off her attempted attack on the invasion fleet to keep from being sunk by the three small American destroyers.

The USS *Hoel* was mortally wounded but kept steaming in the hope that she would remain a target for the Japanese and keep them busy. She continued to fire her remaining gun at the Japanese. She had been hit numerous times and was finally brought dead in the water when a Japanese shell hit her remaining engine room. Commander Kinterberger ordered the sailors left alive to leave the sinking ship. Nearly two hours after the battle began, the USS *Hoel* sank. Only 86 of her officers and crew survived the first day after her sinking. Many died during combat and after the ship sank. It is thought that 40 sailors died in the sea awaiting rescue, a terrible fate. Some died of their wounds, and sharks ate others. They spent three days at sea awaiting rescue.

The final survivor of the USS *Hoel*, Walter Gammon of Henrico, Virginia, on April 8, 2021, said, "It was terrible. I didn't do too much sleeping that night. I'll tell the world that." Walter joined the Navy during WWII when he was 19 years old. "When I shipped out, I was on the USS *Hoel*." He said that when the order came to abandon ship, "I found half a life jacket. I put it on, and I made it out on my own. I jumped off the bow of the ship." He could not swim, and a shipmate pulled him onto a raft. "Less than 10 minutes after I jumped ship, the USS *Hoel* was gone. I saw it go down. We were out there all night. I did everything I could to help the ones on the raft. When I saw a guy drink seawater, I knew he wouldn't make it. He was delirious. He just lost it, you know? They had to take his life jacket off and say a few words. Over the side, he went. Sharks were eating him before night." Gammon spent three more agonizing days and nights at sea before being rescued.

Oliver Jones correctly said that the USS *Hoel* would never return home. To this day, he is firmly convinced that he would have died on October 25, 1944, but his intersection with fate on the USS *Hughes* in that same theater of battle was now less than two months away.

"FISH HEADS AND RICE WITH CHOPSTICKS"

Emperor Hirohito of Japan (Showa) sometime around 1928.
Japanese public domain photos.

Germany, Japan, and Italy were in the grips of militant national-ism. If left unchecked, America would be in grave peril.

No matter how remote people were, they seemed aware of the war in Europe and the Pacific. In Harold Peterson's book *The Last of the Mountain Men*, the central figure, Sylvan Hart, is a hermit who lives deep in the mountains of Idaho and has little contact with the outside world. Still, he remarks that if the Allies don't do something about the Japanese, the world will soon be "eating fish heads and rice with chopsticks."

What few people understood was how this insanity came to be. Germans were "krauts," and Japanese were "nips," all of whom needed to be killed, and that was that. But in truth, it wasn't that simple. Dehumanizing one's opponent is an age-old tactic that makes it easier to destroy them all. What brought the world to this place in the late 1930s?

Understanding how these events came to pass in Germany and Japan is necessary. Oliver Jones and his shipmates all wanted a chance to "kill Japs" when they joined the Navy in the 1940s. At 97 today and living in Arizona, Jones sees his mortal adversaries during that war differently now. Although he certainly thinks they were crazy to crash their airplanes into American ships in Leyte Gulf intentionally, he now understands that they may not have been all that different from U.S. sailors in many respects. He thinks they were led astray by their leaders. He now wonders how such a cultured and ancient race came to do such things.

To begin with, the leader of Japan was seen as a god. Hirohito ruled Japan and was the head of state under the Meiji Constitution during Japan's imperial expansion, militarization, and involvement in World War II. Japan waged its war of expansion across Asia in the 1930s and 40s in the name of Hirohito and said it was doing so to benefit the nations it conquered. They believed their country was better than all others and overseen by a god. They called this concept the "East Asia Co-prosperity Sphere." Japan was trying to be a colonial power, something it had learned from the West.

This took place at a time when the Japanese were suffering a financial crisis. Times were hard, and the military leaders were taking more and more political power under Hirohito's name. Political violence was rising. A moderate prime minister was assassinated in 1932, leading to the end of control of the military by civilian leaders and the start of control by militarists.

The message was simple: Japan was the greatest country in the world, and God had ordained the Japanese people to run it. Hitler told the German people the same thing. If things had progressed to a conclusion where Japan, Germany, and Italy had prevailed against the Allies, this belief would have led to war between them until only one remained.

A flaw in radical nationalist thinking is that all other groups and races of people are inferior to yours and other people are responsible for hardships you may have in your life, justifying their elimination or enslavement. Again, this was illogical, as the Japanese, Germans, and Italians, signatories of the Axis Pact between their countries, all considered each other's citizens sub-human to some degree. But patriotic nationalists do not allow intelligent, logical thinking by their masses. When they rise to power, they intimidate, kill, or imprison intellectuals, teachers, and scientists. Flag waving, simple slogans, and public demonstrations replace reason.

Things were going well for Hideki Tojo, the actual ruler of Japan, just as they were for Hitler. Still, the militarists needed something more significant to unite the Japanese people. They needed a war. In 1931, they found it.

The "Mukden Incident" was a false accusation against the Chinese, choreographed by the Japanese military, that was used as an excuse to invade China. Militarists brought the plan to Hirohito, and although he later voiced concerns about going to war, he failed to object to it, and China was attacked. The Japanese invaded portions of China and set up puppet governments with leaders loyal to Japan. They were careful to keep from calling it a war, instead calling it an "incident," thereby justifying a departure from the international rules of war. The Japanese carried out atrocities throughout China,

Hideki Tojo - The simple-minded nationalist architect of Japan's war against the world, sometime before 1945. Japanese public domain photo.

including using poison gas, executing prisoners, and raping civilians. The Japanese military directed their army's leaders not to use the term "prisoners of war," thereby justifying execution without due process.

Hideki Tojo began his career in the Japanese Army and eventually became a general by 1934. In March 1937, he was promoted to chief of staff and led military operations in China. In 1940, he became the minister of war. What set Tojo apart from other militarists was that he was an outspoken advocate for a preemptive attack on the United States. Many other members of the military, especially the navy, felt that this was a fool's errand and that the industrial might of the United States would, over time, defeat Japan.

Tojo ran a nationalist patriotism campaign based on loyalty to the emperor and Japan. Slogans, flags, songs, and signs were everywhere in Japanese life. People were encouraged to accept that Japan was the world's greatest country and had the right to rule handed down by God. Religion and politics were mixed. To dedicate oneself to the country was the highest calling for any loyal, patriotic person. Military service was considered holy, and service members were given the highest honors. Questioning the leaders or Japan's position as the greatest country in the world was seen as treason. On this platform, Tojo was appointed prime minister on October 17, 1941. From this position, he oversaw the direction of the war.

Young Japanese men were swept up in this nationalist hysteria. People who thought differently generally kept it to themselves and dared not publicly discuss misgivings. Flags, parades, songs, and patriotic slogans were ever-present reminders to all. It was in this nationalist discussion that the first concepts of self-sacrifice came to the surface among the militarists. Although it was not until October of 1944 that the first official kamikaze attacks would occur against American ships, the first rumors of the concept resulted from this nationalist furor.

The concept of duty, even to death, was a family, community, and national obligation. As much as the American sailors on the USS *Hughes* wanted to "kill Japs," young Japanese pilots wanted to kill enemies of the Empire of Japan.

One of those who initially opposed the idea of self-sacrifice or kamikaze was Admiral Takijiro Onishi. He graduated from the Imperial Japanese Naval Academy in 1912. He worked his way up in the naval officer ranks, serving on several different types of ships. He was also a pilot and flight instructor. As he progressed in his career, he took an assignment on a seaplane tender called the *Wakamiya*. From this assignment, he helped to develop the Imperial Japanese Naval Air Service. He was sent to France and England to study combat aircraft development as they were used in WWI. He continued to be promoted and assigned to air combat operations. Once promoted to lieutenant commander in 1928, he was assigned to the aircraft carrier *Hosho* and named commander of the air carrier wing. He became an admiral in November of 1939.

By 1941, he was assigned to assist in developing the technical plan to attack Pearl Harbor, something he strongly opposed. He believed the United States had the resources to defeat Japan and would eventually force it into a humiliating unconditional surrender. Nevertheless, he did his part as ordered, and America was attacked on December 7, 1941.

Onishi was also interested in psychology. He studied the mental aspects of soldiers' responses to combat and stress, and he published *War Ethics of the Imperial Navy* in 1938. Long before this time, though, other militarists had suggested that suicide attacks against an enemy were necessary to defeat opponents of the imperial throne. Onishi was unalterably opposed and even called such concepts "heresy" and not to be spoken of again. He deemed such ideas to be immoral and without honor.

Time and circumstances changed his belief. Onishi, commonly called the father of the piloted kamikaze aircraft attacks, embraced the concept he had once vehemently opposed. In May 1943, when Japan looked like it might be at risk of losing the war, he was again promoted, and in October 1944, he became the commander of the First Air Fleet in the Philippines. He visited the 201st Navy Flying Corps headquarters, where he told his officers, "In my opinion, there is only one way of assuring that our meager strength will be effective to a maximum degree. That is to organize suicide attack units composed of A6M Zero fighters armed with 250-kilogram bombs, with each plane to crash-dive into an enemy carrier. What do you think?" They did not oppose him, and he ordered the attacks to commence.

The pilot who would attack the USS *Hughes* only weeks later was one of the attendees.

On October 20, 1944, Onishi gave a speech to the pilots who volunteered for special attack duty. His voice shook with emotion as he said:

> Japan is in grave danger. The salvation of our country is now beyond the power of the ministers of the state, the General Staff, and lowly commanders like me. It can come only from spirited young men such as you. Thus, on behalf of your hundred million countrymen, I ask you for this sacrifice and pray for your success. You are already Gods without earthly desires. But you want to know that your crash-dive is worthwhile. Regrettably, we will not be able to tell you the results. But I shall watch your efforts and report your deeds to the Throne! You may all rest assured on this point. I ask you all to do your best.

By then, Onishi had been ordered to destroy the American aircraft carriers. He felt that this was now the only chance of doing so. He harbored no belief that Japan could prevent invasion without catastrophic losses. Close to the war's end, he urged the country and emperor to fight on and said that he thought the invasion of Japan by America could be avoided and that the Allies could be defeated by sacrificing 20 million more Japanese lives. He believed that if the nation embraced "nobility of spirit," Japan, as a culture, would survive.

Under Admiral Onishi's command, these pilots would begin the attacks on October 25, 1944. Over three thousand kamikaze missions would be carried out, many in planes with Japanese pilots in their cockpits. Roughly 14% would hit ships. The first such mission was in Leyte Gulf, where the USS *Hughes* was deployed. Kamikaze attacks sank 34 ships and damaged hundreds of others during the

Admiral Onishi - Father of the Special Attack Forces —
photo taken before 1945. Japanese public domain photos.

war. At Okinawa, they inflicted the most significant losses ever suffered by the U.S. Navy in a single battle, killing almost five thousand
men. At Leyte Gulf, they sank three U.S. aircraft carriers. This was
the Japanese Navy's most significant win against American ships
during the war. An A6M Zero fighter hit the aircraft carrier *St. Lo*
and sank it in less than an hour, a devastating loss to the Americans,
who had never seen or imagined anything like it.

One of the pilots was Yukio Seki. As a young man, he wandered
the displays of his parents' antique shop in Shikoku, which sold tea
ceremony supplies and utensils. This was a traditional and disciplined
Japanese household. He was an only child, and as he grew up, he
listened to the messages about duty to Japan and the emperor. His
parents knew of his interest in the navy and flying. Because Yukio
was an only child, they adopted a daughter in case he lost his life
in military service, something the nationalist messaging in Japan
required of all who served. Yukio studied and eventually joined the
navy and aviation service. From the beginning, he and his parents

Lieutenant Yukio Seki & Chiran High School girls waiving to kamikaze pilots on April 12, 1945. Japanese public domain photos.

were told that he would be required to die in battle and would never return from his military service. Kamikaze pilots were not mentally deranged or insane but carefully indoctrinated young men from ordinary Japanese life.

The first kamikaze attack on October 21, 1944, was unsuccessful. But the attack on October 25, 1944, did succeed, becoming the first successful deployment of a suicide attack by a manned aircraft. Lieutenant Seki led five Mitsubishi Zero fighters, who sank the USS *St. Lo* by crash-diving their aircraft into her flight deck.

The process of nationalism led the pilot who dove his plane into the USS *Hughes* to take a similar action. That process took time to develop. Thousands of young Japanese men volunteered, believing it was a symbol of holy and patriotic commitment to their emperor. This mix of religion and politics was dangerous.

When told of these attacks by the Japanese, Oliver Jones initially refused to believe the stories were true. That would change once he saw the attacks for himself.

I saw Jap planes circling American ships many times. This didn't happen every day, but it happened a lot. If they were close enough, we shot at them with the guns on the deck, including mine. I saw quite a few Jap planes get shot down into the water. I thought that they were dropping bombs on the American ships. People said they were diving intentionally on our ships, but I could not believe it. I initially thought it was an accident, but I was wrong. That is exactly what they were doing.

Well, they were trained. There were enough kamikazes that it was a known thing. They were taught to do it. It seemed way out of line to me. I wouldn't do it. I don't know what was done to those people or what happened to them. At first, I didn't believe it. I figured what they had done was parachute out, and the plane hit the ship at the last moment. Then I saw a couple of them happen. Then, I believed. When I saw it for myself, I thought he'd lost his mind. It was tough to defend against, for sure. This all started in October of 1944. If you think about it, they were dead before they did it. They couldn't survive. After a while, I knew darn well what was going on. I talked to the other sailors I worked with, and they said that they were damn sure that no one would get them to do that. Most guys thought it was nuts. After a while, we didn't talk much about it.

"THE DESTROYER OF WORLDS"

J. Robert Oppenheimer - Father of the atomic bomb.
Ed Westcott photo. U.S. Archives.

"Now I am become Death, the destroyer of worlds." At 5:30 AM on July 16, 1945, at the first detonation of a nuclear explosion on planet Earth, in the desert near Alamogordo, New Mexico, along the ancient "Jornada Del Muetro" trail, Spanish for "Journey of Death," Robert Oppenheimer turned to Hindu scripture to express what was almost impossible to describe. President Roosevelt's dream of a weapon that could vaporize Japanese cities and quickly end the war with Japan had finally emerged. Its power was unimaginable. Admiral Onishi, the father of the kamikaze air attacks, would soon cross paths with Robert Oppenheimer, the father of the atomic bomb. The USS *Hughes* would forge the path for this to happen, but it would be a long and challenging journey for each of them.

Atomic fission occurs when a neutron slams into a uranium or plutonium atom, forcing it to excite and split into two. The release of additional neutrons can initiate a chain reaction. When each atom splits, a tremendous amount of energy is released.

Fission was discovered on December 19, 1938, not in America but by German chemist Otto Hahn and his assistant, Fritz Strassmann. At the time, this posed an unprecedented danger to the world. Had this research continued in Germany and had Albert Einstein stayed in Germany along with other Jewish scientists, Hitler would have created the first atomic bombs before America and likely won WWII. The "Thousand Year Reich" might have become a reality. But Hitler and the Nazis hated intellectuals, not to mention all Jewish people, which ultimately led scores of them to flee Germany, many to the United States. This became a primary reason America developed nuclear weapons before any other country. America's original plan was to drop the first atomic bomb on Berlin and Hitler, but that was not accomplished before Germany was defeated with conventional weapons.

Although much research and work lay ahead, Hahn understood that a "burst" of the atomic nuclei had occurred. The implications of this event were staggering to the imagination. Explaining it to those not versed in science and mathematics was virtually impossible. But not all atoms could be spit in such a way. Only the heaviest and lightest elements are unstable enough for fission, with the heaviest elements, like uranium, and fusion with the lighter elements, like hydrogen.

The potential release of energy by these processes was beyond the imagination of the public at large and even many scientists. It seemed possible to unlock the secrets of science and physics in a way that could destroy the world. Initially, the scientists faced the problem of getting people to understand what they had discovered and then quickly feared the potential consequences. German scientists were very aware of what Hitler planned for the world. German Jewish physicists, many of whom were among the most brilliant in the world, were deeply concerned.

Although the material for the first atomic bomb that exploded at Hiroshima had several pounds of nuclear material in its core, the amount that blew up was less than the size of a third of a penny. Had the entire fission material at the center of the bomb detonated, more of that part of Japan would have been instantly vaporized.

Fortunately for the world, Albert Einstein and other brilliant Jewish physicists fled Germany and other European countries to the United States. As work progressed, the physicists grew more alarmed by what their research indicated. Enrico Fermi and Leo Szliard felt that the United States government needed to know the risk of what would happen if Hitler created an atomic bomb. But as scientists unaccustomed to public speaking and, in many cases, almost devoid of social graces, they were convinced no one would take them seriously. Although eccentric, Einstein had a significant following and was a popular public personality. So, they decided to take the issue to him and have him contact President Roosevelt.

Leo Szliard wrote a letter to Einstein and met with him on August 2, 1939. Einstein reviewed the data Szliard brought with him and concluded that the assumptions were correct and the

Albert Einstein and Leo Szilard with letter to President Roosevelt, August 2, 1939. Creative Commons License. Time Life Pictures 1946.

consequences were staggering to the imagination should Hitler gain control of such a device. The letter begins:

> Some recent work by E. Fermi and L. Szilard, which has been communicated to me in manuscript, leads me to expect that the element uranium may be turned into a new and important source of energy in the immediate future. Certain aspects of the situation which has arisen seem to call for watchfulness and, if necessary, quick action on the part of the Administration. I believe therefore that it is my duty to bring to your attention the following facts and recommendations:
>
> In the course of the last four months it has been made probable—through the work of Joliot in France as well as Fermi

and Szilard in America—that it may become possible to set up a nuclear chain reaction in a large mass of uranium by which vast amounts of power and large quantities of new radium-like elements would be generated. Now it appears almost certain that this could be achieved in the immediate future.

The letter was sent to President Roosevelt, whose administration considered it and examined it further. On October 9, 1941, just as the USS *Hughes* was operating in the North Atlantic against German U-boats and two months before the Japanese attack on Pearl Harbor, President Roosevelt approved a crash program to build the first deliverable nuclear bomb. In June of 1942, President Roosevelt ordered the United States to make a bomb to potentially drop on Germany and Japan. They called this the Manhattan Engineering District Project. General Leslie Groves was placed in command, and he, in turn, hired physicist Robert Oppenheimer to oversee the development.

Roosevelt did not think the U.S. would avoid a war with Germany and Japan. Churchill was thrilled that the United States might enter the war. Even if it meant Britain's destruction, its people would never be slaves to Nazi Germany. With the commitment that England would see the battle through to the end, Roosevelt knew that America now had the potential to hasten the end of that war with a devastating new weapon that could vaporize entire cities, but the problems of the size of the bomb and how to deliver it needed to be solved.

Few people were aware of the project at the time. Roosevelt knew these problems needed solutions if the Manhattan Project were to produce the results that now seemed probable. The USS *Hughes* would become a critical part of the policy to assist in getting nuclear bombs to the doorstep of Japan. America needed bases to assemble and launch atomic strikes at the heart of the Japanese Empire.

Oppenheimer had assured Groves, and Groves had assured Roosevelt that bombs were not only possible but highly likely once the technical problems were solved and America had bases near Japan.

Compounding the problem for General Groves and the U.S. Army was the choice of Robert Oppenheimer. Groves didn't understand nuclear physics but was a master at marshaling large projects and picking the people necessary to complete them. Bringing together some of the greatest but also some of the most independent and complex minds in the world under the tightest secrecy imaginable was no small task. Oppenheimer was highly controversial. He had ties to left-leaning groups at Berkeley, where he was a professor, and was thought by many in the intelligence community to be a communist. His longtime girlfriend, Jean Tatlock, was a communist, and he never broke off his relationship with her, even after his marriage to another woman.

Oppenheimer was not a communist, but this cloud of controversy never left him and was a constant irritation for Groves. Groves battled the Army and national security intelligence agents who wanted to withhold and later revoke Oppenheimer's security clearance. Army OIC agents denied a security clearance for Oppenheimer for months and only issued one under the direct order of General Groves. Even after that, they tapped Oppenheimer's phones, office, and house and followed him constantly throughout the war years. They never stopped pressing General Groves to abandon Oppenheimer for his left-leaning politics, even though he was no threat to national security at any time. General Groves knew Oppenheimer and understood he was a loyal American of the highest order. He also knew that without Oppenheimer, there would be no atomic bomb project.

Compounding these issues, no one had ever created an atomic bomb, and the whole thing was only a theory at the time. In the beginning, Oppenheimer thought only a handful of scientists might

Admiral William "Bull" Halsey. USN Official Photo.

solve and unlock the secrets of the atom and fission. However, thousands of scientific, support, and Army personnel would work there only a short time after the Los Alamos lab was created. Tens of thousands would work in other locations to make the materials necessary for the first bomb.

Another challenge was the Pacific Ocean. The vast oceans were a significant barrier when navies put to sea. The Pacific Ocean was not only a barrier but also a battlefield. Admiral Halsey once said, "Nothing has happened since V-J Day to shorten the eight thousand miles of water between us and the enemy." Aircraft could not cover that distance and deliver a nuclear bomb.

Halsey knew America needed time to focus and understand the dangers ahead. The Navy needed time to clear the islands of Japanese bases so America could bomb the Japanese main islands. Halsey provided constant reminders of who the enemy was. American resentment of Japan was strong, but Halsey felt it was essential to keep that feeling, so he reminded them of the mission. "Kill Japs, kill Japs, kill more Japs" was his motto. He never let the American public forget it.

Admiral Halsey captured the imagination and support of American citizens. He deftly articulated his position that carefully orchestrated, extreme violence against the citizens of the Empire of Japan was not only justified but necessary. Halsey won the adoration of his subordinates and the public at large. Halsey convinced Admiral Nimitz of this vision and the value of messaging it to the American people. If Americans were going to lose loved ones overseas, they needed to feel it was worth it.

At Halsey's urging, Nimitz gave a speech to the National Geographic Society, saying, "Sea power has its roots deep in the core of our country. They draw nourishment from the farms and ranches that feed our men. They derive from our mines, logging camps, mills, and factories. There is scarcely a village in the geographical center of the continent which does not contribute in some way to America's sea power."

These words moved the nation, especially rural areas, where families and young men felt the pull to do their part in a war to save America and the world from radical nationalism. They were young men like the sailors who signed up and set out on the USS *Hughes* to fight the enemy in the Pacific. They would clear the islands of the Pacific so Americans could drop bombs on the Empire of Japan until it either surrendered or was wiped off the surface of the Earth, and they didn't care which happened first.

When the USS *Hughes* set sail into the Pacific, Oppenheimer was still a theoretical physicist at Berkeley, California, soon to join and take over the Manhattan Project to build an atomic bomb to drop on Japan. Admiral Onishi was marshaling the naval air forces of the Empire of Japan to hold the Pacific bases Roosevelt needed to take so he could drop an atomic bomb on Toyoko. In the coming years,

Onishi would have a new job commanding the kamikaze forces to stop those American ships.

The sailors of the USS *Hughes,* coming from the heartland of America, would meet them both in the epic battle between these desperate efforts at Leyte Gulf in the Philippines. The USS *Hughes* herself would help write the final chapter in this story in 1945 at Bikini Atoll.

CHAPTER SIX

"YOU PISS YOUR PANTS, BUT DON'T WRITE THAT"

USS Hughes starboard view. Chester Bradley Collection.

Americans heard Nimitz's call to arms. One of those young men was Glen Edmonson, the only child of Denizal and Anna Edmonson of DeKalb County, Missouri. He attended the University of Missouri and graduated with a teaching degree from Missouri State Teachers College. He taught high school classes until WWII, when he joined the Navy. Edmonson served for over three and a half years in the South Pacific and was the gunnery lieutenant in charge of weapons, ammunition, and combat training on the USS *Hughes*. Edmonson grew up during the Great Depression.

Edmonson explained that times were hard for everyone, especially in the rural heartland of America, where opportunities were few and far between. The pay was low, and so were expectations. Simply surviving was difficult enough, and adventure and entertainment were rare. Those joining military services were patriots, but that was not the only reason. Edmonson selected the U.S. Navy in part because of the food.

Some people in the heartland didn't get three meals a day, but the Navy generally offered good meals every day. The best was reserved for submariners, but the rest of the Navy ate far better than most Americans in the late 1930s. Once the wartime economy kicked in, all of that changed, but in the beginning, not worrying about where your next meal would come from was a luxury.

Oliver Jones from Montana said, "Oh, the food was excellent. We always had good food, except when we were too far away from re-supply ships in combat. But for the most part, I always remembered getting great food on the USS *Hughes*." It is one of his fondest memories of serving on the USS *Hughes* in the Pacific, even today.

Edmonson and his fellow sailors also had a luxury in the Pacific that service members in other military branches could not have imagined: fresh bananas, mangoes, papayas, and, especially, pineapples. Although often in combat, the USS *Hughes* would sometimes be approached by the native populations of Pacific Islands in canoes, who came out to greet the sailors. Most locals were already aware of the brutal repression by the Japanese Imperial Army and were happy to see the Americans. The locals were a great source of intelligence on where the Japanese were. They brought fresh fruit, which they knew the sailors loved. The sailors of the USS *Hughes* also gave gifts in return.

One day, Edmonson went below to find a suitable gift commensurate with the treasure of fresh fruit. He came upon a standard Navy-issued wool blanket. He climbed back to the deck and threw it down to the locals in their handmade outrigger canoe. They passed it around, looked it over, discussed it, and threw it back to him on the deck. The climate in Leyte typically varied from 75 degrees to 89 degrees Fahrenheit and was rarely below 73 degrees. There was never a time when someone needed a wool blanket, and the locals, although appreciative, were puzzled about why Edmonson had thrown them one.

After the war, the USS *Hughes* famously had one of the most active reunion organizations of any U.S. ship from WWII. The survivors and their families gathered yearly to remember fallen comrades, renew old friendships, and tell war stories. But at these later events, the families often remarked on how so many sailors on the USS *Hughes* came from the center of America to serve in the Pacific Ocean, a place most had never seen. The heartland of America could not be more different than the West Coast or the waters of the Pacific. Was it patriotism? Or maybe, like in Glen Edmonson's case, the food was part of it.

The recruits craved adventure. Having survived her attacks on German U-boats and the attempt to sink the German pocket battleship *Bismarck*, the USS *Hughes* met up with the aircraft USS *Yorktown*, destroyers USS *Sims* and *Walke*, and guided-missile destroyer *Russell* and sailed from the Atlantic through the Panama Canal, leaving behind the cold waters of the stormy North Atlantic and

Officers on the USS Hughes - Glen Edmonson seated in the center.
Glen Edmonson collection.

entering the tranquil, warm waters of the Pacific. They arrived in San Diego on December 30, 1941. Ships were desperately needed to combat Japanese advancement throughout the Pacific after the attack on Pearl Harbor.

Oliver Jones fell in love with the USS *Hughes.*

Everyone welcomed me on board. They put me on the Fo'csle crew, that's on the ship's bow. I was glad to get on the bow. They assigned me to that crew. We all slept in the same area, towards the back of the ship called the fantail. I was in the third bunk up from the bottom. Four beds were hooked to the wall of the ship. I got lucky. It was a big problem to get into the bottom or top ones. If you were on the bottom one, you had to bend over and almost crawl on the deck to get into your bunk. It was only six inches off the deck. But even in my bunk, I could take my elbow, hold it up, and touch the springs on the bunk above me. It was very close, and a fellow would not have wanted to be claustrophobic on a WWII ship.

The bed was about two feet wide, and we stored our gear in a nearby locker. After getting out of the Navy, I could sleep on anything. I can sleep on a hardwood floor now. We had a mattress that was maybe three inches thick. That was all you had between you and that spring. I also had my clothes, shoes, and personal property. When I entered the Navy, I didn't bring much stuff as I thought it could end up on the bottom of the ocean. No, I'm just kidding and storying now. I never felt anything like that. Being on the ship was a joy. I just wanted to get over there and shoot at Japs.

There were a lot of guys on the USS *Hughes*, and you didn't get to know everyone all that well from different parts of the ship. I got to know the guys from the front of the ship. But men from the middle and back of the ship were on their own crews. On the front of the ship, we were all like brothers. Someone was on watch. No matter the weather or time of day. Usually, we had six or seven guys on watch in the front of the ship all the time. We had four-hour shifts on deck duty. We used to eat in the same place except when we were in battle. Then, we would try to get loose occasionally to grab something to eat if we could. But when we were not in battle, we got to eat three times a day, which was usually excellent food! As long as they could get it anyway. But way down south, we ran out of supply ships when we were in battle. Then it got tricky.

We cleaned, painted, and kept the ship in shape. When not on duty, we washed our clothes and tried to get some sleep. There was not much free time and none when we were in battle areas. When on watch, we saw a lot of ships and submarines that we had to report immediately. One time we reported a Jap submarine near Pearl Harbor that had to be sunk. You could find them anywhere and always had to be careful on your watch. We had guns and depth charges.

The depth charges made considerable explosions in the water and blew it high into the air.

When asked how it felt when they dropped depth charges, he said, "Well, I was just hoping that we got the Japs. We didn't think about much else. You would throw that depth charge and then try to escape it. You did get a pretty good concussion from it, though."

When asked about seasickness, Jones said, "Seasickness is something everyone sometimes gets, but I never did. I still can't believe it to this day. I was the only one who never did. No matter how rough it got, I never got seasick on any ship. Usually, when some got it, they would be seasick for about a day. Then, they would get over it, and it was pretty miserable."

The regular routine was abandoned in combat areas.

When you were in combat, you were up and at your station or gun for what seemed like forever, sometimes three days at a time. In New Guinea, we would go in and right up to the beaches and strafe the Japs hanging in the palm trees. They would be up in the tree and have a machine gun. We would make a circle and shoot at them when they shot at us. We were trying to get them out so our troops could land without being killed by the Japs. In some areas, we shot anyone moving. Their machine guns hit our ships. We could hear their bullets hit our ship, and we had shields on our gun mounts. Sometimes, some of our sailors got hit. It sounded like a hammer was hitting steel. Usually, the bullets hit below me when I was manning a machine gun, and I was shooting back at them. I was on the 20 mm machine gun. We had a shield with a plastic cover, but the bullets could hit you if you were not careful. Sometimes, we did this for two straight days at a time. I felt pretty good shooting at the enemy, but I guarantee it wasn't very comforting. You never knew if you were going to get it or not.

When asked about his first combat experience when someone shot at him, he said:

Well, you piss your pants. That isn't good. But don't write that.

No one ever froze up in combat, even their first time. Everyone shot at the enemy. The thing about it was you couldn't see what everyone else was doing. You just did your job. You followed your orders. We also used our guns to shoot at Japanese airplanes. You never knew whose bullets hit the planes when they were destroyed and crashed into the sea. When we were trying to protect the aircraft carriers, we did our best to shoot the Jap planes when they came in to get them. That made us a target. Sometimes I got so scared I just shot the hell out of the Jap planes as best I could. That was the job of the destroyers. We circled the aircraft carriers to protect them.

Usually, two destroyers would be out front in the lead, one on each side and the back. They tried to have six if they were available. Most of the time, there would be two or three aircraft carriers with our tin cans all around them. That is what they called us, "Tin Cans." We were expendable. No one liked to do this, but we were proud of what we did. I did see aircraft carriers get hit by the Jap planes. Sometimes, they were further away. On the ocean, over a distance, you can lose sight of a ship, but it is just over the horizon, but we knew they were there. You could tell where other ships were because of where the Jap planes were going. The Jap planes could see them from the air.

Al Tysoe, in the center, was transferred out of the area of the ship that was destroyed by a kamikaze plane, saving his life during the attack. Chester Bradley Collection.

The Japanese advances were staggering in scope and speed as the USS *Hughes* sailed into the Pacific Ocean. To protect her home waters, the Japanese Imperial Navy attacked and defeated Pacific targets and landed Japanese Army forces with remarkable quickness. Every attack met with almost instant success in the early parts of the war, and the prospects for America were frightening. Manila and Cavite in the Philippines fell on January 2, 1942, and Bougainville on the 22nd. Rabaul and Balikpapan were captured on January 23, 1942.

It was believed that the Japanese Imperial Navy planned to attack Samoa soon. If successful, the Allies feared that Australia would fall. This would deprive the Americans and British of essential bases and re-supply routes to the Pacific fleet. At the time, America was out-gunned in the category of the ship that made the most difference in attacks against forward bases: aircraft carriers.

Although America would more than overcome this deficit over time, in 1941, Japan had the resources to defeat the United States Navy in the Pacific. Japan had aircraft carrier superiority. If they maintained it and sank the remaining U.S. carriers, Hawaii and the West Coast would be vulnerable to daily Japanese attacks. People from Seattle to Los Angeles would be bombed by Japanese air-craft-carrier-based planes.

One of the initial keys to countering the Japanese carrier advan-tage was reinforcing the troops on Samoa. This could counter the Japanese advances in the Marshall Islands. America needed some-thing to slow the Japanese down and divert resources from other American targets. One of the first missions was carried out by the USS *Hughes*. On January 12, 1942, the meager US Naval Forces left the West Coast, and the USS *Hughes* escorted the *Matsonia*, *Lurline*, and *Mariposa*, full of Marine reinforcements, to Samoa. They com-pleted this mission on January 25, 1942. The Marines raided Japa-nese installations immediately.

Soon, the USS *Hughes* joined the carrier striking force built around the American carrier USS *Yorktown* under the command of Admiral Jack Fletcher. This task force was ordered to attack the Japanese at Jaluit, Makin, and Mili in the Marshall and Gilbert Islands. A second carrier-based force, led by the American carrier USS *Enterprise*, was to attack Kwajalein and Roi.

The attack began on February 1, 1942. The USS *Hughes* steamed west at 2:00 AM with a light northerly swell. The Pacific Ocean's

Seamen Chester Bradley & Malcolm Riker from the USS Hughes
on leave in San Francisco. Chester Bradley collection.

deep, clear blue water was a hot 84 degrees Fahrenheit, and the air temperature was a humid 80 degrees.

The visibility was 25 nautical miles that morning, but a sailor on watch could not see enemy vessels at that distance. The old ways of naval combat, perfected throughout centuries of human conflict, would be forever changed in WWII. In the past, ships and sailors had to see each other to fight and sink the other's ships. A person standing on the ocean's surface can only see a little over three miles due to the Earth's curvature. A sailor high up on a mast, looking for a tall ship in the distance can improve that, but not considerably.

Due to radar and ship-based aircraft, America and Japan would fight a new type of naval war. Radar could detect ships at longer distances, at night, and in poor weather. The USS *Hughes* was one of the first ships with such a top-secret device, a remarkable development in naval combat operations. Ships could now be detected when they could not be seen. Airplanes from carriers would expand naval battles to distances where navies never saw each other. That is how this current battle began.

The USS *Hughes* was screening the carrier *Yorktown* when it was noted in the log, "On station 2,000 yards 45 degrees on the starboard bow of *Yorktown*. Course 090 True and Gyro. 9:40 AM—Plane crash on the port quarter. All engines stopped. *Walke* proceeding to the rescue." The destroyer USS *Walke* rescued the two airmen from the plane that crashed on takeoff from the *Yorktown*. Quickly underway again, at 11:09 AM, it was noted in the log: "Made radar contact bearing 350 degrees True, and Gyro, distance eight miles. Japanese enemy four motor patrol bomber sighted, coming out of a rain squall on the port side and, a few seconds later, disappeared back into the squall. *Russel* and *Sims* opened fire on the plane. The plane dropped bombs, which landed approximately 2,000 yards astern of the *Sims*. Various changes to course and speed to maintain radar contact with the bomber."

Not long after, the battle was over. The USS *Hughes* log notes, "5:09 PM Ceased zigzagging. Cut speed to 15 knots. *Yorktown* recovering aircraft. 5:42 PM increased speed to 25 knots and resumed zigzagging." The task force ships had orders to keep changing course as a group to prevent Japanese submarines from having a steady target. This was called zigzagging. But an aircraft carrier could not recover her planes when changing course. This was a time of heightened danger for the fleet, and they returned to evasive tactics as soon as all aircraft were safely on board.

USS Yorktown (CV-5) during the Battle of the Coral Sea,
April 1942 - U.S. Navy Photo.

As American planes from the two carriers attacked the Japanese, Fletcher lost seven aircraft and a light cruiser in the raids. The USS *Hughes* had been assigned to protect the aircraft carrier at all costs. The USS *Enterprise* also lost aircraft in the raid, and a Japanese bomb almost hit her during the encounter.

The raids by this task force had little long-term strategic impact. The Imperial Japanese Navy sent two aircraft carriers to chase the two American task forces. However, they quickly left this pursuit and returned to their ongoing successful conquests of the Philippines and other Pacific islands. The only real value of the raids was the morale improvement among American sailors and the public, who were still reeling from the attack on Pearl Harbor. But these raids also provided actual combat experience in carrier air operations. This would benefit the U.S. carrier groups in future combat against the Japanese. It was also a wake-up call to the Japanese. For the first time, they realized that resupply would be at risk with their far-flung bases around the Pacific unless the American carriers could be sunk.

Although the setbacks were only modest for the Japanese, the militarists nonetheless convinced Japanese Admiral Isoroku Yamamoto, commander of the Japanese Imperial Pacific Fleet, that the time had come to trick the Americans into a battle at Midway Island, where they planned to destroy their fleet. The USS *Hughes* and the carrier task forces returned to Pearl Harbor while Japanese troops poured into Dutch and British possessions in the South Pacific Islands almost unabated. Despite America's combat experience and minor victories, it was a dark time for the country's prospects in the war against Japan.

During this early part of WWII in the Pacific, many of the eventual sailors on the USS *Hughes* were completing their eight weeks of basic training. Within two months of Pearl Harbor, the number of recruits grew from 2,869 in four battalions to over 15,000 in 13 divisions. But the Navy wasn't interested in just anyone who applied. No matter how grim the prospects were in February 1942, the wrong person serving on an American ship could doom the entire crew. Many of those volunteering never made it to a ship.

A sailor manning a gun had to be reliable, even in his first encounter. Oliver Jones, a gunner on the starboard bow of the USS *Hughes,* recalled, "You hear bullets hitting the metal around you. It's deafening. You would die if you didn't do your job, and everyone knew it. It didn't matter how scared you were. You had to do your job. We trained a lot. Everyone knew his job. After a while, it got easier." The Navy was looking for that, and they knew how to find it in young recruits. Every sailor's life was in each other sailor's hands.

One sailor on the USS *Hughes* was Alfred D. Wright of McAllen, Texas. After initial training, he shipped out on the USS *Hughes* and participated in early battles, passing ammunition to the deck guns for firing at the Japanese. He was in combat in the Marshall Islands and Samoa. When a routine check indicated he was only 14, he had already earned two battle stars. He looked older and presented himself well, but his deception was discovered because he had two other brothers who had joined the service. He was the first of them to see actual combat. An officer advised him that his combat days were over. At 14 years old, Wright was the youngest sailor in combat during the early days of WWII and the youngest ever to serve on the USS *Hughes*. The Navy sent him home to his parents in Texas with an honorable discharge. He was proud of the two battle-awarded stars he received on the USS *Hughes*.

"I WOULD NOT SMOKE, CURSE, DRINK, OR BE UNFAITHFUL TO MY WIFE"

Seaman and radar operator Chester Bradley on the USS Hughes - Chester Bradley collection.

An attacking Japanese bomber could be "seen," tracked, and attacked due to radar on the USS *Hughes*. The USS *Hughes* could also direct aerial attacks on other Japanese targets. It wasn't until May 1941 that the U.S. Navy developed and installed the first S-band Navy search device (radar) on a ship. With a gyro-stabilized mount, it could detect large ships 15 miles away and a submarine periscope at five miles. About a thousand of these sets were eventually built, but they were still relatively new in February 1942. Sailors on board were not supposed to know about radar, but it was one of the worst-kept secrets on the ship.

Two of the radarmen on the USS *Hughes* were Chester Bradley and Malcolm Riker. Bradley explained:

Unlike many others on the USS *Hughes,* I was drafted into the Navy at age 23. I always thought I was drafted to be a radarman because I had taken Morse Code in college. I served as Radarman 2C 43-45 and remained until the war ended. When the war ended, I returned home to my wife, Lamesa, and my business in Trinidad, Texas. My wife ran the business in my absence. When the USS *Hughes* was in dry dock for repairs after the kamikaze attack, the married shipmates were given a Quonset hut at Hunters Point. Lamesa came out and stayed with me and would cook for me and the radarmen. After that, we returned to the war and the Aleutian Islands to fight the Japanese and then on to Japan for the end of the war and occupation.

When I got into the war, I promised God if he would get me home safe, I would not smoke, curse, drink, or be unfaithful to my wife. I was never so afraid of anything than to be a floating target for the Japanese in the middle of the Pacific Ocean.

Malcolm Riker and I were radarmen on the USS *Hughes.* We became lifelong friends. Ever since 1939, Malcolm had monitored the war in Europe on his shortwave radio and reported to his family each evening at dinner. He felt that life was passing him by, and each day he was at Episcopal High School, he listened in the study hall for more news of the war. Then, after only six hours of the summer semester, he left school and joined the Navy in 1943. The war couldn't wait for him any longer. He began the long train trip to San Diego and would not return home for 30 months.

After basic training, Riker shipped off for Pearl Harbor and specialized training. His camp overlooked the harbor. At the time, the Americans were still trying to raise the USS *Oklahoma*, which the Japanese had sunk in the Pearl Harbor raid.

Riker also solemnly vowed to remain a virgin in the Navy. He was convinced that he would survive the war if he did so. He was pretty sure that few, if any, of his shipmates would adhere to this standard for a young man, but he was determined to uphold it. This

Officers of the USS Hughes. Glen Edmonson collection.

path would be seriously challenged in the coming years, but he said he fulfilled it. He told everyone about the pledge, leading to no small amount of ridicule from his shipmates. After the war, he would go on to be a priest. But with all the visits to ports filled with bars and brothels, it is unlikely that many of his shipmates followed his path.

Bradley continued:

A member of the radar gang was an atheist. We all told him about our faith and wanted him to be saved. He was not having it and would shrug us off when the topic arose. One day, the ship came under attack, and there seemed little hope of survival. Then, suddenly, over the radio, we heard "Bong Here," and my shipmates were elated. Major Bong was an ace pilot, and we knew our fate would change when he arrived. Bong shot down three Japanese planes to save the USS *Hughes* that day. American pilots were not supposed to fly over the ships, but on that day, Major Bong made three revolutions over the bow of the USS *Hughes*. All my shipmates were standing on the deck when Major Bong flew over. Everyone was cheering for him, but I was so emotional that I could not make a sound. Next to me stood the atheist, and he was cheering, and then he shouted at the top of his lungs, "Thank God!" I guess he had his come to Jesus moment, and all was well with his soul.

Riker was initially assigned to the USS *Luce*, a *Fletcher*-class destroyer. In another remarkable decision that, like Oliver Jones, saved Riker's life, he decided to leave that ship, and he would go on to serve on the USS *Hughes*. He didn't like the USS *Luce*. He had a bad feeling about her. Just like the ship Oliver Jones initially shipped out on, she was sunk in battle, losing much of her crew. Riker was then assigned to the USS *Liscome Bay*, but he didn't like that ship either and asked for a transfer. The USS *Liscome Bay* would also be

24-year-old Major Richard Ira Bong, America's highest-scoring "Ace of Aces," shot down a remarkable 40 Japanese aircraft in WWII, and was awarded the Congressional Medal of Honor, and saved the USS Hughes. U.S. Army photo

sunk in battle by the Japanese, losing over six hundred men. Riker later said he had been lucky to get off those ships.

Riker was then assigned to the destroyer USS *Morris*, but he was still waiting for a ship where he could use his skills as a radarman. He was assigned a series of duties on the *Morris* and hated every task. He cooked and cleaned the vessel. Riker also hated the man he reported to, a 50-year-old ignoramus who hated all educated sailors. He got off the *Morris*, and right after he did, it was hit by a Japanese aircraft in the number two gun-handling room. The sailors in this area of the ship were killed. This was the third time he had narrowly escaped death. Riker had worked in that area of the vessel when it went to general quarters and was under attack.

Upon his return to Pearl Harbor, he found that the USS *Hughes* needed a radarman. He jumped at the chance. He wrote a letter to his father telling him the good news.

Riker had finally found the home he wanted, and just like Oliver Jones, he loved the USS *Hughes*. He became a lifelong friend of Bradley, a married Texan six years older than him. Bradley was also a radarman on the USS *Hughes*. Their friendship would last the rest of their lives.

Much of the equipment on the USS *Hughes* was new and secret. However, many on the ship knew quite a bit about it. Not only did they have radar, but they also had sonar to see beneath the waves. This was handy in searching for submarines, but the sonar also frequently detected whales, larger schools of fish, and dolphins. Bradley recalled that it was hard to discern if what they detected was a submarine, a school of fish, or something else. "The sound would bounce off them and give us false readings." Due to the height of the mast, the radar would detect ships and planes at long distances. American planes also sent the "IFF" signal: "Identification Friend or Foe." That way, if a plane did not correctly respond with a radio signal back to the USS *Hughes*, they knew a Japanese plane was approaching them.

Bradley reported:

When we first received radar aboard the USS *Hughes,* no one knew how to operate it. We taught ourselves how it was used. We created coordinates using a fixed point called "Point Molly" as a reference point. After that, we could locate and identify other contacts. My shipmates in the communications room were almost in a different WWII than everyone else. We lived in our little world in the radar shack and were constantly alert for danger.

We were more aware of the dangers we were facing as enemy planes were approaching or just being nearby. Malcolm and I saved many ships one day while we were docked to refuel off Samar. We kept hearing chatter on the radio about some Japanese planes being spotted flying at a low altitude. Our ships were refueling then and were sitting ducks for the attacking Japanese planes. We used their coordinates and determined the planes were headed right for us. I sounded the General Quarters alarm, and the ships cut the fuel hoses and backed away from the docks. The USS *Hughes* helped fight off the bogies with the others, and 500 lives were saved that day. I kept a copy of the radar chart we made that day to identify the attacking Japanese planes and took it home with me from the war.

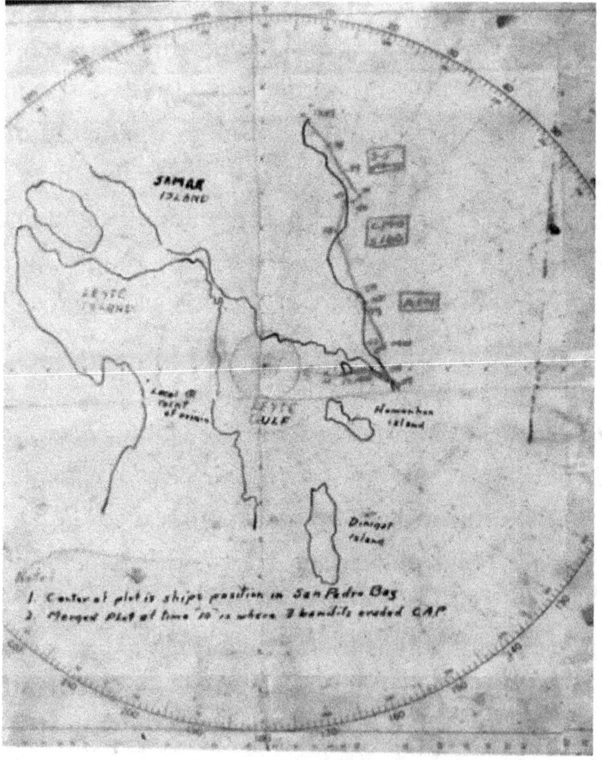

Chester Bradley kept the radar track log that saved over 500 sailors one day off Samar. Chester Bradley collection.

Riker and Bradley didn't like the morning shift from 4:00 to 8:00 AM. It was challenging to get back to sleep. Working in the cramped area sometimes made them seasick, as the ship would roll as much as 30 degrees from side to side. If they got sick, they had to clean it up themselves. There were no seasickness pills back then, but the sailors knew the nausea would usually pass quickly if they went outside, even in heavy weather, and breathed the fresh air. They couldn't afford to get anything on the sensitive equipment that everyone's lives depended on.

The crew generally got along well, but on one occasion, a crewman in the radar room was a bully. Once the team had had enough of him, they went to the communications officer, who threw the troublesome crewman off the ship at a foreign port. They did not see him again for two months. Bradley said, "Some guys got in trouble when we were in port. I once told another sailor that he wasn't even in the war as he spent so much time in the brig after being caught fighting!"

Although unthinkable today, Bradley and Riker noted that six black crewmen waited on the officers, cleaned their quarters, and were segregated from the rest of the crew. Three groups were separated: officers, men, and black sailors.

Like others, Bradley and Riker recalled eating very well most of the time when they could get resupplied. The food and cooks on the USS *Hughes* were excellent, depending on what was available. But at times, they ate what was on hand. "The worst was the Australian rabbit, fried like a chicken. They cut it in the middle, and you got either the front or the back half. It was unpleasant." But most of the time, the food was good, and this helped morale. Bradley remembered they even had an ice cream maker aboard the USS *Hughes,* a popular addition to a ship at war in the hot Pacific Ocean.

CHAPTER EIGHT

"A TERRIBLE RESOLVE"

Japanese Admiral Isoroku Yamamoto, a few hours before
his death, saluting Japanese naval pilots at Rabaul, April 18, 1943.
Official Japanese photo - public domain.

After the American aircraft carriers survived the attack at Pearl Harbor on December 7, 1941, Japanese Admiral Isoroku Yamamoto, who planned the attack, wrote in his diary, "I fear all we have done is to awaken a sleeping giant and fill him with a terrible resolve."

America wasn't off to a great start in the war. Pearl Harbor was a significant defeat. America lacked large ships, aircraft, and adequately trained men, and Americans didn't have much combat experience. Even a tiny increase in these areas could be a significant improvement. What the United States did have was virtually unlimited manufacturing resources.

Shifting into a wartime economy was a top priority. It was a new way of doing business. The employment opportunities as the country emerged from the Great Depression presented jobs and wealth that many Americans had thought might never return. Extra work hours replaced soup lines in the country's heartland. Young men signed up to fight in Europe and the Pacific, so much so that women soon entered the workplace in large numbers, a significant change in American culture. Women were just as efficient at the jobs that once were solely reserved for men. Their motto was "We can do it!"

Japanese Imperial Admiral Onishi, who would soon be director of air operations, faced the opposite problem and was acutely aware of it. At the beginning of the war, he had the best pilots in the world. The Zero fighter, although without armor to protect the pilot, was lighter and more maneuverable than the American fighters. His pilots were experienced after fighting in China and were supremely confident in their skills. However, they were limited in number, and a long war would exhaust the reserves of planes, pilots, and aircraft carriers.

The whole point of the attack on Pearl Harbor was to eliminate the American Pacific Fleet, particularly the aircraft carriers. But the carriers had been out to sea on the day of the attack and were now roaming the Pacific Ocean, threatening Japanese advances in the Marshall Islands.

In retribution for the Pearl Harbor attack, America had sailed her aircraft carriers close enough to Japan to launch an attack on Tokyo. Emperor Hirohito could hear the bombs drop from his home in the Imperial Palace and was whisked to safety. The Japanese militarists had promised that nothing like this could ever happen. The American "Doolittle" raid did minor damage but was a blow to the Japanese and a massive boost to Americans back home.

The flyers from this daring American mission were to land in China. However, the planes were launched after the American aircraft carriers were detected far from their initial launching point. After launching so early for this raid, most pilots expected they would not survive, and they did not have enough fuel after the attack to reach their intended landing bases in China. Many crashed into the ocean. The Chinese, who were already suffering from brutal repression at the hands of the Japanese Army, paid a terrible price for helping the downed American flyers. A staggering 250,000 Chinese citizens were executed for assisting the American flyers who survived the raid on Japan.

Admirals Yamamoto and Onishi were deeply troubled by the failure to eliminate the aircraft carriers at Pearl Harbor. With the Doolittle raid, they had demonstrated their worth against Japanese targets. Yamamoto and Onishi knew it was only a matter of time before America, with its almost limitless industrial capacity, would begin to make more of them.

On December 7, 1941, the Americans only had three heavy aircraft carriers in the Pacific: the *Enterprise, Lexington,* and *Saratoga.* It wasn't until March of 1942 that America's newest heavy aircraft carrier, the USS *Hornet,* would enter the waters of the Pacific. The Imperial Japanese Navy started the Pacific War with ten aircraft carriers. Americans would class six of Japan's first-line aircraft carriers, the *Akagi, Kaga, Soryu, Hiryu, Shokaku,* and *Zuikaku,* as "heavy" aircraft carriers. America only had three in that class, giving Japan a two-to-one superiority.

Japan would build six more aircraft carriers in the next three years, while the Americans would make 17. However, aircraft carriers were only part of the equation. Planes and pilots were equally important. Japan was at its peak of pilot deployment and aircraft production. In the next four years, America would produce 297,000 aircraft for combat operations.

In an extended war, Japan could never hope to defeat America in the race to recruit and train men or the race to build ships and aircraft. Japan staked its hopes on the inventory it had on hand. Japan needed a short war. Pilots were ordered to keep flying until the war ended or they died in combat. This would prove to be a fatal error. Americans implemented a different policy. Their air crews would fly a set number of combat missions and then be shipped home to be instructors at flight schools and train new pilots. Newly minted American fighter pilots were trained by veterans of actual combat. New Japanese pilots were being trained at regular flight schools not run by combat veterans. Simply put, Japan could only afford to lose a few ships, planes, or pilots.

Japan also staked its fortunes on a concept that was proven wrong repeatedly. They believed in Japanese racial superiority over all other nations, something common among fanatical nationalist regimes. They were convinced Americans could never have their level of bravery or commitment to battle, even unto death. But American sailors and soldiers were just as brave as the Japanese, albeit more cautious in how they risked and spent their lives.

As America began to recruit and train men to serve on the USS *Hughes*, she went to sea again against the backdrop of the country ramping up to fight a protracted war. Throughout February and early March 1942, the USS *Hughes* had set out with a task force as part of the *Yorktown* battle group. She was in almost constant combat as the Americans chased the ever-increasing Japanese advances throughout the Pacific. Their mission was to slow these advances and land American troops for shore combat on hot, humid, desolate islands. Five other destroyers were in the contingent with her. Three of the five, the *Sims, Hamann,* and *Walke,* would soon be sunk and lying at the bottom of the Pacific Ocean.

Protecting the American fleet was a hazardous duty. Every sailor on the USS *Hughes* was fully aware of their mission. Their job was to "screen" the capital ships, especially the aircraft carriers. That meant they were to sail along the outside edges of the larger ships and subject themselves to enemy aircraft before an attack could hit and sink the larger vessels. Their most important duty was to ensure Japanese attacks could not reach the carriers, even if it meant being sunk by a shell, torpedo, or bomb. It was like stepping before a bullet to keep it from hitting someone else, and they always did this in combat. The American "tin can" destroyers were often little more than inconvenient barriers for the Japanese.

CHAPTER NINE

"THE IDEA STRAINED HIS INTELLECTUAL CAPACITY"

Albert Speer and Nazis officers after being captured in Europe by the Allies May 23, 1945. UK Forces public domain photo.

In 1942, President Roosevelt and British Prime Minister Churchill were deeply concerned that Germany had the scientific capability to develop a nuclear bomb. Many of America's best theoretical nuclear physicists came from Germany. The Allies felt they had to beat the Germans in this race. They also wanted to use the bomb to destroy Berlin and Tokyo. It wasn't until years later that they learned that this fear about Germany was unfounded, mainly due to Hitler's lack of primary intelligence and short attention span. In the end, it was discovered that Japan was far closer to creating an atomic bomb than Germany, which was a complete surprise to the Americans. Japanese physicists had been making significant progress toward the concept of nuclear weapons.

In February 1942, as Robert Oppenheimer raced to create a team for the American bomb development, Hitler appointed Albert Speer as Reich minister of armaments and war production. Essentially in charge of the development of a German atomic bomb, Speer met with German nuclear physicists, and they informed him that building such a bomb was not only possible but probable with the expenditure of the proper funds to construct the infrastructure to create the necessary fissionable materials.

Speer met with Hitler and discussed the findings. "Hitler had sometimes spoken to me about the possibility of an atom bomb, but the idea strained his intellectual capacity. He was also unable to grasp the revolutionary nature of nuclear physics." Speer added, "Occasionally, however, he joked that the scientists, in their unworldly urge to lay bare all the secrets under heaven, might someday set the globe on fire." Hitler's childlike intellect kept the Americans and British from any real risk of a German atomic bomb. Fortunately for the Allies, Hitler and the Nazis had little use for intellectuals, particularly Jewish scientists.

On March 9, 1942, presidential nuclear adviser Vannevar Bush wrote to President Roosevelt, "I cannot indicate the status of the enemy program," but at the same time, he reported that assessments were coming in that the American program might deliver a bomb of staggering proportions, a single blast exceeding that of two thousand tons of TNT, which proved to be low once the program got underway. The first blast would be equal to 17,000 tons of TNT.

Robert Oppenheimer, ever the poet, saw scientific physics and mathematics as universal truths and the building blocks of the universe itself: "It is a profound and necessary truth that the deep things in science are not found because they are useful; they are found because it was possible to find them." He knew it was only a matter of time before the atom's secrets would be discovered and used. Oppenheimer was brilliant and deeply intuitive. Fellow Berkeley Professor Haakon Chevalier said of him, "He was always, without seeming effort, aware of, and responsive to, everyone in the room, and was constantly anticipating unspoken wishes."

Oppenheimer was born to wealthy German-Jewish parents and grew up in New York. He watched what was happening in Germany and Europe in the 1930s. "I had a continuing, smoldering fury about the treatment of the Jews in Germany. I had relatives there and was later to help extract them and bring them to this country." Although any sane person could not help but have reservations about using nuclear bombs on other humans, Oppenheimer was resigned to the fact that an atomic bomb would become a reality simply because it could and thought it better that Americans built and controlled them. He would have no qualms about using it on Hitler's Third Reich.

General Groves considered several scientists before settling on Oppenheimer to lead the project to build a bomb. The intelligence establishment opposed the choice, but Groves told the Military Policy Committee, "After much discussion, I asked each member to give me the name of a man who would be a better choice. In a few weeks, it became clear that we would not find a better man, so Oppenheimer was asked to undertake the task."

Groves needed a remote site where no one could discover the work. Oppenheimer knew of a location from his earlier years, high up in the mountains of New Mexico, an old boy's school. It was at a place called Los Alamos in the Sangre de Cristo Mountains (Spanish for the "Blood of Christ"), on a plateau at 7,200 feet. No one would find and spy on it, and there was no location from where it could be seen from above. On a personal note, Oppenheimer also wanted the area to have an excellent horseback riding view. The Los Alamos Boy's Ranch satisfied Oppenheimer's needs. Groves purchased the land, school, and improvements, including 62 horses, two tractors, two trucks, 50 saddles, eight hundred cords of firewood, 25 tons of coal, and 1,600 books for $440,000. The top nuclear scientists were recruited and brought to this remote and seemingly desolate location from densely populated cities and universities. They were not happy.

Oppenheimer once wrote, "My two great loves are physics and desert country. It is a pity they cannot be combined." Now they were, but not everyone agreed on the location. Coming from the urban cities, Leo Szilard, who authored the letter from Einstein to President Roosevelt, said, "Nobody could think straight in a place like that. Everyone who goes there will go crazy." But Groves loved it. The solitude and isolation were everything he felt necessary for secrecy. There were also a few distractions from the scientists' work.

Oppenheimer then began to recruit his colleagues from universities around the country. Some came, and some did not. Military secrecy was abhorrent to many in the scientific field who were used to free-flowing information between colleagues. Others did not like the idea of such seclusion. A few, like I. I. Rabi, who was already working on the development of radar at MIT, had concerns about the bomb itself. He told Oppenheimer he was concerned that "the

Robert Oppenheimer and General Leslie Groves at Ground Zero of the nuclear test site. Digital Photo Archive, Department of Energy, courtesy of AIP Emilio Serge Visual Archives.

culmination of three centuries of physics would result in a weapon of such destructive power." These comments foreshadowed some deep concerns by other physicists later in the project.

But many did come, and Oppenheimer got Groves to gradually reduce the security and compartmentalization requirements on different scientific tasks and replace them with a free flow of information. But the hot, dry summers and cold, snowy winters burdened many scientists and their wives, leading Groves, with his characteristic temper, to be annoyed at one of the results of such seclusion. Oppenheimer wanted scientists to bring their families with them because he thought they would be happier and more productive. He convinced Groves that scientists would not come to the remote, high desert location to work on a secret project for an unspecified amount of time without the comfort of their families.

The average age of these recruits was 25, and many were just out of college. After bringing their wives to such a lonely place, 208 babies were born at Los Alamos during the early part of the war, and nearly a thousand would arrive between 1943 and 1949.

Said historian Jon Hunter, author of *Inventing Los Alamos*, "These were a lot of young couples, and young couples do what young couples do, and all of a sudden, there was a baby boom at the maternity ward in Los Alamos." He added, "Groves wasn't too happy about that. He thought it took away from the mission, at least of the hospital. Now they have to have pediatrics, and they had to have childbirths, and all that."

Groves believed all this sex and childbirth was wasting time, taking away from the project, and wasting military resources at the hospital that he felt should be used for scientific research. He told Oppenheimer to do something about it. But Oppenheimer's wife was also pregnant, and he had little inclination to discuss sexual habits with his scientists. On top of that, it was a good deal. Rose Bethe, the wife of Nobel Prize-winning physicist Hans Bethe, recalled spending 83 cents a day for the hospital stay when her children were born.

A limerick swept through the community:

The General's in a stew.
He trusted you and you and you.
He'd thought you'd be scientific;
Instead, you're just prolific.
And what is he to do?

So, the scientific work on developing the first atomic bomb began earnestly at Los Alamos. At the same time, scientists and their wives had children at the Army's expense, Oppenheimer got to mix his favorite two things in life, science and the desert, and General Groves had to accept the consequences of scientists he deemed out of control having babies when he thought they should be spending time on critical atomic work. The American effort to build an atomic bomb was underway.

Meanwhile, out in the Pacific, the USS *Hughes* was learning aircraft carrier combat techniques and testing itself in battles against the Japanese so that one day, the bombs built at Los Alamos could eventually be dropped on Japanese cities.

"SCRATCH ONE FLAT TOP!"

The Japanese aircraft carrier Shoho was torpedoed during attacks by U.S. Navy carrier aircraft in the late morning of 7 May 1942. US Navy photo.

In March 1942, things would grow even darker for the Americans. The Japanese began bombardments and landing of troops on the Islands of Salamaua and Lae in New Guinea, further entrenching their hold in the Pacific. The Americans decided that they must attack these locations to try again to slow the Japanese advances.

A task force was sent to carry out the mission, centered around the aircraft carriers *Lexington* and *Yorktown*. The USS *Hughes* was dispatched to cover carrier operations and intercept any Japanese forces that might move south to attack Port Moresby, the capital of Papua New Guinea.

For the next month, the USS *Hughes* would be on patrol with the *Yorktown* in the vicinity of New Caledonia, located in the southwest Pacific Ocean, approximately 746 miles east of Australia and 932 miles northwest of New Zealand. The island nation of Vanuatu lies to the northeast. During this mission, they made no contact with the enemy and returned to Pearl Harbor for resupply and refueling, where they arrived on April 17, 1942. The *Yorktown* left almost immediately for what would become known as the Battle of the Coral Sea.

The USS *Hughes*, which usually traveled with the *Yorktown* as part of Destroyer Squadron Two, was detached to escort the USS *Platte*, with badly needed fuel oil, to Noumea, thereby missing much of *Yorktown's* engagement.

Her sister ship, the destroyer *Sims*, DD-409, would not return from this fight and would be the first of many losses to Destroyer Squadron Two. Only four of the eleven ships initially assigned to this group would make it to the war's end.

The Japanese task force was sent to begin operations supporting moves toward taking Australia, a primary objective of the militarists. It consisted of an Imperial Japanese naval group to protect landing forces on Tulagi and Port Moresby and a strike force to attack Allied shipping in the Coral Sea. As strike force commander, Japanese Admiral Takeo Takagi commanded the aircraft carriers *Shokaku* and *Zuikaku*. The American destroyer USS *Sims* was escorting the USS *Neosho*, a *Cimarron*-class oiler providing crucial fuel to the big ships. The task force refueled on May 5 and 6, 1942. The USS *Sims* was then assigned to go with the *Neosho* to the next refueling mission.

But early in the morning of May 7, 1942, a search plane from the Japanese force sighted the oiler and destroyer and mistakenly reported them to Admiral Takagi as an American aircraft carrier and a heavy cruiser. Takagi was thrilled at the prospect of catching an American aircraft carrier off guard and ordered them to be attacked.

Initially, 78 Japanese aircraft from the two carriers searched high and low for the American carrier task force, but of course, they could not find them, as they were never there. They eventually gave up the search and returned to sink the USS *Sims* and *Neosho*. At 9:30 AM, 15 high-level bombers attacked the ships but did not hit them. At 10:38, ten more Japanese planes attacked the USS *Sims*, but she evaded the nine bombs the Japanese dropped on her location. A third attack against the two ships by 36 Japanese Val dive bombers hit them both. The *Neosho* was severely crippled and burning aft due to seven direct hits and one suicide bomber that dived into her deck.

Three 250-kilogram (551-pound) bombs hit the destroyer, causing devastating damage. Two exploded in her engine room, and within minutes, the ship buckled and began to break apart. Sailors recalled a colossal explosion that thrust the ship out of the water, but she quickly sank below the waves.

Survivors of the *Sims* were picked up and taken to the *Neosho*, and she was kept afloat for four more days until she was spotted by a British plane and an American seaplane. The destroyer USS *Henley* rescued the remaining 123 survivors from the two ships and sank the *Neosho* with fire from her deck guns.

The rest of the Battle of the Coral Sea, from May 4–8, 1942, became a significant battle between America and Australia against the Japanese Imperial Navy. This was the first time a major naval battle occurred where the ships never fired on each other. They never even saw each other. Aircraft sent by each fleet carried out the entire action. Radar and aircraft were replacing sailors with binoculars and range-finding equipment. The naval warfare era of ships shooting it out with each other was almost over.

In the Battle of the Coral Sea, the U.S. learned, via military intelligence and code-breaking, of the Japanese plan to invade and occupy Port Moresby and Tulagi in the Solomon Islands. Admiral Fletcher was dispatched to oppose those plans. The *Yorktown* surprised and sank several Japanese warships during the invasion of Tulagi.

The *Yorktown's* attack let the Japanese know that aircraft carriers, targets that they desperately wanted to find and sink, were now in the Coral Sea. On May 8, 1942, both sides finally located and attacked the other's carriers, leaving the Japanese carrier *Shokaku* damaged and the U.S. carrier *Lexington* mortally wounded and soon sunk. The *Yorktown* was in serious trouble after a bomb penetrated four decks and set her on fire. Japanese pilots returned and reported that they had sunk both American carriers, but the USS *Hughes* would see the USS *Yorktown* again as she limped back into Pearl Harbor.

Before losing the *Lexington*, the Americans sank the light Japanese carrier *Shoho*. Planes from *Yorktown* hit the carrier with 13 bombs and seven torpedoes. She went down at 11:35 AM with six hundred of her crew. In what would become a line often used in movies in the years to come, Lieutenant Commander Robert E. Dixon of *Lexington's* "Scouting Two" sent his classic report to the task force: "Scratch one flat top!"

Both sides of the battle suffered heavy aircraft losses, and each had carriers that were either sunk or damaged. The Japanese and Americans retreated from this battle to their bases of operations, fearing more losses and not knowing the status of the enemy. Although the battle was a tactical success for the Japanese, it was the first time they had been turned back from a land attack. A second, yet-unknown

A mushroom cloud rises after a heavy explosion on board the U.S. Navy aircraft carrier USS Lexington (CV-2), 8 May 1942. U.S. Navy photo.

impact of the Battle of the Coral Sea was the loss of aircraft and ship damage that would prevent the two Japanese carriers from participating in the battle at Midway Island.

The loss of the *Lexington* was devastating for the Americans. Initially, American Admiral Nimitz, commander of the Pacific Fleet, heard radio reports from the Japanese that two American carriers had been sunk. He was devastated but soon heard from Fletcher that his ships were damaged but okay and that a heavy Japanese aircraft carrier was in bad shape, but this was wrong. Nimitz sent Fletcher a message saying, "This was a red-letter day for our forces operating in the Coral Sea." It was a premature message. Nimitz was shocked by Fletcher's subsequent message about the loss of the *Lexington*. A staff officer observed that the news "was a terrible blow to Nimitz;

he was visibly jolted and muttered several times that Fletcher should have saved her."

The USS *Hughes* would soon return to battle at Midway Island with the *Yorktown*. She could not be blamed for losing the USS *Lexington* at the Battle of the Coral Sea. Her sailors were deeply saddened by the loss of her destroyer shipmates on the USS *Sims*. New sailors were now about to board the *Hughes*.

"DO YOU DESIRE EARNESTLY?"

Tsutomu Hayakawa, Yukio Araki, Takamasa Senda back row
Kaname Takahashi, Mitsuyoshi Takahashi. At 17, Yukio Araki is
the youngest known Kamikaze pilot to die in the war.
Photo taken 26 May 1945. Japan public domain.

Admiral Yamamoto was furious that the Japanese carriers had not pursued the American carriers and destroyed them all at the Battle of the Coral Sea. Upon hearing of their retreat, he ordered the Japanese fleet to reverse course and attack. The fleet initially followed these orders but quickly retired from the chase. The Americans were already gone. The *Lexington* was sunk, and the *Yorktown* was on its way back to Pearl Harbor, a heavily defended area that was, by now, almost impervious to attack.

Moreover, Yamamoto and Nimitz were both angry at the outcome of the battle they had not been able to see unfold. Historians of the naval battles of the Pacific between America and Japan have left out a vital feature of these engagements. In the past, naval battles had been fought by surface ships that could see each other. Radar and airplanes threw that playbook out the window. No one was safe if they were within the fuel reserves of an aircraft that could drop bombs or torpedoes. Yamamoto and Nimitz hadn't seen this in person, so they did not initially understand.

The commanders on the scene were unnerved by what they had seen. No one was safe anywhere, no matter what they did. It was the same for both sides. At any moment, survival was governed as much by luck and the clearing of a single cloud as anything else. Radar even began to remove that safety. The Japanese and the Americans retreated to lick their wounds and reassess how to fight the next battle.

One fact rose above all the rest: any fleet with functioning aircraft carriers would pose a threat that could destroy the enemy fleet in a single lucky encounter. Additionally, Japan knew now that America had demonstrated that it could use aircraft carriers to bomb Tokyo and even Emperor Hirohito's home.

Admiral Onishi had helped Yamamoto plan and execute the air attack on Pearl Harbor to destroy the American carriers, but this was no longer an option. Onishi was quite controversial among some of the fleet commanders. He was often impulsive and simple-minded, but as Captain Rikihei Inoguchi remarked, "However right or wrong his decisions might be, he never shirked responsibility for their consequences." When he sided with Admiral Nagano against the Pearl Harbor attack and the declaration of war against America, he shared the concept of the Americans' ability to build and deploy aircraft carriers quickly. This effort was now underway, and the clock was ticking. The only solution was to destroy the remaining American aircraft carriers in the Pacific and sue for peace.

Yamamoto chose what he planned to be the showdown in the Pacific, calling it Operation AF. American carriers would be tricked into a fight at Midway Island and then sunk by the Japanese fleet, but two damaged Japanese carriers from the Battle of the Coral Sea would not be sent to the battle.

Admiral Onishi was aware of the unofficial suicide attack on the *Neosho*. Some officers advocated for such attacks to be standard policy, but Onishi opposed them as immoral. Damaged planes on both sides had been used this way occasionally, and the tactic was not new. But Onishi began to understand that if the American carriers were not destroyed quickly, the islands of the Pacific would fall to them. He began considering directed suicide attacks if the coming battle at Midway Island failed.

In 1941, Onishi was named chief of staff to Japanese Air Fleet Vice Admiral Eikichi Katagiri, and he began to develop the concept of kamikaze air attacks to defend Japan from American heavy bombers. He did not know that America was building a new atomic bomb. If he had, Onishi might have begun these efforts much sooner. New pilots would be screened to gauge their interest in joining this mission.

Onishi created and documented two systems for assessing pilots. Experienced pilots were needed for carrier operations at sea. They were not subject to the new system, but young naval aviation cadets were asked if they were willing to fly suicide missions. College graduates were deemed less likely to agree to such a concept, as they generally knew more about the world and had not been so profoundly brainwashed as less-educated and often less-advantaged Japanese men off the streets. So, to get them to join, college graduates who entered the Naval Aviation Corps had to complete a survey. The question it asked was straightforward:

> ***"Do you desire earnestly/wish/do not wish***
> ***to be involved in the Kamikaze attacks?"***

College recruits had to circle one of the three choices. Surveys had to be completed in front of a Japanese recruiting officer, and college graduates were often forced to circle the proper answer. The appropriate response was always "desire earnestly." Most college graduates marked this selection.

Japanese young men were not all that different from those in America. They all had families and dreams for the future. None of them wanted to die. They all felt patriotic devotion to their country based on their beliefs and community standards. Public indoctrination was critical to getting young Japanese men to hate Americans enough to volunteer for this new mission.

American newsreels were adept at forging public opinion. Movies were a top diversion during the war, featuring short news stories and featurettes. One of the most popular in 1943 was the original *Batman* serial. It was nothing like today's movies. Batman battled the evil Japanese agents of Emperor Hirohito.

The original villain was Dr. Daka, a secret agent of the Japanese Imperial government, played by J. Carrol Nash, who also went on to play Charlie Chan. Although the serial first appeared in 1943, the public was already aware of the power of the atom—the evil Dr. Daka planned to steal an American city's radium supply to fuel his

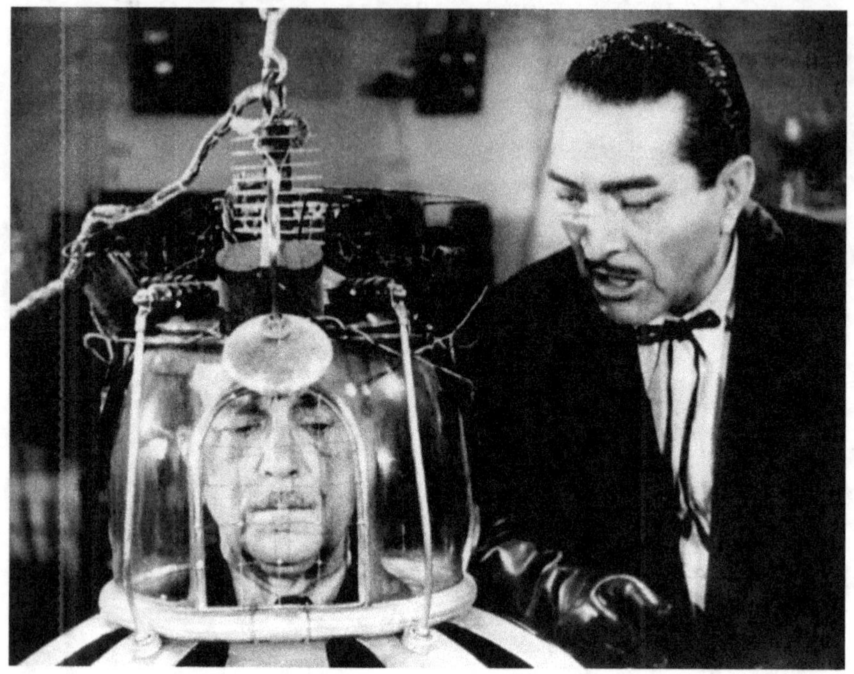

The evil Dr. Daka uses nuclear power to create weapons and turn
Americans into Japanese Zombie slaves in 1943. Alamy licensed image.

invention. The beam of his hand-held ray gun could dissolve anything it hit. In truth, this was close to what was being developed
at Los Alamos at the time. Dr. Daka was a sinister "Nipponese,"
adept at turning Americans into zombies and making them Japanese
Imperial slaves. Batman referred to them as "little yellow men." Two
early episodes were titled "Mark of the Zombies" and "Slaves of the
Rising Sun."

This was not far from the mark, as the Japanese militarists, led
by Prime Minister Tojo, would have made most, if not all, Americans
into slaves. These movie stereotypes were intended to get Americans
to believe that the Japanese people were a sinister and dishonest race
that needed killing.

These propaganda efforts kept American civilians in the fight. Americans needed to hate the Japanese enough to go to war and kill them, but the war would end someday. There were a lot of Americans of Japanese descent who were in the United States military, fighting Germans in Europe. Japanese were the neighbors and friends of many American families. Their kids attended school together. America couldn't hate the Japanese forever.

Some military leaders of the United States, like General Curtis LeMay, said they had few qualms about killing Japanese civilians. When he later led fire-bombing raids on Toyoko, he remarked, "We scorched and boiled and baked to death more people in Tokyo on that night of March 9-10 than went up in vapor at Hiroshima and Nagasaki combined." This ended up not being true since far more people would die of the effects of radiation poisoning than died due to the firebombing of Japanese cities. Still, his comments reflected a widespread belief among many Americans that all Japanese people deserved to die.

This thinking led to the internment of Americans of Japanese descent in detention camps for the duration of the war. No one could know how it would all end and how the world would move forward after the war if America won. For now, it was about the next battle and the newsreels back home in American theaters.

That next battle in the Pacific would be Midway Island, where a new group of sailors reported to the USS *Hughes* for action.

"IF THERE WERE JAP SURVIVORS, WE DIDN'T BOTHER TO LOOK FOR THEM"

The USS Yorktown (CV-5) in Pearl Harbor Naval Shipyard, 29 May 1942, receiving repairs for damage from the Battle of the Coral Sea. U.S. Navy photo.

Seaman Ollie Stine joined the USS Hughes at Pearl Harbor on May 26, 1942. Seamen were strictly prohibited from keeping documents or journals of any kind for fear that they would fall into enemy hands, but a few did keep diaries, Stine being one of them.

Ollie Stine's daughter, Laurie Finger, said of her father:

My dad was born in New Orleans, Louisiana, in 1924. He and my mother grew up around the corner from each other. My dad's father was a telegraph operator, so during the Depression, my dad's family was "well off," but my mother's family was destitute. My dad, my Uncle Charlie, and Uncle Manuel went hunting and fishing, and whatever they caught or killed, my mom's family got to eat. If they didn't get anything, my mom's family ate rice or, sometimes, nothing. My dad and uncles hunted rabbits, ducks, deer, squirrels, and alligators. Once, they killed an owl. My mom's sister cooked it, but it didn't taste good, and they couldn't eat it.

"My dad was on a hunting trip with his "uncle" Chips (Chips was a good friend of his father's and not his uncle) on December 7, 1941. My dad said they stopped for a bite on the way home and heard the news. When he got home, he told his parents her wanted to enlist. He was only 17, and my grand-mother said, "No." We were told that his father convinced his mother to sign as he would be 18 years old that January, but there was some thought that he may have forged his mother's signature.

My dad told us several stories about his experiences in the war, but the following were my favorites. He said when he enlisted and finally got out of boot camp and training and got on the ship, he "couldn't wait to kill some Japs." He was bored with training and routine days at sea. Once he saw his first action in the battle of Midway, my dad said he thought, "Go away Japs, go away." He was not a coward, but once he saw war and experienced it himself, he didn't want to see it anymore.

Another story was that one day, he was trying to climb a ladder from one deck to the other, and another guy was trying to come down the same ladder. They both saw each other, and they both got off, then they both got back on, then they both got back off. This happened several times before my dad lost his very short temper and reached up and pulled the other guy down by the ankles. Once the guy stood up, my dad punched him. Then the guy decked my dad. My dad was only about 5 ft 8 in and 18 years old, and the guy was 6 ft 2 or 3, broad-shouldered, and in his mid-twenties. The man's name was Eugene Erpenbeck from California. The Executive Officer fussed at them both for fighting but told Erpenbeck shame on him for "decking this kid." His punishment (job) was that he was responsible for the kid from now on. My dad wasn't happy about being referred to as a "kid," but what could he say? So the both of them, though initially not happy about the "punishment," eventually became best friends—they even stayed in touch after the war. "Erp," as he was known to us, was Catholic (as was my dad), and my dad said from that point Erp made him go to Mass at every opportunity. That wasn't too demanding for my dad, except at the beginning—he didn't like being told what to do—especially by a guy who decked him. My dad said that "Erp" saved him many times when he got into trouble.

My dad was a torpedo man but had duty on the bridge and drove the ship. He said they let him drive the ship because they knew he could drive a boat—but I don't know if he was joking—my brother said dad wasn't joking. On the day the *Hughes* was bombed and hit by a Kamikaze (December 10, 1944, in Leyte Gulf), my dad was on the bridge. He received a commendation for "cool courage under fire." At one point, he ran down to Erp's gun as Erp was coming out—he had blood and intestines all over his clothes. My dad said his heart caught in his throat, and he said, "Oh God, Erp, you're hurt." But Erp said, "It's not mine, Ollie"—they hugged, and my dad cried.

In his diary, Stine recalls, "Reported aboard the USS *Hughes* (DD410) for duty. I got squared away with my bunk and locker and became acquainted with members of the torpedo gang. This ship participated in the Gilbert Islands and Marshall's raid, operating with the U.S.S. *Yorktown,* so I should see some of the action I'm craving."

May 28, 1942, Stine noted, "Got underway from Pearl—destination unknown. Rumors have it we will deliver planes from *Yorktown* to Midway Island. Forces consist of *Yorktown,* Heavy Cruisers

Seaman Ollie Stine and his wife. Ollie Stine family collection.

Portland and *Astoria*, Destroyers *Hughes, Morris, Anderson,* and *Hamman.*" The next day, Saturday, May 30, 1942, Stine recorded, "At sea, very rough today. Destination still unknown." But on Monday, June 1, 1942, their mission became clear: "At sea, read the captain's night order book, and now I know why we're out here. We are cruising Northeast of Midway in anticipation of a Japanese attack on Midway or Hawaii." Seaman Ollie Stine was about to see enough battle action at sea to last a lifetime.

Admiral Yamamoto had a well-laid-out trap for the American carriers: take Midway Island by surprise and then attack the American carriers at will with this new base. Unbeknownst to the Japanese Imperial Command, the plan had a fatal flaw. That flaw was a man named Joseph John Rochefort. Although a naval officer, he was one of the most un-military-looking men ever to serve in the United States Navy.

Rochefort was good friends with Edwin T. Layton, a fellow cryptanalyst who had traveled with him to Tokyo some years earlier to learn Japanese. By 1941, Layton was the chief intelligence officer to the then commander of the Pearl Harbor Fleet, Husband E. Kimmel. As commander, Kimmel was held responsible for the surprise attack by Japan on December 7, 1941. Part of this failure centered on Layton and Rochefort being denied access to critical intercepted Japanese diplomatic documents that could have foretold the attack.

Rochefort and Layton became expert codebreakers and were assigned to the intelligence division at Pearl Harbor to decipher a Japanese code called JN35. This was the system by which the Japanese encoded and decoded their messages. It was thought impossible for anyone else to read. Rochefort hand-selected the staff at this office and recruited many of the best-known cryptanalysts in the business.

Rochefort, simply put, was a slob. Although brilliant, he didn't like military discipline and was despised by his superiors. The

Joseph Rochefort & Edwin Layton of Naval Intelligence Service.
Unclassified National Security Agency and U.S. Navy photos.

cryptanalysts worked 12-hour shifts and seldom came out of their basement office for days, even to take a bath or put on clean clothes. Often wearing bathrobes and slippers, he and his group were a constant irritation to other naval officers. But after the colossal failure of intelligence that led to the Pearl Harbor attack, no one wanted to upset the men who might discover the next Japanese offensive.

For a while, after much of the earlier JN25 code was broken, daily intelligence provided information about Japanese operations critical to the war effort. Then the Japanese changed the code, and the code breakers returned to step one.

Rochefort and his team cracked the new code, even if only tiny bits here and there. While the Americans and Japanese were reeling from the Battle of the Coral Sea and trying to find a path to destroy each other's aircraft carriers, the team came upon a thin piece of evidence that seemed to indicate an upcoming operation the Japanese called "Objective AF." As Rochefort considered other intelligence concerning the movement of Japanese naval resources, he began to believe that AF was Midway Island, where the Japanese would sink the American carriers. His superiors were skeptical.

The cryptanalysts developed a plan to test the idea that AF was, in fact, Midway Island. Midway Island sent a message in the open indicating their freshwater plant had failed. The Japanese intercepted the message. Due to this reported deficit, the Japanese took the bait and ordered the invasion fleet destined for AF to load additional fresh water. This proved that AF was Midway Island. The Americans determined that the raid would occur on either June 4 or 5, 1942. Rather than sailing into a trap, they would go there ahead of time, lie in wait, and ambush the Japanese at Midway Island.

By Wednesday, June 3, 1942, Ollie Stine on the USS *Hughes* could see the fighting tops and the masts of the carriers *Hornet* and *Enterprise* just over the horizon. The deadly game of waiting for the enemy would not last long, but on June 3, 1942, the Americans needed to know exactly where the Japanese attack fleet was. They sent out scout planes.

Japanese Admiral Nagumo was sailing his strike force down from the north. This force would be followed by an invasion fleet that would take over and occupy the island and airfield for Japanese use. But Nagumo was not necessarily the best choice to lead the force, and many of his contemporaries had reservations about him being in command. Many thought he was physically and mentally past his prime. He was also a relic from the past regarding his understanding of air operations—his expertise was in destroyer and torpedo techniques. He did not have up-to-date knowledge of carrier air-attack operations.

Admiral Nishizo Tsukahara recalled, "Nagumo was an old school officer, a specialist of torpedo and surface maneuvers... He did not know the capability and potential of naval aviation." Yet the battle at Midway Island was intended to be the most significant clash between aircraft carriers in history. Nagumo, who initially opposed the attack at Pearl Harbor and the declaration of war against the United States, had already made a severe tactical error in not launching a third attack at Pearl Harbor. As Nagumo sailed his striking force south, the USS *Hughes* and the American carriers, vastly outnumbered by the Japanese, were waiting. The Japanese were shocked to find the *Yorktown* had been repaired after extensive damage at the Battle of the Coral Sea and was with the American carriers *Hornet* and *Enterprise* at Midway Island. The USS *Hughes* would be at her side.

Both forces sent out scout planes to search for enemy carriers. Meanwhile, the Japanese sent out small attack forces to divert the Americans by striking Australia and Alaska. However, the United States was sure of the pending attack at Midway. Planes from the *Hornet* located the Japanese main force. Luck favored the Americans as the battle began.

Thursday, June 4, 1942, Ollie Stine wrote:

We went to general quarters just before dawn. The *Hornet* and *Enterprise* have left us. The Jap force was in range of our planes, and *Yorktown* sent off her dive bombers and torpedo planes to attack them. At 10:00 a.m., the signal "Prepare to repel aircraft" was hoisted, and the *Yorktown* sent off her fighters to intercept them. Shortly afterward, we spotted two columns of smoke on the horizon made by Jap planes that our fighters had shot down. The Jap dive bombers came in over the *Astoria*, who opened fire and shot down two almost immediately. Then all ships commenced firing with everything they had.

As the Americans attacked the Japanese carriers, the Japanese planes located and began their attack on the American carrier *Yorktown*. The USS *Hughes* was screening her.

While Admiral Nagumo's planes bombed Midway Island, the American torpedo planes reached *Akagi, Kaga,* and *Soryu.* This was a devastating event for Nagumo, who did not know that the Americans were waiting for him. At first, he thought the planes were from Midway Island, but soon it became clear they were coming from American aircraft carriers. Nagumo was almost paralyzed with fear and began to make a series of fateful and terrible mistakes. He went back and forth about what to do and how to arm his planes. Bombs or torpedoes? Was he fighting land-based planes or aircraft from carriers? The response would be entirely different. If the carrier-based dive bombers got to his aircraft carriers, they would be in peril.

Minutes would determine the battle's outcome, but as time ticked by, Nagumo's decks were covered with fully fueled and armed aircraft. Highly experienced officers around him urged him to act; he seemed indecisive and unable to grasp what was happening. The other commanders and pilots knew what would happen if American dive bombers got to the carriers and caught them with their fully loaded and fueled aircraft on deck. The Japanese aircraft would provide the means for their own destruction if this happened.

Before the arrival of dive bombers, the Japanese would face American torpedo planes. However, the American torpedoes had a severe flaw. Many of the planes were shot down before launching their torpedoes, and many of the torpedoes launched failed to detonate.

The Japanese fighters protecting the carriers descended to water level to defeat these American planes. This left the skies above the aircraft carriers unprotected, and it took time for a fighter to get back to altitude. While Nagumo decided to change all the weapons on his planes, a lengthy process, the American dive bombers arrived at 20,000 feet above the carriers. The pilots were stunned to find a lack of proper fighter aircraft cover and the Japanese decks loaded with planes and bombs, just waiting to be ignited.

The Japanese heavy cruiser Mikuma, photographed from
a USS Enterprise (CV-6) Douglas SBD-3 Dauntless during
the afternoon of 6 June 1942. U.S. Navy photo.

This also violated the orders of Admiral Yamamoto, who told
Nagumo not to take such a risk. Yamamoto was concerned that they
might have been wrong about the location of the American carriers
and wanted to keep a force on board the ship to attack them should
the American carriers arrive. But in this confusing process, Nagumo
ordered all his planes to be stripped of those weapons and re-fitted
with bombs to bomb Midway Island once again, a fateful mistake.

Looking skyward, Nagumo saw the horizon filled with American Douglass SBD Dauntless dive bombers. The destruction of the
Japanese carriers was at hand. The American planes carried five-hun-
dred- to thousand-pound armor-piercing bombs with delayed fuses

so they would detonate once inside a ship. They could dive at an astonishing 80 degrees and were challenging to shoot down. The dive bombers descended on the aircraft carriers at four hundred feet per second, dropped their deadly load on target, and pulled out of the dive at only 1,500 feet.

Soon, all three carriers were engulfed in flames. Standing on the bridge of the *Akagi*, Nagumo was nearly killed when a mortally wounded American plane almost crash-landed on the bridge. He went into shock as he saw the destruction. His officers urged him to give the order to abandon the sinking ship and transfer his command to another vessel, but he muttered to himself about it not being time. Finally, with tears in his eyes, Nagumo ordered all hands to abandon the *Akagi*.

The Japanese fleet's flagship was lost, but the battle was far from over. The Japanese forces had located the Americans, who were at risk of a similar fate. Both commanders were unaware of what was happening to the other in this new type of war.

Back on board the USS *Hughes*, Stine wrote in his diary, "The noise was deafening! I was knocked off my feet by the muzzle blast from Gun 2. The 'Big Y' [the *Yorktown*] turned and twisted like an eel, but she couldn't dodge all the bombs. Most of the Jap planes were shot down before they reached the carrier, but two got in and made direct hits, which stopped the carrier."

The USS *Hughes* was in the thick of trying to save the USS *Yorktown*. Seaman Ollie Stine wrote, "One plane dropped its bomb just astern of the carrier and followed it into the sea. Another crashed on her flight deck just forward of the Island, killing the crews of two 1.1 batteries there. Two Jap lives for 14 Americans, not so good. In about twenty minutes, *Yorktown* got underway again. It made fifteen knots when Jap torpedo planes were spotted coming in. Our fighters were on the job and shot down several before they got in. The rest attacked the carrier from all sides."

The USS Hughes is just alongside the mortally wounded
Yorktown at Midway Island 4 June 1942. U.S. Navy photo.

The Japanese planes seemed to be coming from everywhere. The USS *Hughes* helped protect *Yorktown* and shot down Japanese planes, but too many were getting through the screen to save her. Stine noted, "One cut in across our bow, and we cheered when he burst into flames and hit the water. None of the torpedo planes got away, but they had hit *Yorktown* with two fish [torpedoes], and she was abandoned." The *Yorktown* seemed lost.

Stine added, "We picked up 400 survivors. About this time, the *Yorktown's* planes returned from attacking the Japs. Some circled the carrier, but others tried to find and land on the *Hornet* and *Enterprise*. Many of them were low on gas and crashed into the sea." The sailors on the USS *Hughes* did not yet know the fate of the *Hornet* and *Enterprise*. All hands were painfully aware of the consequences of what unfolded with the *Yorktown*. They could hardly believe it. But then a small glimmer of hope ran through the ship, noted by Stine: "It appears the *Yorktown* isn't going to sink, so we have been designated to guard her tonight, with orders to sink her if Jap ships approach."

The *Yorktown* could never be allowed to fall into enemy hands. The Japanese had the same policy. Friendly forces would sink a badly wounded ship before allowing this to happen. But then the news for the sailors on the USS *Hughes* turned very dark. All the other ships left to give chase to the enemy. The *Hughes* was suddenly ordered to go on a suicide mission of her own. Stine wrote, "We expect the Jap planes to return in the morning, and if they do—goodbye *Hughes!*" Without additional help, the crew of the USS *Hughes* could never hope to survive if the Japanese fleet and planes returned. The seamen spent the night expecting to die in battle sometime in the morning.

They waited by the stricken *Yorktown* throughout the warm and humid night, rolling slowly with the waves in the now lonely waters of the central Pacific Ocean. Their friends would not be around to save them. The Pacific Ocean, crowded not long ago with planes and ships, had become vacant and oddly quiet. American and Japanese ships, aircraft, and sailors now littered the bottom of the ocean below in over three miles of water. That depth is a cold grave for all who ended up there, a dark thought for seaman Ollie Stine that night. But with the light of dawn unfolding across the sky, things began to look up. The Americans could see no Japanese planes or ships on the horizon. Stine remarked, "Dawn broke with no air attack at sea, and we were relieved!" The daylight brought a new lease on life.

Stine wrote in his diary: "Friday, June 5th. We patrolled around the carrier all last night and noticed a light on her hanger deck, which kept flashing on and off. It was very eerie. At about 10:00, we noticed splashes in the water near the 'Y' [the *Yorktown*] and sent our boat to investigate. It was a wounded sailor firing a machine gun to attract our attention. We went aboard and removed several wounded men from her sick bay." This lucky sailor had been left on board but was seriously wounded. He managed to drag himself from deep inside the ship to the deck and found a machine gun to fire into the water in front of the USS *Hughes* to get her sailors' attention. A search discovered a second wounded sailor. Both were taken to the USS *Hughes*, along with a pilot found floating on the ocean in a life raft.

In the meantime, the Americans had located and sunk the fourth Japanese aircraft carrier. The *Enterprise* and *Hornet* survived the attack. Although devastating, the pending loss of *Yorktown* was far offset by the loss of four Japanese aircraft carriers. Equally alarming to the Japanese Imperial Navy was the loss of many aircraft and the best of their pilots. The battle of Midway Island was a staggering loss for the Japanese, one from which they would never fully recover. The attack force was defeated, and the invasion fleet turned back home. But the battle was far from over.

Direct orders were sent to the USS *Hughes* from the commander of Task Force 17:

050500 June 1942 DIRECT HUGHES STAND BY YORK-TOWN X DO NOT PERMIT ANYONE TO BOARD HER X SINK HER IF NECESSARY TO PREVENT CAP-TURE OR IF SERIOUS FIRE DEVELOPS X

The next day, on June 6, 1942, the USS *Hughes* got help protecting *Yorktown*. According to Stine, "Three more cans [American destroyers] and a tug joined us this morning. The tug took the *Yorktown* in tow. We were supposed to go alongside to assist in salvage operations, but the USS *Hammann* went instead."

Soon, the tell-tale crease across the water's top signaled doom for *Yorktown*. It was the wake of multiple Japanese torpedoes headed in their direction. They came from Japanese submarine *I-168*, commanded by Lieutenant Commander Yahachi Tanabe. There was no better prize for the captain of a Japanese submarine than an American aircraft carrier.

Ollie Stine wrote, "Late this evening, a Jap sub sneaked in and fired four torpedoes; two hit the *Yorktown,* and two hit the *Hammann,* which was tied up alongside, sinking her in about 45 seconds." The USS *Hammann* was a sister ship of the USS *Hughes* in Destroyer Squadron Two and now the second of their group to be sunk in combat. It was heartbreaking to the sailors of the USS *Hughes* to see her slip below the surface.

The only option left to the USS *Hughes* was to attack. Stine wrote, "All destroyers commenced dropping depth charges, and soon, the sub surfaced on the horizon, smoking badly. We steamed toward it at 35 knots and destroyed it with shellfire. If there were any Jap survivors, we didn't bother to look for them."

In truth, the USS *Hughes* did not sink *I-168* that day. Even though the *Monaghan* reported detecting the sounds of a sub breaking apart, the *I-168* was sunk the following year by another American submarine, the USS *Scamp,* on July 27, 1943, north of Rabaul in the Bismarck Sea. On that day, the *I-168* spotted the *Scamp* on the surface and fired a torpedo at her. The *Scamp* dove and avoided the incoming torpedo but soon came up to periscope depth and located the *I-168* still on the surface. The *Scamp* fired four torpedoes and sank the *I-168* with all 97 men on board. The Japanese confirmed this sinking and removed her from that October's list of active ships.

There is no doubt that the diary entries of Seaman Ollie Stine accurately described what he saw and felt, and the USS *Hughes* may have sunk a Japanese submarine that day, but it wasn't the *I-168,* the submarine that torpedoed the USS *Yorktown.*

In his diary, Seaman Ollie Stine recorded the final act of the Battle of Midway Island: "Sunday, June 7, 1941. Just before dawn, it became apparent that *Yorktown* would sink. She rolled over and, on her side, slowly, like a tired old lady, and as dawn broke, she slid beneath the waves. She was a fighting ship! We left soon after and headed for Pearl with what was left of Task Force 17. From the reports we have received, we have dealt the Japs a hard blow."

The remnants of the Japanese fleet returned to Japan. Admiral Nagumo, sailing back without his flagship, contemplated ritual suicide, but he was talked out of it by a friend. However, he never recovered from the devastating loss at the Battle of Midway Island, which haunted him for the rest of his life.

Cryptanalysts Joseph Rochefort and Edwin Layton were heroes for discovering the Japanese plot. Americans were overwhelmed at the prospect of an American naval victory at sea in a battle against the seemingly invincible Imperial Japanese Navy. The tide of the war seemed to be turning. With this crystallizing in the minds of the sailors on the USS *Hughes,* she sailed back into port at the now-tranquil waters of Pearl Harbor. They returned to a hero's welcome. Stine wrote, "Arrived at Pearl Harbor, and Task Force 17 was commended for excellent work at Midway. When we entered port, the flag flying from the Aloha Tower said, 'Well done!' Everyone working in the yard and on the sunken battleships gave us three cheers."

The dirty, bloodied, battle-hardened, and weary sailors of the USS *Hughes* entered the port's routine, went swimming at Waikiki Beach, and got drunk. The scuttlebutt was they might return to the West Coast soon. In the meantime, the seamen enjoyed themselves. Stine wrote, "We stayed overnight at the Royal Hawaiian Hotel! Millionaire tourists used to pay 20 bucks a night for the room I had, but I got it for 50 cents!" (That millionaire room that Ollie Stine stayed in and paid 50 cents for on Saturday, June 13, 1942, would cost over $3,000 a night in 2023.)

"THE WINTER OF DISASTER"

SS Pennsylvania Sun burning after being torpedoed amidships by U-571 on July 15, 1942. U.S. Navy Photograph, in the collections of the National Archives.

The good news from the Battle of Midway Island was a relief, but the Allies suffered other setbacks on many fronts. At least English Prime Minister Winston Churchill had gotten his wish that America would enter the war the previous December. Although long and dark, Churchill could see a path to victory due to the United States' industrial capacity.

After Midway, Churchill congratulated America on June 7, 1942, saying, "The annals of war at sea present no more intense, heart-shaking shock than this battle, in which the qualities of the United States Navy and Air Force and the American race shone forth in splendor." But Churchill and President Roosevelt knew the world faced relentless hardships in the coming years. Both agreed it would be best to temper any good news with the truth or risk making things worse for Americans and the British if they expected victory to come quickly or without considerable cost.

Even when a victory did come, Churchill tempered it with reality and lowered expectations. Later, in 1942, after a win against the Germans in Africa, he told the British people, "Now, this is not the end. It is not even the beginning of the end. But it is, perhaps, the end of the beginning." He remarked in 1942, "There is no worse mistake in public leadership than to hold out false hopes soon to be swept away. The British people can face peril or misfortune with fortitude and buoyancy. Still, they bitterly resent being deceived or finding that those responsible for their affairs are themselves dwelling in a fool's paradise." Roosevelt told the American people, "The news is going to get worse and worse before it begins to get better."

The immediate impact of the Pearl Harbor attack ended up being the opposite of what Churchill had in mind. When England needed every available ship to defend convoys of critical supplies to their shores, the USS *Hughes* and other warships were diverted to the Pacific. Then, the Japanese sank the British battleship HMS *Prince of Wales* and battle cruiser HMS *Repulse* with torpedoes at the Battle of Malaya, causing Churchill to ask Roosevelt who these Japanese were. Before that time, he was almost entirely obsessed with the Germans. The land-based and ship-based torpedo bombers of the Imperial Japanese Navy had dealt a devastating blow to the British and their sense of naval superiority. Submarines and aircraft, a relatively new addition to combat on the world's oceans, could sink anything floating on the water. The battles of Malaya and Midway Island drove that point home.

It was time to define what type of war this would be. Only two and a half years earlier, Roosevelt had tried to verbalize the feelings of most Americans, who found the concept of attacks on civilians repugnant. On September 1, 1939, he said, "The ruthless bombing from the air of civilians in unfortified centers of the population during the hostilities which have ravaged in various quarters of the earth during the past few years, which has resulted in the maiming and the death of thousands of defenseless men, women, and children, has sickened the hearts of every civilized man and woman, and has profoundly shocked the conscience of humanity." He called on nations to condemn and prohibit such civilian collateral damage.

But then Germany bombed Warsaw only 17 days later, killing innocent civilians. Nationalist regimes, who convinced their populations that they were superior to other nations and peoples, had no qualms about bombing, killing, and enslaving others as a first right, often ordained by God. But even darker were the reports of concentration camps for enemies of Germany. The systematic murder of European Jews was just beginning. It was not long before England and America faced the concept of a much wider war against far-right nationalists. Defeat would not be enough. They would have to be exterminated from the earth. These were the early days of what would become "total war."

Social order was falling apart. The concept of civilized war quickly faded. Churchill remarked that although some Nazis might be "fixable," it mattered little as the rest were all "killable." Germany and Japan seemed destined to fight to the very last man, woman, and child. This was the "winter of disaster."

The rules of war were changing, and Hitler and Tojo were devising new weapons, inventing and building them rapidly. Three were most notable. One was the rockets Hitler created to use on England, what he called his "Vengeance Rockets." The V1 and V2 rockets horrified civilians in London. They were devices of terror. Japan created the concept of kamikaze attacks. These would change and rewrite the rules of warfare forever. The third piece of the puzzle, on the side of the Allies, was the harnessing of the atom by the United States. The atom bomb was well into development before America and England embraced the concept of total war.

Two options for the American project emerged. One used uranium, and one used plutonium. Plain uranium is called U-238 because it has 238 neutrons in each atom, which will not make a bomb. A uranium bomb can only contain U-235, an isotope making up only 1% of naturally occurring uranium. No one knew an easy or inexpensive way to make U-235 for a bomb. Plutonium did not exist, except in theory, until the first sample was created on December 14, 1940. The only known quantities of each consisted of millionths of a gram. The first atomic bomb detonated at the Trinity Test Site would use 13 pounds.

The government needed to decide which type of bomb to make. No one gave much thought at the time to vaporizing civilians by the hundreds of thousands, but everyone on the project knew what this device could do. By 1942, it was clear that such a bomb was worth building for the war against Germany and Japan.

Alexander Sachs was an economist and banker. He was also the man who brought the Einstein letter to President Roosevelt. He told Roosevelt, "There is no doubt that sub-atomic energy is available all around us and that someday man will release and control its almost infinite power. We cannot prevent him from doing so, and I can only hope he will not use it exclusively to blow up his next-door neighbor."

Roosevelt got the point, replying, "Alex, what you are after is to see that the Nazis don't blow us up."

"Precisely," said Sachs.

Roosevelt saw that vaporizing Germany and Japan from the face of the Earth might be the only way to keep them from doing it to the rest of the world first. The stakes were enormous. He decided the project must be completed at any cost, which turned out to be $2.2 billion. The entire United States spending in 1940 was only $9.5 billion. In 2023 dollars, the project cost would have been $37 billion for three bombs.

Oppenheimer and his scientists at Los Alamos were tasked with developing a U-235 and a plutonium bomb to ensure success. The two processes would go on simultaneously. The uranium bomb was a relatively simple process. The scientists were confident that if they took two pieces of U-235 and smacked them together quickly, the result would be an atomic blast. The design was a simple gun. At one end was the projectile, or the U-235 bullet. It would be shot toward the other end, where it would hit a "slug" of U-235. In a millionth of a second, they would go critical, heat up several thousand degrees, and release deadly radiation, vaporizing everything in the area.

But they had to make the U-235 first. This was done at Oak Ridge, Tennessee. It would take two years for over 80,000 war-time workers to produce a few pounds of the material.

Groves was also aware that the processes of making the fissionable U-235 and the plutonium isotope P-239 could present risks for the American population. The P-239 required a nuclear reaction to create it. The scientists had to keep that under control. Initially proposed for Tennessee, Groves thought the risk too high: "While I thought that the possibility of danger was slight, we could not be sure; no one knew what might happen if anything when a chain reaction was attempted in a large reactor." He said such an accident could "wipe out all semblance of security in the project." Covering the Eastern United States with a radioactive cloud seemed risky, so the project was moved to the desert country in eastern Washington State at Hanford.

The other problem with plutonium was how to explode it. The gun-type device would not work. The scientists at Los Alamos came up with a new idea called implosion. A ball of plutonium would be crushed like an orange from the outside. But no one knew how to make an explosion go in, not out. This was but one of the hundreds of theoretical problems that Oppenheimer's scientists were working on, all under the watchful eyes of General Groves, who was still unhappy they were creating so many babies at the government's expense.

Both devices also faced the problem that an airplane could only carry a limited amount of weight, and then only so far. Dropping an atomic bomb on Berlin, only an hour from London, would not be all that difficult, except that a B-17 could only carry six thousand pounds. The U-235 bomb, code-named "Little Boy," would weigh 9,700 pounds. The plutonium bomb, code-named "Fat Man," would weigh 10,800 pounds. Roosevelt approved the creation of an aircraft that could haul atomic bombs to both Berlin and Tokyo. Although Berlin was close enough, the Japanese had to be cleared from the islands of the Pacific to get the new B-29s close enough to bomb Japanese cities.

Meanwhile, the sailors of the USS *Hughes* inched closer to their goal of capturing an airfield from the Japanese that could support a B-29 carrying atomic bombs to Japan. That would prove to be a bloody and slow process.

CHAPTER FOURTEEN

"WHAT'S THE MATTER WITH THE DAMN FOOLS?"

The USS Hughes underwent many changes during WWII, and those modifications helped her survive the war. U.S. Navy photo.

After losing her aircraft carrier at the Battle of Midway Island, the USS *Hughes* was sent to escort a convoy of civilian ships. On June 15, 1942, she sailed with three other destroyers from Pearl Harbor. Ollie Stine wrote in his diary, "Left for the states with a large convoy. There are 37 merchant ships, and the speed is 9 knots! This will be good hunting for Jap submarines here. Some decrepit hunks cannot make even 9 knots, and the stragglers are strung out for 10 miles."

The crews of the destroyers despaired of working with the undisciplined civilian sailors. "We guard the main body of the convoy all day," wrote Stine. "Then at dusk, we go back to check on the stragglers, rejoining the main body after dark. Several times, we've cautioned some of them about showing lights. What's the matter with the damn fools? Don't they know there's a war on?"

Lighting a cigarette on the deck of a ship at night could bring swift consequences, like a torpedo from a Japanese submarine. But on convoy duty, they would find ships with lights turned on, an easy target for a Japanese submarine skipper. Stine noted, "If there are any Jap subs around, some of these merchant skippers will get a big surprise. It'll serve them right." The battle-hardened and experienced sailors of the USS *Hughes* could only do so much.

The slow going was irritating. The USS *Hughes* was used to zig-zagging and fighting at 40 knots. Escorting careless merchant ships and sailors was not something the seamen enjoyed. They began to miss the excitement of shooting down Japanese airplanes. Stine wrote, "Monday, June 22, 1942, still at sea—WILL WE NEVER ARRIVE?" Saturday, June 27, 1942, Stine made a single entry in his diary: "Still at sea—Monotonous, isn't it?" as if asking a question to no one in particular.

The USS *Hughes* reached the Golden Gate Bridge near San Francisco on June 30, 1942, but the ship was stuck in the fog and not

Battle-tested and ready for the next mission, the torpedo sailors
of the USS Hughes. Glen Edmonson collection.

allowed to enter the bay. After three days, the crew got sick of waiting and decided to go in anyway, but this was not without incident.
"We rammed the dock while coming to our berth and tore a hole in
our bow," wrote Stine. His description of the visit would be concise:
"Went to the Union Iron Works to have our bow repaired. When
repairs were completed, we stood out to sea, and do we ever feel low!
Who knows how long it will be before we see the States again? Soon,
we overtook the Battleships *Pennsylvania, Maryland, Colorado, Tennessee,* and *Mississippi* and proceeded to Hawaii. We met Task Force
17 and the carrier *Hornet* and began maneuvers."

At sea, the USS *Hughes* continued to develop a reputation as one of the finest shots in the Navy. Time after time, the ship proved to have the best guns and gunners. On August 12, 1942, Seaman Ollie Stine noted:

A drone was sent out from Pearl Harbor for AA firing. It made one run down the battle line, with all the battleships firing at it, and it came through unscathed. It then cut across our bow. We turned broadside to it and opened fire. Our sixth round burst directly underneath, and the seventh made a direct hit in the motor and blew it up. We were then congratulated on our "excellent shooting" and were barred from firing for the rest of

Hunters Point in California when the USS Hughes was in dry dock for repairs. Officers and shipmates could be joined by their wives while on shore leave. Chester Bradley collection.

the day. Another drone came out soon after, but the battleships failed to shoot it down, and it finally ran out of gas and crashed. Bum shooting by the BB's [battleships].

The USS *Hughes* was detached to escort the oil tanker *Guadalyse* to New Caledonia, 750 miles east of Australia. The ship stopped in Espiritu Santo, where the sailors were allowed to go ashore and pick oranges, a welcome addition to their diet.

Soon enough, the ship returned to Pearl Harbor and was assigned to protect the USS *Hornet*. The seamen resolved not to lose another aircraft carrier on their watch.

"THESE ARE HOSTILE WATERS"

Japanese Battleship Nagato in Brunei 21 October 1944. Although the battleship era was coming to an end, U.S. sailors still feared these ships. Public domain Japanese photo.

After the victory at Midway Island, America faced a difficult decision. The Army, Churchill, and Roosevelt wanted to make a push in Europe, but the Navy felt the time had come to stop

Japanese expansion in the Pacific. The Navy believed that if Japanese expansion plans could be halted, the United States could go on the offensive toward Japan. Ultimately, the Navy got the go-ahead to attack the Japanese at Guadalcanal in the Solomon Islands.

The Solomon Islands is a country that lies Northeast of Australia at the edge of the Coral Sea. Guadalcanal is the largest island in the territory, 2,047 square miles, and in 2023 had a population of 155,500. People there are remarkably diverse, and even though English is the primary language, over 120 languages are still spoken throughout the islands. Peaceful and friendly, the islanders were stunned by the arrival of the Japanese soldiers. They were told they were being liberated but were treated as slave labor. If the Americans could stop Japanese expansion here, it would mark a turning point in the war in the South Pacific.

The war at Guadalcanal was not a single battle but a series of land and naval sea battles that extended for months. The initial primary objective was an airfield that the Japanese had been constructing. The Americans seized it, but the Japanese attempted to retake it. This introduced the Americans to how the Japanese would fight on land. Soldiers on both sides would be tested to the limits of human endurance. Seventy thousand American Marines would fight here, over seven thousand would die, and another 20,000 would be wounded. Over 18,000 Japanese troops fought in the Battle of Guadalcanal. The American Marines would capture just 216 of them. The rest died because they would not surrender.

Guadalcanal also marked a brief return to the past for the naval fleets of America and Japan. There would only be two more battleship-to-battleship fights in maritime warfare, and part of the encounter at Guadalcanal would be one of them. Aircraft carriers and planes had forever changed the face of naval warfare, but on this occasion, the Americans and Japanese would test battleships against each other. Even though battleships were becoming obsolete, they

USS Hughes sailors hand-loading ordnance from trucks to their
ship in combat zones. Chester Bradley collection.

could still bombard shore facilities at 20 miles with reasonable accuracy. In contrast, a plane from an aircraft carrier could hit a target on
land with pinpoint accuracy hundreds of miles away.

The Americans came to call Guadalcanal the "Island of Death."
Two-thirds of the shore forces got tropical diseases. Malaria was
rampant. Marines heard that the malaria medication caused sexual
impotence, and although that was not accurate, many spit out the
pills after the medics walked away. Malaria ravaged their units, seriously impacting their effectiveness. Re-supplying by sea was difficult,
and for weeks, they relied on eating worm-infested rice they captured from the Japanese troops. Navy ships faced considerable risks
in trying to resupply the troops on land. Most battles in the Pacific

were fierce but short. The battle for Guadalcanal seemed to drone on forever.

An early loss for the Allies at Guadalcanal was the Battle of Savo Island. On the night of August 8–9, 1942, the Japanese fleet sank one Australian and three American cruisers. An additional American cruiser and two destroyers were seriously damaged. The Japanese only suffered moderate damage to one cruiser. However, the Japanese commander on the scene, Vice-Admiral Gunichi Mikawa, miscalculated. He had an opportunity to attack the American transport ships, intent on landing troops. He was unaware that Admiral Fletcher was already withdrawing his aircraft carriers for fear of a Japanese assault. Adequate air cover was not provided, leaving the landing forces and ships alone when he departed. Mikawa's failure to destroy the American transport ships was a severe tactical mistake and missed opportunity.

When Fletcher left with his aircraft carriers, the landing fleet commander left after landing Marines without the necessary supplies for basic survival. This was a significant error by the Americans. The Marines would pay a heavy price for this mistake as the days droned into weeks and months of horrible conditions.

Both sides were off to a bad start. There would be months of confusion at war. The Marines initially took the airfield at Guadalcanal and renamed it Henderson Field, after airman Lofton R. Henderson, a Marine aviator killed at the Battle of Midway Island. But the Marines only had five days of food left. To make matters worse, they developed severe dysentery, a debilitating illness.

The Japanese forces left alive were not faring much better. They had moved to a remote part of the island and were subsisting off of coconuts, but the Imperial Japanese Navy destroyers began to land reinforcements. The Americans needed to stop these landings, and the American troops desperately needed help and support of their own.

Deceased Japanese soldiers on the beach after Battle of the Tenaru,
Guadalcanal, 1942. U.S. Army photo.

Japanese Admiral Yamamoto saw that the Americans were committed to stopping Japanese expansion in the Solomon Islands. He sent Nagumo and his two fleet carriers, the *Shokaku* and *Zuikaku,* along with the light carrier *Ryuio* and 177 carrier-based aircraft, to attack the Americans. Fletcher had the American carriers *Saratoga* and *Enterprise*, with 176 aircraft. The two forces clashed on August 24, 1942. The Japanese light carrier was sunk. The *Enterprise* was hit and damaged, and neither Japanese fleet carrier was hit. The *Enterprise* would be so damaged that she would not return to action for two months. This encounter proved a more serious loss to the Japanese than initially thought due to the loss of dozens of Japanese aircraft and their crews. The Japanese could not replace these experienced flight crews.

The USS *Hughes* was on the way to Guadalcanal. On August 18, 1942, she headed for the Western Pacific. Seaman Ollie Stine noted in his diary, "Saturday, September 6, 1942. The reports say Guadalcanal is bombed on the average of twice a day. We should have some fun!"

The next day, they discovered the periscope of a Japanese submarine on the surface of the water nearby and attacked, but the attack's results were unknown.

The Japanese had perfected a process of nightly runs of destroyers dropping off men and supplies to augment their land forces. The route was called the "Tokyo Express" down the "slot" that ended at Guadalcanal. The Americans called it "rat transportation." Although the Japanese could not land heavy equipment or much in the way of meaningful supplies, they did land over five thousand new troops. Initially, the Americans were reluctant to challenge these operations at night but retained control of the sky during the daytime due to the use of Henderson Field.

Stine noted, "Monday, September 8, 1942. We arrived off Guadalcanal and proceeded to patrol while the ships unloaded. All hands are set as these are hostile waters. The air is heavily scented by the perfume of some flowers growing on the beach. I've never smelled anything quite like it before. Two Jap cruiser planes attacked, but no damage to either side of the ship. We got underway as a message came in that two Jap cruisers and six cans were heading this way."

On Tuesday, he wrote, "Spent the night cruising the Indispensable Straights. Twenty Jap high-level bombers attacked us but scored no hits. The *Hughes* shot down three bombers, and I saw two P-40s [American aircraft] fall in flames. After the attack, we went in and finished the unloading. We had to sneak out to sea at dark, as those Jap cruisers were shelling the north side of the island. Lucky, they didn't spot us!"

Stine was getting the action he craved when he signed on board the USS *Hughes* at Pearl Harbor. As they left and went out to find Task Force 17 so they could rejoin the *Hornet*, they couldn't find her right away. "Saturday, September 13, 1942," Stine wrote. "At battle stations searching for TF 17, we are alone, so I hope that Jap carrier doesn't find us at sea. If she does, we're dead ducks!"

The next day's entry was the same as fear gripped the crew: "Sunday, September 14, 1942, still at General Quarters. Still searching for TF 17. No sign of the Japs, thank goodness." Being caught at sea alone by a Japanese aircraft carrier would mean certain death. Their only hope would be to inflict some damage to the enemy before dying, a chilling prospect that ran through the minds of everyone on board for the seemingly endless hours of searching at sea for their lost battle group.

This location was also known as "Torpedo Junction" to the navy sailors. The waterway between Guadalcanal and Espiritu Santo was a dangerous place, constantly patrolled by Japanese submarines. This was no place for the USS *Hughes* to wander around alone.

The next day, the USS *Hughes* discovered Americans. Stine wrote, "Sighted planes from the USS *Wasp* and followed them by radar to TF 18. We arrived to find the aircraft carrier USS *Wasp* had been torpedoed and burning! She made a pretty sight after dark and sank at 8:00 PM. Another carrier lost!" As depressing as it was to be away from their carrier task force and alone at sea, it was devastating to see another American aircraft carrier sinking. But on September 17, 1942, they finally got some good news. "Sighted TF 17 at 5 PM, 100 miles east of N.H., and the *Hughes* rejoined. It's good to be back again!" There was safety in numbers, no matter how dangerous it was to screen an aircraft carrier.

That safety did not last long. They were sent away from the carrier *Hornet* battle group the next day. Stine wrote, "We left formation to search for seven men in a life raft and found them. They had been in the water for seven days." The following day, they found and rejoined Task Force 17. "Transferred the seven Army B-17 men to the *Hornet,* where they can receive better medical attention. Heading out of the Coral Sea now and into the Pacific, cruising around and looking for trouble. Today is the third birthday of the USS *Hughes.*"

The USS *Hughes* would patrol the waters and keep looking for "trouble," but seaman Ollie Stine began to think of home when things slowed down. "Thursday, October 1, 1942. We are at Noumea—Today is the opening of the rabbit season at home. How I'd like to be there!" Soon, they headed out to sea again. "At sea—Destination unknown, but we're headed north towards the Solomons." On October 4, 1942, Stine noted that they would attack two Japanese aircraft carriers in the morning, "We will hit them at dawn tomorrow. If their patrols don't spot us, we have a surprise for them!"

The Task Force was not spotted, but the Japanese carriers had escaped to Rabaul, New Guinea, fearing an American attack. Transport ships and a cruiser were damaged, along with an airfield used by the Japanese. In the coming days, they would have intermittent contact with and shoot down Japanese bombers trying to get to the *Hornet.* On October 16, 1942, Stine noted in his diary, "*Hornet's* fighters shot down another patrol bomber. Tojo's going to be mad! *Hornet's* dive bombers and TBDs attacked two more Jap bases. We sank 12 Jap seaplanes, destroyed AA batteries, set fire to landing barges, and made direct hits on a seaplane tender and two transport ships, breaking their backs."

The next day, due to the loss of the *Wasp* and damage to the *Enterprise,* things were once again looking grim to the sailors on the USS *Hughes.* Stine reflected this mood, writing, "Got word that a Jap carrier is heading our way. TF 17 is the only carrier task force we have here. If the Japs only knew how little Navy we have here, he'd retake Guadalcanal." This fear materialized a few days later: "We went to General Quarters this morning. Radar contact by carrier on a large group of planes. Thought that Jap carrier might have sneaked in and caught us with our pants down, but our fighters identified them as our American B-17s." During this month, the Japanese kept landing more troops on land. Japanese battleships bombarded Henderson Field with giant shells, and their explosions could suck the air out of the lungs of the Marines defending it.

By Sunday, October 25, 1942, it was clear to everyone that an epic battle was on the horizon. Stine wrote:

> Got the word that a large Jap force is coming down. This is no false alarm, and we're steaming at 27 knots to meet him head-on! Monday, October 26, 1942. We went to battle stations at dawn, and at about 9 AM, enemy planes attacked. Four dive bombers were shot out of the sky before they got in, but several made it and scored three direct bomb hits. One tried to dive down the stack but didn't make it and crashed on the signal bridge. A torpedo plane attacked simultaneously and scored two hits, stopping the *Hornet* dead in the water. One torpedo plane crashed into the hangar deck and started a large fire. The *Northampton* took her in tow but had to cut loose when planes attacked again. We went alongside to assist and took off wounded men. Three more dive bombing attacks, one more torpedo attack, and the *Hornet* was abandoned. We picked up about 450 survivors, meanwhile keeping an eye open for returning Jap planes. Next came a high-level attack, and they scored one hit, which exploded with a cherry red burst. We had to sink the *Hornet* to keep her from the Japs. The end of the "Blue Ghost." She was a gallant lady.

By the end of October, the *Enterprise* was back in action. The day after the loss of the *Hornet*, the USS *Hughes* caught up with her. Stine wrote, "Met *Enterprise* today after being separated all night

USS Wasp (CV-7) burning on 15 September 1942 (fsa.8e00768).
U.S. Navy photo.

from our group. We transferred 10 of our wounded and dead to the USS *Pensacola*. We have three holes in our side. Also, shrapnel holes all over the topside, and the starboard wing of the bridge is smashed."

Anything except actual combat now seemed "routine" after so much time in battle. On the next day, October 28, 1942, Stine wrote a single entry to his diary, "Routine day at sea, entering Noumea," and on the 29th, "Transferred 200 *Hornet* survivors to the USS *San Diego* as we are overcrowded two or three times over." The next day, he noted, "Entered harbor of Noumea. Our losses for the Battle of Santa Cruz are the *Hornet*, the destroyer *Porter*, the destroyer *Mahan* damaged by collision, and the *Smith* damaged by a torpedo plane which crashed into the foc'sle."

A few days later, Stine noted, "Halloween! Transferred some *Hornet* personnel. Tied up to the USS *Whitney* to be patched up." Then, on November 1, 1942, he wrote, "Transferred the last of the *Hornet* survivors and continued repairs to the ship." The next day, he followed with "Monday, November 2, 1942. Still alongside the tender, but the duck season opens today back home, and I wish I were there!" The USS *Hughes* had to remove her deck boat and davits after they were crushed while coming alongside the *Hornet* to rescue survivors just before her sinking.

On November 9, 1942, the USS *Hughes* was back at sea to find and rescue sailors from a torpedoed ship. Stine noted, "Got underway and went out to pick up survivors of a torpedoed ship 80 miles away. The name of the torpedoed merchantman is *Edgar Allen Poe*. She did not sink and is being towed back to Noumea by a Limey army trawler while we screen her against further attack." After returning from this mission, on the 11th, he wrote, "Task Force 16 got underway today. The *Enterprise* is replacing the *Hornet*. At battle stations all day. Shot down a PBY [float plane] manned by Japs sending reports on our position. This little trick has cost us at least two carriers."

The primary naval battle of Guadalcanal was now underway. "Saturday, November 14, 1942. Operating east of the Solomon Islands. At battle stations all day. Shot down two Jap patrol bombers. *Enterprise* attack groups put three 1,000-pound bombs on a Jap battleship." This entry by Stine turned out to be a mistake as the ship was a Japanese heavy cruiser, but the USS *Hughes* also sank seven Japanese transport ships.

The Japanese desperately needed to get reinforcements on Guadalcanal. Admiral Halsey desperately needed to stop them but was now short of undamaged ships. The USS *Hughes* was joined in this battle by two American battleships, the *Washington* and *South Dakota*, and three other destroyers from the *Enterprise* strike force. Before this fight was over, the Americans would lose three destroyers from

Destroyer Squadron Two, of which the USS *Hughes* was an original member: the *Walke* (DD-416), *Barton* (DD-599), and *Benham* (DD-397). Six of the original 11 destroyers in her battle group would soon sit at the bottom of the deep blue waters of the vast Pacific Ocean.

Retired Commander Alan S. Evans recalled, "During the next five days, the USS *Hughes* was part of the screen for *Enterprise*. At 8:10 AM on November 13, 1942, the attack was launched, which sank the Japanese Battleship *Hiyei*. On 14 November, the main Japanese transport group was located, and *Enterprise* planes sank or damaged nearly all Japanese transports. On November 14, 1942, the great battleship night action took place, which completed the smashing of the Japanese drive and ensured that Guadalcanal would remain ours."

Evans also pointed out something often missed in stories of battles from WWII: "With all the ships firing at the same targets, it is almost impossible to determine where the credit might go for any individual kill of a plane or ship." He noted that attacks against reported subs or submarine "contacts" often happened in this area of Torpedo Junction. Still, following up to ensure a kill was difficult and dangerous. He said the USS *Hughes* could claim at least partial credit for many Japanese losses during these months of close combat in the Solomon Islands.

That night, battleships and heavy cruisers delivered devastating blows to each other with shells from their massive guns. The shells would hit solid steel and liquefy it in milliseconds as they penetrated hulls and decks. Anyone nearby would be showered by molten metal. It was terrible to see, hear, and smell. The exploding shells also spread shrapnel. Heat would explode the boilers used to power the ships' turbines. The steam would instantly cook nearby sailors, turning the dead men a ghastly white, a horror many would never forget. Blood covered the decks, and men slipped and fell to injury or death in the carnage. Body parts had to be tossed into the sea to make way for battle. As news came to the USS *Hughes,* Seaman Stine often feared for his friends from other ships: "Heard *Monssen* was sunk. Hope Joe Porter is O.K." Stine would not find out the fate of his friend until December 24, 1942, Christmas Eve: "I learned that Joe Porter was killed by a 20 mm slug when the *Monssen* went down. He was a swell guy."

On Friday, November 20, 1942, the USS *Hughes* was back at port to refuel and get refitted. Stine wrote in his diary, "Standing by to get underway again for Guadalcanal. Our Captain was decorated for action up there last time. Here's his chance for another medal. USS *San Francisco, Helena, Gurn,* and *Buchanan* entered port today! *Frisco* is shot to pieces." The USS *Hughes* returned to sea and resumed patrol of the waters off Guadalcanal.

For entertainment, the seamen used a telescope called a "long glass" to watch artillery duels between Marines and Japanese forces. At the same time, American planes bombed and strafed the Japanese lines, but submarines were a constant threat. Stine noted, "Saturday, November 28, 1942. We brought the *Barnett* and *Alchiba* over from Tulagi, where we've anchored every night. At 6:15 AM, *Alchiba* was torpedoed and beached. The *Barnett* got the hell out of there and designated us as an escort. We never did find the sub. Fires started by fish [torpedoes] finally reached her cargo of bombs, etc. There was a terrific explosion, and the *Alchiba* was no more." On December 2, 1941, the *Hughes* tied up alongside the USS *Dixie,* a USS destroyer tender, where the crew was treated to a concert on the ship's fantail, which Stine reported as "Not bad!"

For the next month, the Japanese struggled with supplying their forces on land while the Americans continued to make gains, but at a considerable cost. The military initially attempted to hide the casualty lists because they were high, fearing a public backlash. Accurate totals of servicemen lost were not released for several years. The USS *Hughes* would continue patrols with intermittent combat against a shrinking Japanese presence. Dropping depth charges on remaining Japanese submarine contacts became routine and of little note. On Sunday, January 24, 1942, the USS *Hughes* participated in a battle off Guadalcanal. Stine noted, "The bombardment came off perfectly! Huge fires were started, which were visible a long way off. About 15 Jap torpedo planes attacked us; two were shot down. No damage to us and no other enemy opposition. Proceed to Tulagi and fueled from USS *Helena*. We received a 'well done' from Admiral Halsey!"

Soon after, the sailors of the USS *Hughes* were getting bored by the remaining Japanese engagements. "A lone Jap seaplane bombed the fighter strip tonight but did no damage," Stine wrote. The next day, he added, "Went to General Quarters at 1:30 AM. Another Jap plane bombed the fighter strip again. If they're bombing this place for nuisance value, they're being successful, as far as we're concerned." The most significant action was on the 30th when she sped out at 30 knots to help rescue the heavy cruiser *Chicago* when she came under attack. "Covering the *Chicago*," wrote Stine, "we went to General Quarters for an air attack by 20 Jap bombers. Fighters shot down two, but nine torpedo planes attached the *Chicago*. Believe the *Chicago* may sink because of torpedo hits." Then, the next day, he noted, "*Chicago* did sink."

During the next few nights, the Japanese destroyers evacuated the remaining Japanese forces on Guadalcanal, and the bloody fight ended. This would be the end of Japanese expansion in the Pacific. The sailors of the USS *Hughes* had lived every second of it. Guadalcanal and Tulagi became major Allied bases for operations to retake the other islands and get closer to Japan.

During the Solomon Islands campaign, the Japanese lost 31,000 men, 38 ships, and 683 aircraft. Tojo would now turn to the defense of Japan's home islands. The idea of Americans and their allies, whom the Japanese extremists saw as sub-human, setting foot on Japanese soil was suddenly possible. The shame and humiliation of such an idea had to be avoided at all costs. The next phase of the war would bring the USS *Hughes* closer to Japanese shores, and a few new members would soon join her to replace those lost in battle. The Japanese would double down on protecting their emperor and pay any price to avoid surrender.

CHAPTER SIXTEEN

"FUELED BY THE USS *SAN FRANCISCO* IN A SNOWSTORM"

The USS Hughes sets sail for Alaskan waters to fight the Japanese.
U.S. Navy photo.

The USS *Hughes* got a break after the Battle of Guadalcanal and the Solomon Islands campaign. Stine noted, "Wednesday, February 24, 1942. We will probably enter Santos tomorrow. *Hughes* and

Mustin are supposed to go to Australia. I hope we do!" The sailors hadn't had a decent break for months, and the thought of Australia and the bars, brothels, and women was intoxicating. Their minds were swimming with the idea of time off in Sydney. Soon enough, they got their orders to head for Australia. Stine wrote, "Left Noumea in company with USS *Mustin* en route to Sydney, Australia!" They got to stay there for ten days, during which time, Seaman Ollie Stine reported, "Liberty is swell here. The girls are nuts about the Yanks!"

It didn't take long for the sailors to get into trouble. The deck logs during that time show many sailors not returning to the ship on time and being absent without leave (AWOL). Gunnery Lieutenant Glen Edmonson recorded in the ship log, "Wednesday 10 March, 8:15 AM, Held quarters for muster, absent Shandor, Steve, AWOL since 12:00 on March 8th." But this wasn't to last much longer as he was apprehended by a Canadian shore patrol and brought back to the *Hughes*: "8:10 PM—Shandor, Steve, was delivered aboard by shore patrol AWOL since 1200, March 8, 1943, a period of about two days, 10 hours and 10 minutes, confined to the brig of the USS *Dobbin* for safe keeping."

Being AWOL was a common offense when the ship was in port. The sailors weren't always sober enough to return to the ship when assigned. Sometimes, they were stuck in jail. For the most part, the punishment was light. Often, a significant sentence would be imposed, but at the end of the proceedings, most of it would be suspended, and the violator would be let off with a warning, loss of a bit of pay, and sometimes confinement to the ship while in port. These proceedings were called a "captain's mast."

Occasionally, there would be a full court-martial, but this was usually reserved for more serious offenders. A sailor could be dishonorably discharged from the Navy and face significant fines and long terms of confinement, but this was uncommon. On March 12, 1943, several sailors were reduced in rank and pay, and one received ten days in the brig. Missing out on further shore leave was deemed the worst punishment.

The sailors needed to blow off steam. The crew was weary from almost constant combat during their time in Guadalcanal. The officers needed a "rested" and motivated crew, as well as a group that understood military discipline and would follow orders. It was a careful balance. One sailor was sentenced to six months' confinement on short rations, but in the end, he only paid an $18 fine and had a couple of days of extra duty on the ship while his shipmates lived it up on shore. The officers and Navy couldn't afford to lose good, battle-tested seamen, as the war against Japan would last for years.

Things were entering a time of consolidation and planning in the Pacific. Many decisions had to be made, and there was enough time to plan things properly and avoid mistakes made in haste. As part of the Midway campaign, the Japanese had landed troops in Alaska as a diversion to hide their true intent. They knew any attack on the West Coast would alarm the Americans, Canadians, and British. The Americans found this a source of irritation, though the threat to the US mainland was insignificant. Still, something had to be done.

The USS *Hughes* got a new mission: attack the Japanese on Alaska's Aleutian islands. This was a dangerous and tricky thing for the USS *Hughes*. Although she had radar for detecting enemy aircraft, like many ships at that time, none of the vessels in Destroyer Squadron Two had accurate surface radar. This was a problem with heavy, cold fog for days on end, requiring a high level of seamanship and navigation. Still, this was a far cry from the daily bombardment from Japanese airplanes at Guadalcanal.

Retired Commander Evans recalled, "Despite this cool climate, the lack of the nerve-wracking imminence of enemy action made the duty pleasant compared to the South Pacific." Plus, salmon were waiting for the crew of the Hughes—lots of fresh, tasty salmon.

When not fighting the Japanese, sailors of the USS Hughes enjoy salmon fishing in Alaskan waters, a welcome addition to their diet. Glen Edmonson collection.

On Sunday, April 11, 1943, the ship crossed the equator at 11:20 AM, heading north to Alaska. Soon, the crew got used to the cold temperatures and adjusted to the ship's frigid conditions. Gunnery Lieutenant Glen Edmonson recalled the heavy, fur-lined jackets the crew was issued for the cold, snowy weather of the Aleutian Islands. Although the jackets might warm a sailor, they were sure to quickly drown anyone falling overboard. The sailors thought them funny.

If the crew needed any reminder of how far from the equator they were now, they only had to look at the water temperature, which dropped from a daily average of 80 degrees *Fahrenheit* near Guadalcanal down to 38 degrees as they traveled north. A downed pilot or the survivor of a sinking ship would die quickly. This also cooled the ship's hull, a relief after the stifling and humid climate in the tropics. Suddenly, they needed their Navy-issued wool blankets.

The ship's job was to find, attack, and kick the Japanese out of the Aleutian Islands. Seaman Ollie Stine remarked, "Thursday, April 22, 1943. Fueled by the USS *San Francisco* in a snowstorm. We entered Kuluk Bay, Adak Island, in the Aleutian group, 250 miles from Kiska. This will be our operating base, a barren-looking place! The snow-capped mountains are pretty, however. Occasional snow flurries today."

The Americans had located the main Japanese force on the islands of Attu and Kiska. The initial Japanese attack in Alaska occurred in June 1942 when two aircraft carriers launched bombers against American bases at Dutch Harbor and Unalaska. Due to bad weather, half of the Japanese strike force became lost in the fog and never made it there. Many returned to the carriers, and even more crashed in the North Pacific's freezing water. Only 17 planes reached the target and faced anti-aircraft fire and American fighters. The surprised Japanese inaccurately dropped their bombs and left, doing almost no damage.

The Japanese returned a few days later, set some storage tanks on fire, and damaged a hospital. The raids were so unsuccessful that they left without landing the 1,200 soldiers they'd brought with them, which would have constituted an invasion force. This was due to the bad weather and the resistance of the Americans. However, the bad weather also kept the Americans from finding and attacking the Japanese carriers. Neither side knew how to fight in Alaska.

The Japanese returned and invaded the islands of Kiska and Attu. There were no American bases there, only the villages of the Native

Alaskans called the Unangax, more commonly referred to at the time as "Aleuts." The Japanese eventually took the Unangax people back to Japan and put them in an internment camp.

The USS *Hughes* was also tasked with keeping any new supplies from getting to Japanese bases in Alaska. Seaman Ollie Stine wrote, "Tuesday, April 27, 1943. Cruising 500 miles from the Kurile Islands, where the Japs have an extensive naval base. Our job is to intercept and destroy any supplies or reinforcements headed for Attie or Kiska. Our ship is rolling through an arc of 60 degrees! Occasional snow flurries. An ordinary day. We are trying to draw the Japs into a fight. Four light cruisers are patrolling southward as bait."

On May 10, 1943, the USS *Hughes* assisted in bombarding Attu in preparation for landing American troops. Stine noted, "Very foggy, but today is the warmest day since we've been here. The temperature is 48 degrees!" The next day, American troops landed and faced terrible conditions. A Japanese submarine snuck into the waters and almost sank the USS *Pennsylvania*.

The troops battled deteriorating weather and snow drifts. Approximately 549 Americans were killed, 1,148 were wounded, and over 1,200 got frostbite. The battle continued until May 29, 1943, when the Japanese made a "banzai charge" deep into the American lines. This resulted in the killing of most of the Japanese soldiers. Only 30 were taken prisoner, and thousands died, many killed by a naval bombardment by the *Hughes* and other ships.

The crew of the USS *Hughes* returned to chilly and rough days of patrolling at sea near Attu. The crew was pleased to be able to catch quite a few salmon. Fresh fish was a welcome addition to their diet. Occasionally, there was a Japanese attack, like that on May 22, 1943, when 12 twin-engine planes attacked the fleet, but no damage was done. On July 6, 1943, Ollie Stine noted that the USS *Hughes* had returned to combat duty: "Went in today and bombarded Kiska. *Hughes* fired 300 rounds at the main camp area. Cruisers fired at

Captured Japanese Zero - Dutch Harbor Alaska - June 1942.
U.S. Navy photo.

their seaplane base, camp area, and submarine base. Numerous direct hits were scored on all of the above. A submarine was sighted in the inner harbor before it submerged, but we did not go in after it as the Japs were returning our fire with six-inch guns. All their shells fell short and did no damage to us. Aerial photographs of Kiska proved our bombardment to be a success!"

While preparing for the land invasion against the Japanese on Kiska, the USS *Hughes* participated in what became known as the "Battle of the Blips." At 12:13 on July 26, 1943, ships discovered radar readings that showed a Japanese fleet closing in on them. The official log notes, "Went to Battle Stations tonight. Radar picked up three targets. Cruisers and battleships opened fire." The bombardment lasted 45 minutes, and a staggering amount of artillery rained down on the enemy targets. But there were no Japanese ships. The "targets" were false echoes on the radar screens caused by an unknown source near Kiska, probably a snowstorm. The embarrassed naval forces called it a great "training exercise."

On August 11, 1943, Americans landed on Kiska, expecting a tough fight, but the Japanese were gone. By the 13th, not a single Japanese soldier was found. "Our forces have completely occupied Kiska," wrote Stine, "and there are no Japs there. It is believed that submarines evacuated them, as naval and air bombardment had made the place untenable." Soon after, he reported, "With no Japs left here to fight, I guess we'll be leaving soon."

The Japanese had left on July 29, 1943. The Navy was embarrassed about the size of the landing force and the lack of resistance. The intelligence reports were not accurate. They missed the opportunity to catch the Japanese leaving the area. Although it was easy to blame the weather, which was partly true, these military efforts were heavily criticized.

Retired Commander Alan Evans noted, "One unusual event before our arrival was a collision with a whale on our way to San Francisco, which caused considerable damage to the whale and wrecked our sound gear." During September and October of 1943, the USS *Hughes* underwent an overhaul at the Hunters Point Naval Drydocks in San Francisco. The ship would soon be rushed to Pearl Harbor to join a Task Force to invade the Gilbert Islands.

"A BLACK DAY IN THE HISTORY OF MANKIND"

Heinrich Himmler inspects a German prison camp - Soviet prisoners of war. Public domain German acrhives photo.

Although there was good news in the Pacific, where the USS *Hughes* was fighting, dark times were coming to Europe. A small contingent of American troops had landed in England to help with the war effort, but it was the supply of materials that Churchill needed most. The actual conquest of Europe was a long way off. Germany had invaded Russia, and Stalin kept asking when the main European invasion by the Allies would begin. Russia was reeling under the staggering losses of her troops battling on the Eastern Front. The stream of supplies heading to Europe had to face the German Atlantic U-boat fleet, now without the destroyers America had sent to the Pacific, including the USS *Hughes.*

The Americans were building more ships than ever to bring these supplies to England, but on average, they were sunk on their fourth voyage, a staggering loss in both lives and ships. By the end of 1942, there were 212 German U-boats in the North Atlantic, and another 181 were in production. The merchant ships supplying England were easy pickings for the Germans. Churchill had his English codebreakers working on the German Enigma cipher system of communications. They had some success, but the Germans were constantly changing the codes. Over time, the British cryptanalysts could identify where most U-boats were in general terms, and the convoys steered around them as best they could. However, the sheer number of U-boats and convoys crossing the Atlantic left significant supplies at the bottom of the ocean.

No one was immune to these painful and dark times. The families of the crew members of the USS *Hughes* were not alone. By the end of the year, Churchill was ill from fatigue. Everyone now relied on Roosevelt and Churchill. They had to be nothing short of supermen defending democracy on Earth. But the pressures and stresses on both were taking their toll. America also faced an election in 1944, and Churchill feared that Roosevelt might not run again. He told Roosevelt in a letter, "I simply can't go on without you." As their friendship continued to develop, Churchill also began to take a back seat to Roosevelt on the world stage. America emerged as the dominant power that could end the war over time. England and America agreed that although British scientists had done some work on nuclear weapons, America would take the lead on the atomic bombs.

Reports of German and Japanese atrocities and British and American losses were moving both countries towards a concept of total war. This would justify using anything available, including destroying civilian populations with atomic bombs, but no one could grasp what a city destroyed by a nuclear bomb might look like. Civilian and military leaders could only imagine it. The bomb raised moral questions that were yet unanswered.

Scientists working for Robert Oppenheimer better understood the implications, but the whole topic was new, and there had never been a nuclear blast on Earth. Still, the gravity of what they might create had begun to set in, and they became uneasy as they proceeded. Some decided to leave the project on ethical grounds. Others began to debate the use of the bomb on civilian targets. General Groves would soon have his hands full with what would become a small mutiny by some of his scientists.

The fundamental question of whether a self-sustaining nuclear reaction would exist had been solved in late 1942 by a group of scientists at the University of Chicago led by Enrico Fermi. Although the Manhattan Project was headquartered in Los Alamos, New Mexico, many parts were done remotely. Fermi and his team decided to build this test under the stands of the university football field. They avoided asking permission from the college president, Robert Maynard Hutchins. Their reasoning? "The only answer he could have given would have been no," Fermi wrote. "And this answer would have been wrong." Fermi didn't want to ask a lawyer and college president a question about testing a nuclear reaction at the school. Their mission was a top military and presidential priority.

That is not to say that this test was without risk. They were reasonably sure they could contain this nuclear reaction once they got it started, but they were not entirely certain. The process involved a considerable pile of graphite bricks interspersed with uranium balls. They had control rods set into the "pile" that they would remove to get the self-staining atomic reaction underway. This, in essence, would be a slow-developing nuclear bomb.

Once the neutrons bombarded other uranium atoms and released more neutrons and energy, they planned to re-insert the control rods before the reaction got out of control and the city of Chicago was covered in a cloud of deadly radiation. If something failed, they had a person stationed above the nuclear pile with an axe to break open a container of cadmium-sulfate water, which, it was believed, would stop the chain reaction. However, Fermi wanted the test to be completed, and he told the person with the axe not to break the container if Fermi was still alive.

People living in Chicago were unaware of this test, as were the students at the University of Chicago. On board the USS Hughes, Seaman Tony Skic had more at stake in this test outcome than he could have imagined. His entire family lived in Chicago, near the university. If the test went wrong, the control rods failed to go back into the atomic pile, or the person with the axe waited too long and was killed by the radiation before breaking the bottle of cadmium-sulfate water, his family would probably be killed.

On the day of the test at the University of Chicago, the United States government announced that the Nazis had killed two million Jews in Europe, and millions more were now at risk of the same fate. The USS *Hughes* was in the process of shooting down Japanese aircraft attacking American ships at the Battle of Guadalcanal. So that the warships and planes in the war in the Pacific would have enough fuel, people in Chicago were walking to work instead of driving their cars. The streets were eerily silent that day. While scientists watched closely from a balcony overlooking the squash courts, Fermi directed the removal of the control rods slowly from the atomic pile to begin the self-sustaining nuclear reaction. If successful, it would prove that an atomic bomb could be created to drop on Berlin and Tokyo.

One of the witnesses, Herbert Anderson, noted, "At first, you could hear the neutron counter, clickety-clack, clickety-clack. Then the clicks came more and more rapidly, and after a while, they began to merge into a roar; the counter couldn't follow anymore." Suddenly, Fermi raised his hand. "The pile has gone critical," he announced. No one present had any doubts about it. An atom bomb was a theory no more. It was a certainty.

Another scientist, Eugene Wigner, remembered, "Even though we had anticipated the experiment's success, its accomplishment deeply impacted us. For some time, we knew we were about to unlock a giant; still, we could not escape an eerie feeling when we knew we had done it. We felt as, I presume, everyone who has done something that he knows will have far-reaching consequences that he cannot foresee."

To celebrate the success of the test and the dawn of the nuclear age, Wigner had brought a bottle of Italian wine in a brown paper bag and gave it to Fermi. Another scientist at the event, Albert Wattenberg, later recorded, "We each had a small amount in a paper cup and drank silently, looking at Fermi. Someone told Fermi to sign the wrapping on the bottle. After he did so, he passed it around, and we all signed it, except Wigner."

As the scientists began to leave, Fermi was alone with Leo Szilard, who was equally responsible for the project's success. Szilard became sullen and downcast, deep in his thoughts. He had always felt that unlocking nuclear secrets could positively impact the world's development but also posed dangers for mankind. He later recorded the encounter with Fermi, "There was a crowd there, and then Fermi and I stayed there alone. I shook hands with Fermi, and I said I thought this day would go down as a black day in the history of mankind."

The closer the scientists got to producing an actual deliverable atomic bomb for use against Germany and Japan, the more they began to think of its use in absolute terms and what that might mean for the people it was used on. It was becoming clear that it could never be used on only a military target. This type of weapon was far too large. A new concept was emerging even then: to stop people in a country from wanting to support their nation at war or wipe them off the map entirely. Everyone in Berlin and Toyoko might have to be killed to stop Hitler and Tojo. If there were to be total war, there would no longer be civilians—everyone would be targets of these new, powerful weapons.

Some scientists kept their heads down and left these decisions to the elected leaders of Britain and America. Many had come from Europe and were aware of what was happening to their families and friends under Hitler. Although not entirely sure about using atomic bombs against Japan, they had no qualms about using them on the Nazis, who were trying to kill every living Jew across Europe. The German people might have to pay for the sins of the leaders they had placed in power. In the Pacific, the crewmembers of the USS *Hughes* would have welcomed any weapon that could have gotten them home to their families and friends alive.

The project's fate was in the hands of Robert Oppenheimer, now 39 years old. Brilliant, charismatic, and often eccentric, he was once described by a fellow professor at Berkley, Haakon Chevalier, in this way: "Oppenheimer was tall, nervous, and intent, and he moved with an odd gait, a kind of a jog, with a great deal of swinging of his limbs, his head always a little to one side, one shoulder higher than the other. But the head was the most striking: the halo of wispy black curly hair, the fine, sharp nose, and especially the eyes, surprisingly blue, having a strange depth and intensity, and yet expressive of a candor altogether disarming. He looked like a young Einstein and, simultaneously, like an overgrown choirboy." Oppenheimer had a style and charisma that was unmistakable and impossible to ignore. He was a formidable leader. But more importantly, General Groves trusted him implicitly.

With the success of the University of Chicago test, it was now up to Oppenheimer and the scientists at Los Alamos in the high deserts of New Mexico to find a way to build a working bomb, which Roosevelt planned to drop on Japan and Germany. Churchill had no qualms about this objective. He struck a secret deal with President Roosevelt at Quebec in August 1943 that required British and American leaders to approve the weapon's first use. Churchill agreed to its use and never regretted his decision that the bomb could be used against the enemies of the Allies.

But keeping the brilliant scientists on task was a constant headache for General Groves and Oppenheimer. There were many examples, but one of the most notable was that of Leo Szilard. Wigner once said Szilard could have completed the project by himself if only brilliant ideas were required, but Leo Szliard made it his task to drive General Groves nuts. He disliked all military leaders.

Groves once said Szilard was "the kind of man that any employer would have fired as a troublemaker." They were constantly at odds and in one battle or another, often stemming from the military rules of compartmentalization and secrecy. Most of the scientists hated the constraints. In Szilard's case, General Groves was willing to take drastic action. He drafted orders to have Szilard arrested as an "enemy alien" and put him into an internment camp for the rest of the war.

But Szilard had powerful friends, and he reminded people that he and Fermi had brought the letter to Einstein in the first place and that the project might not even be possible without him. Szilard was also profoundly respected among the scientists. Ultimately, Szilard was not arrested and was kept in the project, but he and Groves were constantly at odds.

To be sure, there were obstacles to overcome, but the atom bomb was coming, and the USS *Hughes* had to ensure there was somewhere in the Pacific it could be launched from.

"THE WHOLE THING WAS BLOOD AND GUTS"

Seaman Tony Skic of Chicago, during and after the war, joins the crew of the USS Hughes to fight the Empire of Japan. Tony Skic family collection.

Seaman Anthony "Tony" Skic joined the Navy on December 29, 1941. He would survive the war and serve until December 23, 1946. On October 26, 1943, he stepped aboard the USS *Hughes* in San Francisco and served on it until February 3, 1945. Born to a family of Polish immigrants, he was from Chicago. Most of the kids in his neighborhood were Polish, and many of the department stores in his neighborhood were Jewish. Most of the men in his community worked in the steel mills. His entire family was there when the University of Chicago's first controlled nuclear chain reaction, supervised by Enrico Fermi, went off.

Tony Skic loved fishing and water when he was a kid, so when the Japanese attacked Pearl Harbor, it was natural that he joined the Navy. Skic was only 17 when he and his family were getting ready to eat lunch and heard the news on the radio. Sylvester Jagla, also there at the table, recalled the Skic's reaction:

> I was five years old then, but I remember it very clearly. It was hushed. Tony was distraught when he heard that the Japanese bombed Pearl Harbor. He felt it was his duty to defend our country, so he quit school to join the Navy. The Navy was his first choice. His parents were upset but signed the papers as they also felt it was their duty to do so. They proudly hung the small flag in the front window with one star representing a family member in the service. Tony hated the Japs. He had seen the disaster at Pearl Harbor and the havoc they left throughout the Pacific during the war. When he returned, he did not want to talk about the war as it made him sad and angry.

When Tony Skic joined the USS *Hughes*, the other sailors had been on shore leave in San Francisco off and on for almost two months. Seaman Ollie Stine recorded on September 1, 1943, "Passed under the Golden Gate Bridge at 1:00 PM and proceeded to the Navy Yard at Hunter's Point."

Many sailors were given 20 days of leave. On September 4, everyone was present and accounted for. There was plenty to do, and the sailors took full advantage of their time off. For one sailor, R. H.

Weeks Jr., the pressure of combat had become too much. He was found dead in a compartment of the ship with a .45 and spent cartridge shell by his side. A board of inquiry was convened. The death was suspected suicide.

Other problems developed during this period. Seaman Wesley Hemphill was tried and convicted of striking another seaman and fined $20 a month for two months. Seaman Wilford Willis also got into trouble—the deck log records, "OFFENSE—Assault with a Dangerous Weapon. FINDING—specifications proved by plea. SENTENCE—Solitary confinement on bread and water with a full ration every third day and to lose $25 per month of his pay for (6) months. Approved by Convening Authority. 1:05 PM Willis was transferred to Receiving Ship San Francisco, California for temporary duty while serving the approved sentence of the summary court-martial (under guard)." This severe punishment was uncommon, but a few sailors were near the breaking point.

For the most part, the sailors got much-needed time off as the ship was being repaired after hitting a whale and undergoing refitting for combat. Seaman Ollie Stine noted in his diary, "Sunday, October 26, 1943, we said goodbye to Frisco as we sailed under the Golden Gate Bridge at 9:00 AM. We were gone almost 14 months last time. Wonder how long it will be before we see 'Frisco again . . ."

On the way back to Hawaii, the USS *Hughes* encountered a severe storm that lasted for days. Two hundred soldiers were on board the ship for transportation to combat duty, whom the seamen called "boots." Stine remembered that every single one of them was seasick. When they reached Pearl Harbor, he noted, "This place is full of ships. There are at least 15 carriers, ten cruisers, eight battleships, and more tin cans than you can count here. Something big is in the air, and we arrived just in time to be in on it!"

Northeast of Australia and the Coral Sea lies the island nation of Kiribati. It is about halfway between Hawaii and Papua New Guinea.

This area is called the Gilbert Islands, a chain of 16 atolls and coral islands that are a central part of that nation. Before the arrival of Christian missionaries, the people of these islands were known to be warm and friendly, with a strong sense of community and respectful behavior toward others. It was reported in 1909 that poverty was rare in the islands and most people owned their land. Although initially a British protectorate, the island nation was self-sufficient and provided necessary services to the residents. The islanders produced phosphate and coconut palms as their primary source of income.

War descended on Kiribati when the Japanese landed on the same day as the attack on Pearl Harbor. Within two days, it was under Japanese control. On August 17, 1942, United States Marines landed in a raid to attack and confuse the Japanese about the next steps the Americans were planning. The invasion was a disaster, one of many in the early war. Japanese summarily executed the 19 Marines they captured, violating international rules of war, and the bodies were left for the local villagers to bury. This was a message to the locals and the Americans. These fallen Americans were not recovered until 1999, when a Marine Honor Guard was sent to recover the bodies and return them to American soil.

But this small raid did have an impact. It caused the Japanese to fortify the islands in the area, including those in Tarawa and Makin Atoll. The naval force that the USS *Hughes* was about to embark with was headed to re-take these islands from the Japanese. They would then provide bases for the further removal of the Japanese in the Central Pacific, paving the way for the delivery of atomic bombs.

The American invasion fleet was well-organized and equipped. Gone were the days of Japanese carriers and air superiority. The Americans had so many ships, aircraft, and men at their disposal that the USS *Hughes* was sent as part of a diversionary force to bait the Japanese into a battle that would hide the central portion of the American fleet. Seaman Ollie Stine recorded on November 11, 1943,

"There are three other forces, all larger than this one. The idea is to use us as bait to suck the Jap fleet out of Truk Island. Our other forces will cut off their retreat and force them to fight a grand-stand, free-for-all battle. Their battle fleet is powerful, but we have enough might to cope with it."

On that same day, Seaman Tony Skic wrote in his diary, "Got a hell of a sunburn today! It is getting hot as we are going further south. Got the mid-watch coming in three hours, but it's so damn hot in this compartment it is hard to sleep." Kiribati is about as hot as it gets because the country straddles the equator.

To replace the loss of the fleet carriers at the Coral Sea, Midway, and Guadalcanal, the Americans began mass-producing a much easier aircraft carrier to build by repurposing an older ship design. One of these ships was the *Liscome Bay*, a *Casablanca*-class escort carrier. She was 512 feet long with a 477-foot flight deck for air operations. She had only been in the fleet for three months before this battle. One of seven destroyers with her was the USS *Hughes*. The attacking fleet was so large that the danger of a collision was deemed more significant than a Japanese torpedo attack from a submarine, so the ships were not zig-zagging.

The Japanese submarine *I-175*, skippered by Lieutenant Commander Sunao Tabata, was patrolling off Makin Island when she came across the *Liscome Bay* and the fleet. Early in the morning, a Japanese aircraft dropped a signal beacon, and the destroyer USS *Franks* left the formation to investigate, leaving a hole in the screen around *Liscome Bay*. This was a fatal mistake. Tabata fired three torpedoes. At 5:10 AM, a lookout on the ship saw the incoming torpedoes.

Seamen Ollie Stine and Tony Skic were devastated by what they saw unfolding that morning. Tony recorded:

I was awakened at 5:00 AM this morning by the General Quarters buzzer and, coming to the topside, there was the converted carrier a blazing inferno. She was caught by two fish, one amidship and one forward. She was enveloped in flames. The slant-eyed son of a bitch had done a very nice job. At about 5:30 AM, when we were about a thousand yards away, she blew up and sank fast. Flames were about 500 feet high, small arms were going off, and gasoline was exploding. About two-thirds of the thousand men on the crew went down with her. We picked up 153 survivors, and it was a job picking them up as we were dead in the water for at least three hours. A destroyer with us dropped about a dozen depth charges, but I do not know if they hit anything. I do not wish to write too much about her survivors, as the whole thing was blood and guts.

The explosion was so large that it sent a giant mushroom cloud into the air and rocked the rest of the task force ships. The entire stern of the vessel was sheared off. Burning gasoline poured into the water from the *Liscome Bay's* deck, hampering the efforts of the USS *Hughes* to rescue survivors.

Seaman Ollie Stine wrote, "At 5:15 AM, a Jap submarine torpedoed the *Liscome Bay*. His fish hit their gasoline tanks; I've never seen such an explosion. She burned for about twenty minutes, and there were two more big explosions as the fire reached her bomb and ammunition magazines, which blew her apart. *Morris* and *Hughes* returned and picked up her survivors, about 300 between us. Approximately 700 men were lost."

It was ironic that the USS *Hughes*, a destroyer tasked with defending the heavy ships of the fleet, was present at the sinking of so many of the lost carriers in the war. She had seen more than her share of the battles between the Americans and the Japanese. She had also observed six of the original destroyers in her Destroyer Squadron Two, over half, sink.

Funerals at sea for the dead sailors from the attack on
the aircraft carrier Liscome Bay. U.S. Navy photo.

The Americans landed at Tarawa and fought from November
20–23, 1943. After three days of heavy fighting, the Marines took
Tarawa but paid a heavy price. In this campaign, fighting in the
Gilbert and Marshall Islands cost the Americans 2,459 dead and
another 2,286 wounded. The Japanese lost over 11,000 killed and
358 captured. The Japanese had heavily fortified the islands, as they
were now aware that losing them would bring American heavy
bombers closer to Japan.

The USS *Hughes* would cover additional landings at Makin
Island in the coming days. Taking Makin Island cost far more in
Navy casualties than American ground troops. Roughly 395 Japa-
nese were killed in action, and the Americans lost only 66 dead and

152 wounded, along with 763 sailors, mainly from the escort carrier sinking.

On November 29, 1943, with things wrapping up from the last task force attacks and the Japanese defeated again, the USS *Hughes* joined the USS *Princeton*, a light aircraft carrier, and proceeded with her group back to Pearl Harbor. On November 30, 1943, Ollie Stine noted, "Routine day at sea. We received a message from Admiral Nimitz congratulating us on our capture of the Gilbert Islands. We are en route to Pearl Harbor." Tony Skic wrote, "We are finished with the islands and are headed back to Pearl. We are having bum weather."

They arrived in Hawaii on the second anniversary of the attack on Pearl Harbor, December 7, 1943. Retired Commander Allan Evens recalled, "On December 15, 1943, Destroyer Squadron Two [what was now left of it] received an unexpected message and orders to return to the United States. As the year ended, we were operating on training exercises at San Diego."

Seaman Ollie Stine was back in the United States far earlier than expected. It was a welcome reprieve from battle.

The sailors of the USS *Hughes* made the most of their liberty on shore. Seaman Tony Skic had a good time, writing, "I got shore liberty at 1:00 PM and went ashore with Buff and Neagle. We got drunk as hell and spent the night in the clink." The next night, December 22, 1943, he got off the ship again and returned to the San Diego bars. "We had 32 men in jail last night. I feel lousy after the previous night's drunk." They didn't feel all that bad; the next day, they got off the ship again and, as Skic wrote, "Made liberty again and went to Tijuana, Mexico last night and made out pretty good!" Even on Christmas, he noted, "Christmas Day, I went ashore and went to Tijuana, Mexico, and had a hell of a time."

Such was shore leave for sailors who had been in combat. They had seen horrible things in battle. It was surreal to pick up the body parts of your fellow sailors one day and, not long after, get shore leave and spend the nights in bars, brothels, and jail. A night in jail was nothing compared to having a Japanese plane dropping bombs on your ship and submarines sending torpedoes zipping by just under the ocean's surface.

Life and death were now inexorably mixed on any given day. You had to celebrate being alive and mourn your lost friends whenever you could. The losses were too significant, and the pain too recent to spend much time on reflection. Although there would be time for that later, many of this generation never discussed what they had seen and experienced. Even when they went home on leave, few talked about what they had seen in any detail. Their family and friends could not have understood.

CHAPTER NINETEEN

"HONOR IS HEAVIER THAN THE MOUNTAINS"

Pilots of the Japanese Special Attack Forces, A6M5 52c
Kyushu, Japan. Public domain Japanese photo.

The former general and current prime minister of Japan, Hideki Tojo, had dragged Japan into war against America and her allies. In Japan, he was seen by many colleagues as simple-minded and not all that intelligent but with great passion. His simplistic message was that Japan was the greatest country in the world and deserved to rule over all others. No logic or facts supported this, just nationalist fervor. Uneducated and less-intelligent people often fall for such simple messages, but these beliefs can only go so far.

By 1944, all the slogans, patriotic songs, public demonstrations, and flags would not save Japan from defeat. It was apparent to any thinking person that Japan would never rule the world and that her military forces were losing the war. Tojo doubled down and demanded that every man, woman, and child fight to the death to keep foreigners from Japanese soil, a nonsensical and impractical directive. Japanese civilians could not successfully fight American B-29 bombers with sharpened bamboo sticks. The walls were closing in, but Tojo put a good face on things and promised victory.

In truth, Tojo knew the goal was no longer to win a war of conquest; it was to protect the homeland. Extraordinary times called for special measures, or so Japanese leaders said. Soon, Admiral Onishi was well into developing the new force to keep Americans from setting foot on Japanese soil. The Japanese were used to nationalist slogans by now, so it was time to add some new ones.

"Be resolved that honor is heavier than the mountains and death lighter than the feather." Simply put, this kamikaze slogan meant that death wasn't all that bad and obligation was a crushing weight on all Japanese pilots of the Special Task Forces.

Onishi would read a poem to his men:

Asked about the soul of Japan,
I would say
That it is
Like wild cherry blossoms
Glowing in the morning sun.

Onishi told his men of their "nobility of spirit." He said that if they failed in their duty to Japan and the emperor, the country and their culture would be destroyed forever.

Soon, a new type of letter would be arriving in Japanese homes from pilots of the Special Attack Units who were now in training throughout Japan.

Letter from Special Attack Unit Pilot Toshitaro, soon to die near Luzon Island:

> Honorable Older Brother,
> Once again, orders have come down for the attack from which I will never return. I feel not the slightest regret. Already, I have grown intimate with death, the ultimate character-building passage that we human beings must face. All that is left is to carry out the duties I've been trained in and fulfill the Imperial mandate. I am humiliated that I have been such an unworthy son and younger brother in the twenty-seven years of my life. I will have to leave everything to you. With an untroubled heart, I fulfill the obligations I was born with. I am merely carrying out my duties as a man.

Letter from Captain Furukawa Takao, killed in the sea off Kagoshima, to his wife:

> Recently, in calmer moments, my thoughts are returning to you and our soon-to-be-born child. Please take good care of your health. When we first arrived at our base in Kyushu, there was a sudden change in plans, and we were all ordered into special attack units. I expect to depart at any moment. Every day, as I waited for my first and last attack, I reread the letter you wrote the day you made jelly and gazed at the photos of you and sister Etchan. Surprisingly, my heart was perfectly at peace, as though another me was gazing upon the me that was so calm.

Letter from Captain Adachi Takuya, killed in the Okinawa area, to his parents:

> The war zone is where these beautiful emotions are tested. If death means a return to this world of love, I do not need to fear. Nothing is left to do but to press on and fulfill my duty.

Letter from Second Lieutenant Tomisawa to his family:

> To destroy our enemy, I will summon courage with all my might and will go to strike. We are the ones to deliver the country from the current crises. Taking pride in this, I will surely do it.

What is striking about these few samples is that they are not the letters of raging maniacs or drunken men quickly put into a plane that they had only been taught to take off and not land, as history books have been reporting for decades. Many of the pilots had college educations. The old image of crazed, drunken fools could not have been further from the truth. These letters were from deeply patriotic and thoughtful men. No matter how misplaced their loyalties were, these young men held a deep commitment to honor and obligation that rose above their concern for their safety and survival. Undoubtedly, they shared the same fears as American soldiers, sailors, and pilots. No matter what they wrote home, it is also likely that they would have preferred to live.

Self-sacrifice in war was not new. American pilots and sailors were known to crash their planes or ships in a final act of defiance when they knew they would not survive. America also valued a person intentionally giving their life in exchange for defeating the enemy or saving others. The entire concept of America's highest distinction in combat, the Congressional Medal of Honor, is reserved for Americans who do just that. There is no greater prize that America can bestow. The distinction is that Americans and British servicemen do not plan to make this ultimate sacrifice in advance.

But Japan felt that the war was entering a state where real-time was all-encompassing and that preplanned death by her servicemen would be a new instrument of terror for the enemy. The war was a living thing that they were all in the middle of. It no longer had a beginning and ending point in time. They would all live or die together, or so they were told. To fail in one's duty was to kill everyone you loved and cared about. The nation's needs and national pride outweighed any personal wants or desires. This was a new way of thinking and living out reality. Honor was all that mattered.

Onishi was playing to a captive audience. He and the pilots were also fully aware of Japanese losses in recent battles. At the beginning of 1944, the American forces were steadily progressing toward Japan. The Japanese Imperial Navy pilots of renown were now mostly dead. Their replacements needed the expertise of the American pilots, and the new American planes were soon outclassing the Japanese models that were left. The infamous Japanese Zero no longer ruled the skies. New American fighter aircraft were faster, more maneuverable, and had armor to protect the pilots. The Japanese had to make do with obsolete planes and far-less-experienced pilots. Only older and more experienced pilots had much chance of survival, but they were now rare.

In 1944, the Japanese announced that there would be a new training program led by Captain Motoharu Okamura at the Tateyama Base in Tokyo. Intentional suicide attacks were now openly discussed, and the kamikaze attack forces were to become official public Japanese policy for the first time. No longer a vague, dark concept in the shadows, the idea that Admiral Onishi once called "heresy" was becoming state policy. The Japanese official state news agency, Domei, issued a press release that a flight instructor named Takeo Tagata was to begin training pilots for suicide missions. The Japanese people now became acquainted with something they had long heard rumors of.

Once it was announced to the public, the operation began in the open. Later, Commander Asaichi Tamai would ask a group of 23 of his best student pilots, ones he had personally trained, to volunteer for the Special Attack Units. Each student raised both of their hands in agreement. He then asked one of his lieutenants, Yukio Seki, to lead the attacks. Seki is said to have closed his eyes, lowered his head, and thought for ten seconds before saying, "Please appoint me to the post." Seki became the 24th kamikaze pilot to be chosen for the group. He later said, "Japan's future is bleak if it is forced to kill one of its best pilots," and "I am not going on this mission for Emperor Hirohito, or for the Empire. . . . I am going because I was ordered to." This seemed contrary to the code, but no one who agreed to such a mission would be overlooked.

The essential objective was to cause so much carnage for American families that they could no longer stomach the war against Japan. This would be tested. Japan hoped to keep the Americans out of Japan and force them to sue for peace terms favorable to Japan and its leaders. Japan now wanted the war to end on her terms.

A race was underway, one long in the making. America and Japan had new weapons of terror that they planned to unleash on each other. The only question was who would win this race. Could the Japanese terrorize and kill so many Americans in ships that they could no longer fight, or could America drop an atomic bomb on Japan, forcing unconditional surrender or eliminating the Japanese race from Earth?

The USS *Hughes* would play an integral part in both plans in 1944.

CHAPTER TWENTY

"WE ENTERED PORT TODAY, A BEAUTIFUL PLACE. THE TOWN IS NAMED MAUI"

Chester Bradley on the right in the back, and his shipmates with captured Japanese troops. Bradley collection.

In January 1944, the United States Navy was finally at full strength, far from the minimal forces available at the time of the attack on Pearl Harbor, when the Japanese Imperial Navy seemed unstoppable. The fears of Admiral Yamamoto had finally materialized. The complete industrial might of America was now in place, and the U. S. was building ships, planes, and submarines at a previously unthinkable rate. The next step of the war by the Americans would be a slow, incremental, island-by-island move toward mainland Japan. The only question left was how much war the Japanese would be willing to take before surrendering. It would be far more than the Americans initially thought.

Between WWI and WWII, most civilized countries advocated a more humane war between nations. WWI saw terrible weapons of war that shocked the collective human conscience. Banning certain weapons and limiting civilian casualties seemed the proper course. But suddenly, a new understanding of human behavior was developing. WWII was now simply good versus evil. "Civilized war" was now only a distant dream. The nationalists in Germany, Japan, and Italy were entirely controlled by fanatical personality cults run by Hitler, Tojo, and Mussolini. There were no limits to the evils they would perpetrate on humanity and no cruelty they would not engage in. Their insanity had to be met with a different type of war.

The rules of war continued to change. Hitler had seduced the people of Germany with his motto of making Germany great again. He had promised to create a thousand-year Reich that would dominate the world. Tojo pledged the same to the people of Japan. Their demand for total loyalty ended all conventional governmental limits and constitutional constraints. Death camps to torture and kill opponents were accepted.

This presented a dilemma for the civilized countries of the world, the Allies, and even the sailors of the USS *Hughes*. As the bloody months of the war in Europe and the Pacific dragged on, there arose a new and abiding hatred of the Germans and Japanese. It became so deep that the ideas of the past concerning war were slipping away. There could no longer be rules in a war against fascists and nationalists. This was profoundly concerning to Americans and their Allies. It was becoming apparent that they would have to become, at least to some degree, like the Nazis to defeat Nazism and Japanese nationalism. The dividing line between military and civilian targets disappeared in total war.

However, many Germans and Japanese did not support the governments controlling their countries. At the war's end, Japanese soldiers and pilots could not go out in public without facing ridicule and assault from ordinary people. Soldiers and Nazis met the same fate in Germany after the war. No one wanted to publicly admit that they were a soldier and even less that they had anything to do with the Nazi Party. But for now, Americans deeply hated all Germans and Japanese people. It was time to see them all die, no matter how disturbing this was deep inside Americans' souls.

This aspect of war would be deeply troubling for many of the sailors of the USS *Hughes* in the decades to come. A scar was developing in WWII among civilized people fighting against nationalism and the enslavement of the world, one that would demand a heavy price.

But for now, the USS *Hughes* would set sail again for hostile waters to kill more Japanese. A massive fleet was assembled for the next phase of the war. But their first stop would be Maui and a place called Lahaina Roads. The Navy wanted to hide the new fleet from prying eyes in Pearl Harbor, so they anchored it off the shores of Maui. Their next target was Kwajalein Atoll.

Kwajalein Atoll is part of the country of the Republic of the Marshall Islands, the largest of the islands in the group. Today, it is mainly inhabited by Marshallese and American civilian personnel doing contract work for the military. It is 2,400 miles southwest of

Honolulu, Hawaii. The climate is tropical rainforest. The temperature varies less than two degrees from month to month. The average annual rainfall is 101 inches. Although 2.5 miles long, it is only eight hundred yards wide. The Japanese and Americans both wanted an airfield there.

Before WWII, the Japanese moved onto the islands. Public schools were established in 1935, and teachers from Japan instituted classes. Even though the Japanese saw the Marshall Islanders as racially inferior to themselves, this period was seen by both sides as peaceful at first. Japanese immigration significantly increased until a large contingent inhabited the area, outnumbering the local tribal peoples by a factor of ten to one. The League of Nations had given the Japanese permission to settle and administer the islands if they did not use them for military purposes and respected the rights of the local inhabitants. That lasted only for so long. Combat forces from the Japanese Imperial Navy arrived at the Kwajalein Atoll in February 1941.

The next phase of Japan's attempt to perfect this area as an instrument of war was the relocation of Korean prisoners, who became forced laborers there in the early 1940s. Over ten thousand were sent to build fortifications for the Japanese Imperialists. Their ranks were swelled with the addition of Japanese workers imported from concentration camps for political dissidents. These were the people who began to build the runway for military aircraft. Interestingly, the public schools had to be demolished for this construction, erasing any concept of peaceful coexistence between the Japanese and local villagers. When the nationalist military leaders replaced the civilian government, the Marshallese were shocked to see the transformation from friendly cooperation to slavery. Yet Japan was not the only country that colonized the Pacific.

The Japanese were befuddled when Western countries criticized them as they began expanding and colonizing nations in these waters. Western powers had, for many years, been occupying and claiming these areas throughout the Pacific and other parts of the world for themselves. Japan's East Asia Co-Prosperity Sphere was modeled almost entirely on what they saw other Western countries do. The concept of expanding a country's influence and boundaries to the world's far reaches had been going on for centuries. The Japanese, believing themselves at least equals and even superior to everyone else, didn't want to miss out on this global land grab. This led to some soul-searching at this point in the war. Were the Japanese all that different from the British and Americans? In many respects, they were, but in other ways, they were similar.

One person who was acutely aware of the evils of any country "colonizing" another was Elanor Roosevelt, the wife of FDR. She felt so strongly about it that she demanded that Churchill agree to a process of withdrawing from countries they had colonized over the years before America entered WWII. Churchill agreed that these policies were wrong but felt the issues were complex and could not be addressed during the war. Eleanor disagreed and believed there was a terrible hypocrisy in fighting Germany and Japan for taking over countries when Britain had built their empire on the backs of millions of people in other countries worldwide. The Marshallese were perfect examples of the horrors of the colonization efforts of the Japanese.

Ultimately, no nation or people wants to be invaded and occupied by another country. A big part of the internal debate about what the war was about was a deep introspection by many of the Allied nations fighting against the nationalists in Germany and Japan. They were faced with the guilt of their histories in global expansion, however good they had once thought them to be. This would be a significant reckoning during this period and in the post-WWII era.

In the decades since WWII, historians and Hollywood moviemakers have tended to portray historical battles and clear-cut

Sailors of the USS Hughes were allowed onshore and dismantled a
Japanese plane for souvenirs to take home. Bradley collection.

heroism in epic battles between good and evil. However, this over-simplifies what men at war and nations felt then. Nothing about how humans make war against each other is simple. WWII was a world-wide civil war to address, once and for all, the sins of colonialism and the hundreds of years of incremental conquest by nations.

It now seemed that the words of Abraham Lincoln during America's Civil War were playing out on a world stage: that each drop of blood spilled by the lash of slavery would be repaid by a drop of blood by the sword in war. The sailors of the USS *Hughes* were in a battle to defeat the Japanese but also to define a new world order where all peoples would have a chance at freedom, even though it would still be a long road to get there.

The Marshallese were about to see over 36,000 shells fired on their tiny island from American naval vessels to free them from the Japanese. In January and February of 1942, almost nine thousand Japanese soldiers and forced laborers were killed. Many Marshallese fled the island in canoes during the combat. It is estimated that two hundred were killed in the battles.

Tony Skic knew the risks of the upcoming attack on one of the islands. He wrote, "We will have 30 carriers on this raid. Eight big Battle Wagons [Battleships] will hit Notye. The USS *Hughes* will bombard and attempt to draw fire from the shore batteries. We will be damn good targets for the yellow bitches. If they ever get our range and hit us with a salvo . . ."

January 29, 1944, saw the dawn of a significant battle for the USS *Hughes*. They would start the raid by attacking the shore guns of the Japanese before the landing force came in. The USS *Hughes* would sail close to shore and be used to draw fire from the Japanese gun emplacements so they could be located. Before the attack, Tony Skic noted in his diary, "Breakfast at three AM tomorrow. The bombardment sure sounds nice. The yellow sons of bitches are going to get their asses tanned good."

Ollie Stine noted:

At 6:40 AM, we arrived off Wotze, and the *Louisville* opened the bombardment. We were firing for about fifteen minutes when Jap shore batteries opened fire. One shell hit the bridge of the *Anderson* and killed the captain and several officers on the bridge, so she turned and steamed right for the Jap battery, firing with all guns. The USS *Hughes* fired 350 rounds of five-inch shells. We made three runs on the island. We destroyed one ammunition dump and a radio station, set a hangar on fire, and made direct hits on a pillbox, besides numerous hits on the airfield runways and a camp area. The USS *Hughes* received an 'excellent shooting' from the USS *Louisville* for this. We were straddled twice by 4" fire but escaped injury. Kwajalein is a mass of flames.

On February 1, 1944, Stine recorded, "Just at dawn, our BBGs [Battleship Group] and Cruisers opened bombardment again, starting new fires and rekindling old ones. At 11:00 AM, the first waves of Marines have just left for the beach as I write this. The Marines are meeting only slight resistance so far, and it's no wonder. After our bombardment, I don't see how many Japs could still be alive."

Tony Skic also recorded, "The smoke is so thick that almost nothing can be seen. This is the worst bombardment I've seen. It's savage, murderous, terrific! The fires are big, and all you can hear is the murderous fire, which sounds like thunder. Christ, what a show!"

The United States had learned from the devastating losses in earlier raids and was committed to not making the same mistakes. The Americans now sailed their ships much closer to the beaches when bombarding them, led by destroyers like the USS *Hughes* to draw fire and identify the Japanese gun emplacements on shore. The months of planning were beginning to pay dividends. The islands themselves also provided some benefits. The Navy started to use armor-piercing shells to break into Japanese fortifications on shore before landing Marines. The thin, flat lowlands also left few places for the Japanese to hide their fortifications.

By sunset on the first day, the Marines had taken much of the island with few casualties. Most of the Japanese were already dead from the naval bombardment. The most significant number of Marines killed occurred when they threw an explosive charge into a bunker, not realizing it was being used for torpedo warhead storage. The resulting explosion killed 20 Marines. Ultimately, the area was secured with so few casualties that the Americans would move up the invasion of other islands. But the Japanese were also learning. They would not repeat the mistake of trying to use beach-line defenses in the future.

The surviving Marshallese would face new challenges as well. On February 6, 1944, Kwajalein was claimed by the United States. It was designated, with the rest of the nation of the Marshall Islands, as a United Nations Trust Territory. It was a colony once again but with a new master. It would not be until 1983 that it would sign the Compact of Free Association with the United States, and it would not gain partial independence until 1986. Beginning in 1999, it entered four years of negotiations and signed an amended compact that took effect in 2004, the beginning of actual freedom.

There would be one more dark chapter when the Americans returned to detonate atomic bombs in the area. The environmental impacts of the current battle to retake the islands from the Japanese were horrific. On February 5, 1944, Tony Skic recorded, "Still patrolling off the islands. Large spots of oil were observed on the surface of the water. The smell of oil is heavy."

The next day, Ollie Stine noted, "Routine day at sea. Rough as hell. We are now controlling 19 of the 32 atolls in the Marshall Group. We will probably take the rest of them soon." Those rough waters spread the contaminated oil from sunken ships and planes throughout the island group. The pristine waters and coral reefs would take generations to recover.

The people of the Marshall Islands, now numbering 42,050, had originally arrived two thousand years before the birth of Christ. Once claimed by Spain, the islands were sold to Germany in 1885. They were occupied by the Japanese, initially under a charter by the League of Nations and then the Americans. After centuries of colonial rule, they were finally free again in 2004. The sailors of the USS *Hughes* were witnesses to that final payment of blood in combat.

CHAPTER TWENTY-ONE

"FISHING IS GOOD HERE"

Dublon Island under bombing attack during the invasion of the
Truk and Eniwetok Islands campaign. U.S. Navy photo.

The USS *Hughes* and the fleet moved on to Truk Lagoon and the occupation of Eniwetok Island. Tony Skic never lost his love of fishing from his younger pre-war life. The waters of the Pacific Ocean offered fishing opportunities that were unthought of in his youth. In his journal, he constantly noted his requests for fishing tackle and that he had received boxes of the same from home. On February 15, 1944, he noted, "Anchored as before. I fished till morning and caught a red snapper that was 20 inches and weighed close to 20 pounds! We got underway with two battleships, cruisers, carriers, and transports to take the island of Eniwetok. The *New Jersey, Iowa,* and the other battleships, including five big carriers, will bomb Truk, the Jap Pearl Harbor." The frequent references to fishing, often between battles or even air attacks, show the sailors of the *Hughes* were becoming used to battle as part of everyday life. Even as they prepared for a fight the next day, the sailors often spent much of the night fishing from the destroyer's deck.

That same evening, Ollie Stine noted, "Left the lagoon and headed to sea. The carriers, battleships, and cruisers came out, as did the transports. We are going 300 miles west to occupy the Eniwetok Atoll, the Atoll from which came those planes that bombed us three nights ago."

The Navy began Operation Hailstone, the massive air and land attack against Truk Lagoon. This started on February 18, 1944. The problem for the Navy was that planes from Truk could attack the invasion fleet sailing for Eniwetok Island. Admiral Marc Mitscher's Fast Carrier Task Force (TF 58) comprised five fleet carriers and four light cruisers, carrying more than five hundred aircraft for the assault. The Japanese had long known the weakness in this area and the difficulties of countering the Americans and had removed many of their larger ships.

On February 17, 1944, the American carriers launched their aircraft just before dawn. They flew at low altitude to Truk, evading

Japanese radar, and achieved complete surprise, catching the Japanese planes on the runways. To make matters worse for the Japanese, many of their pilots were on leave when the attack occurred. Only half of the Japanese planes were ready for combat. These 150 Japanese planes and pilots faced five hundred American aircraft. The American Grumman F6F Hellcat planes were much faster and could fly higher than the Japanese Mitsubishi A6M Zero fighters. The Japanese took initial losses of 30 planes versus only four American planes.

With the Japanese aircraft gone from the skies, the Americans concentrated on the Japanese ships in the harbor. Ships that had gotten underway and were headed back to Japan were cut off by American submarines and sunk. American bombers destroyed the airfields and aircraft on the ground. The bottom of Truk Lagoon is still so littered with Japanese vessels and planes that it is now a haven for modern-day SCUBA divers who flock to the battle site.

One of the ships, the *Aikoku Maru*, an ammunition ship, was hit by an American torpedo plane. The explosion was so large that it engulfed the attacking aircraft and the ship and destroyed both, killing the three American airmen on board.

After the battle, it became clear that the Japanese had suffered an enormous defeat. They sent planes back at night to locate and bomb American ships but only hit the USS *Intrepid*, killing 11 sailors but failing to sink her.

Meanwhile, on the USS *Hughes*, Tony Skic noted only light resistance at Eniwetok Island:

Our troops landed on Eniwetok Island with no opposition. I saw about ten torpedo planes drop four bombs apiece on the island. Fighters strafed, and dive bombers also hit them. They are catching hell. They are being pounded day and night, the exploding bombs sound nice, the concussion is thunderous, and they look beautiful when they leave the plane and are coming down. A Jap was seen running down the beach like a madman. The results from Truk have just come in. It was hit for two days; more than 200 planes were destroyed, 150 were shot down in combat, and the others were caught on the ground. Sunk were two cruisers, three destroyers, four cargo ships, two gunboats, one seaplane tender, and many others. Boy, the Japs are humiliated and must have lost face. Fishing is good here! Reagan got a big one, and O'Brien got two big red snappers.

Ollie Stine noted that transitioning from combat to fishing was short: "Several fighters were strafing the beach. We passed 1000 yards from the beach, making five knots. They would make a strafing run, pull out, and zoom over us at about 100 feet. On the third run, they were fired at by the Japs. Eight torpedo bombers were called in, and we watched them dive in single file and release four bombs each. The fourth struck the water, and he had only covered half the distance to our ship when it fell. It exploded 500 yards off our bow, far too close for comfort!" But then, it was time to go back to fishing. This was one of their favorite fishing spots in the entire Pacific Ocean.

On February 23, 1944, the USS *Hughes* got to go back to the harbor for fuel, and Tony Skic notes this was a welcome time for the sailors as they got out their fishing rods again: "Entered port to fuel off the tanker. The crew caught plenty of fish while we fueled. Marines and tanks could be seen advancing along the beach, and fighting was still happening, although on a smaller scale. Mullins was injured seriously when a wave hit him against the depth charge racks."

Ollie Stine recorded, "Rejoined our carrier group last evening and continued our patrol. We watched a torpedo plane crash into the water, attempting a landing on the USS *Suwanee*. We went in, but the *Mustin* got there before we did and rescued all three men."

Swimming from the ship and from shore was popular in the tropical climate of the Central Pacific Ocean. Glen Edmonson collection.

The USS *Hughes* and the American fleet left the Marshall Islands, but scientists would return and conduct 43 nuclear tests between 1948 and 1958. The American servicemen who died in the battle that the USS *Hughes* participated in would be exhumed and returned to the United States before the atomic tests began. The Marshallese, however, were forcibly removed for the tests, and much of this area was destroyed or made permanently radioactive.

Not long after the first atomic bombs had been created, the next step was the development of an H-bomb. This process occurs when hydrogen atoms are fused. The energy released is far more explosive than from a fission nuclear bomb. Robert Oppenheimer, the original father of the atomic bombs used in Japan, was by then reluctant to support these new weapons. The first test of one of these devices was at Eniwetok Lagoon on the island of Elugelab. Oppenheimer attempted to delay the test, hoping they would never be used. He was unsuccessful, and on November 1, 1952, the "Ivy Mike" test was detonated. The island was wiped off the face of the Earth in a millisecond.

The mushroom cloud reached 135,000 feet into the atmosphere. The blast had the same explosive power as ten million tons of TNT, five hundred times as powerful as the bomb at Hiroshima. The shockwave was recorded in California and around the globe. Scientist Edward Teller, an ardent supporter and generally known as the father of the H-bomb, could see the seismometer recording in Berkley, California, as it happened.

The Marshallese were returned to the other islands in the area after the Americans assured them that the remaining islands had been decontaminated. However, soon after, they had to be removed again when they became ill from radiation poisoning. In the end, America spent hundreds of millions of dollars trying to repair the damage to the area. After decades, it is still not safe to go there today.

Tony Skic and the sailors of the USS *Hughes* would be among the last ever to fish the formerly pristine waters of Eniwetok Lagoon.

"IF YOU TELL ME THIS IS MY JOB, I'LL DO IT"

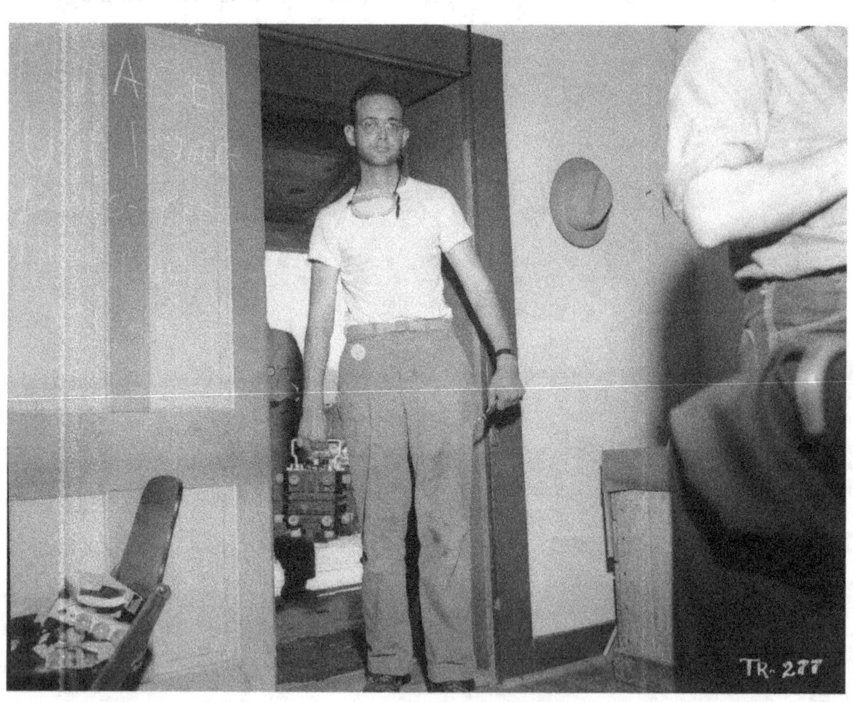

Herbert Lehr delivering the plutonium core for the "Gadget".
July 12, 1944. U.S. Army photo.

As the development of the atomic bomb proceeded in secret, several prominent scientists began asking questions about its use. Unbeknownst to them, President Roosevelt decided to do this project without consulting Congress or the United States courts. As the commander in chief, he had chosen to exercise that power to the maximum extent possible during war. In retrospect, many believed that Congress should have been consulted on the development. This was a remarkable path since it cost an astonishing two billion dollars. Many scientists felt that as the creators of the bomb, they should have a say in how it might be used, but this was never going to happen.

Much was being demanded of the scientists. They were being asked to put everything else on hold and work only on the bomb. One of the top scientists recruited by Oppenheimer was Earnest Lawrence, a man who proved critical in the bomb's development. James Conant, one of the top leaders under Roosevelt on the Manhattan Project and director of the Office of Scientific Research and Development, recalled talking to Lawrence: "Ernest, you say you are convinced of the importance of these fission bombs. Are you ready to devote the next several years of your life to getting them made?" Conant said, "I can still recall the expression in his eyes as he sat there with his mouth half open. It was a serious personal decision." Lawrence responded, "If you tell me this is my job, I'll do it."

But development was all the scientists would ever be allowed to do. President Roosevelt had created a committee called the Top Policy Group. It consisted of Vice President Wallace, Secretary of War Henry Stimson, Army Chief of Staff George Marshall, Vannevar Bush, and Conant. These men were fully aware that they only operated under the strict control of the president, and Roosevelt reserved all nuclear bomb authority for himself. One reason for this was that Roosevelt already knew that the bomb and its impacts would go far beyond its use in WWII against Germany and Japan. The bomb would remake the entire world into a new order.

Roosevelt feared that other nations might obtain one, and he believed that America could not allow any other country to be ahead of the United States in possessing and using the bomb. The next world war would be short if nations used these new powerful weapons. Vannevar Bush recalled a discussion with Roosevelt: "We discussed at some length after-war control." Roosevelt was already developing a concept of a new world order in which nations, faced with such weapons, would collectively meet and solve problems without armed conflict. This concept would someday become the United Nations.

Roosevelt would not allow the scientists to make these decisions. However, as the project developed, the scientists began to think past its development and about its use. Many believed that they should have a proper form of input, or in some cases, veto power, regarding the use of the bomb against cities in Germany and Japan. Some Jewish refugees from Germany and throughout Europe had few qualms about using the bomb on Germany but did not have the same feelings about Japan.

In the meantime, German scientist Werner Heisenberg had been receiving a product called heavy water from Norway. This could be used in a process similar to the one Fermi had used at the University of Chicago to prove the existence of a self-sustaining chain reaction in uranium. He remarked, "It was from September 1941 that we saw an open road ahead of us, leading to the atomic bomb." But in truth, Heisenberg was aware that Germany, under the policies of Hitler and with the loss of so many talented scientists, would not likely build one soon. He was, however, deeply concerned that America would do so and drop them on Germany. He decided to try to share this information with the Danish physicist Niels Bohr.

Bohr was skeptical about the bomb and the path to developing one. But Heisenberg met with him and passed him a paper with a drawing of his heavy water experiment. It is surmised that Heisenberg did this to find out what the Americans knew, hoping to dissuade them from building one and dropping it on Germany. Heisenberg wanted everyone to shelve the concept until after WWII was over. Robert Oppenheimer recalled, "Heisenberg and Weizacker came over from Germany. Bohr had the impression that they came over less to tell what they knew than to see if Bohr knew anything that they did not." Elisabeth Heisenberg had a slightly different recollection of the meeting: "He wanted to signal to Bohr that Germany neither would nor could build a bomb. . . . Secretly he even hoped that his message could prevent the use of an atomic bomb in Germany one day."

After the war, Elisabeth recalled, "Bohr essentially heard only one single sentence: The Germans knew that atomic bombs could be built. This deeply shook him, and his dismay was so great that he lost track of all else." Bohr was also fully aware that Heisenberg was working for the Nazis. Heisenberg felt they were close friends, but Bohr held him in disdain for even being associated with Nazi Germany.

In the end, this convinced the Allies that the risk of Germany developing an atomic bomb was significant. Had the Nazis discovered this meeting and transfer of information, Heisenberg would have certainly ended up in a concentration camp and been executed for his efforts and betrayal, no matter his actual intent.

Vannevar Bush had asked President Roosevelt about money for the project, and the answer was, "The money would have to come from a special source available for such an unusual purpose and . . . he could arrange for this." General Groves and, through him, Oppenheimer were given top priority to spend anything needed to get the project built.

Groves took this literally. He began to build massive cities in Tennessee and Washington State to create uranium 235 and plutonium for the two bombs. Thousands of people were hired, all under the strictest secrecy, but none knew what they were working on. They

Heisenberg and Bohr meet in Copenhagen and talk about the
development of a nuclear bomb in America and Germany.
Creative Commons license.

told their friends they were making the lightning for lightning bugs
or other such stories. When they ran out of copper wire for the giant
magnets that separated U-238 from naturally occurring uranium,
they took 15,000 tons of silver from the US Treasury.

The original letter from President Roosevelt to Vannevar Bush
authorizing the project was concise and to the point. Written on
White House stationery, it reads, "Jan 19—V.B. OK—returned—I
think you should keep this in your safe. FDR." This concise letter
authorized the expenditure of two billion dollars and the creation of
the first American atomic bombs.

Another problem was yet to be solved. Fermi had proven that
a self-sustaining nuclear reaction was possible in Chicago, but no
one knew how much material it would take for a bomb. An earlier

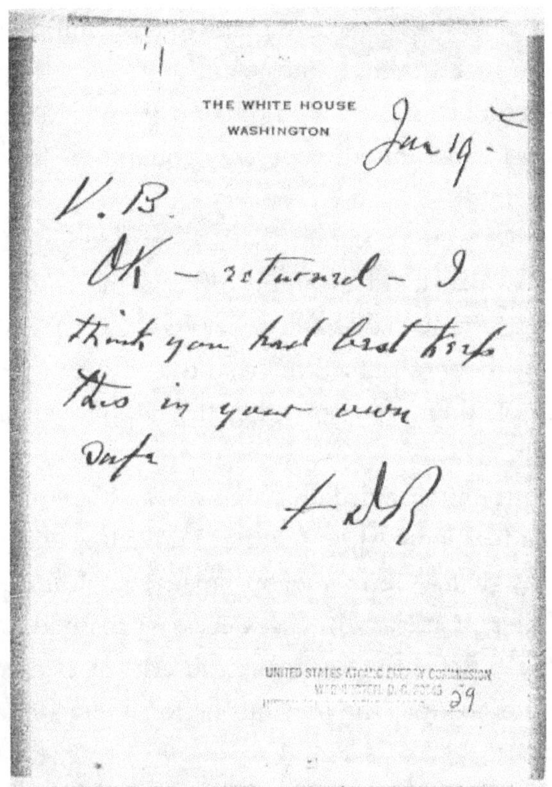

The January 19th letter from Roosevelt to Vannevar Bush approving the creation of the first atomic bombs and the two billion-dollar expenditure. U.S. AEC Archives photo.

report had suggested a considerable range of the necessary U-235: "The mass of U235 required to produce explosive fission under appropriate conditions can hardly be less than 2 kg [4.4 pounds] nor greater than 100 kg [220 pounds]. These wide limits reflect chiefly the experimental uncertainty in the capture cross-section of U235 for fast neutrons."

This was a big problem, considering the difficulty of making even small amounts of the U-235 in Oak Ridge, Tennessee, and plutonium in Hanford, Washington State. Oppenheimer and his team would work tirelessly on these and many other technical problems of assembling the first atomic bombs. As the project progressed, they faced a second problem: there would likely be enough plutonium for two implosion bombs initially but only enough U-235 for a single gun-style bomb.

The scientists were confident that the gun design of the U-235 bomb would work. Rapid assembly of two pieces of sub-critical U-235 by firing one piece at the other in a barrel was considered assured. They did not even feel the need to test such a device, and in any event, they could not do so, as they did not have any material for a second bomb.

But the plutonium implosion bomb was a different story. No one knew if it would explode. Although they hoped it would, a dud posed the problem of giving Germany and Japan a nuclear device for use against the Allies, or at least the core necessary to build such a device. It was not the bomb itself that was the critical element—anyone could make a bomb—but the precious fissionable material necessary for such a device.

So, Oppenheimer recommended that one of the two plutonium bombs should be exploded in a test to see if it would work before dropping it. He proposed that the trial be done at what became known as the Trinity Site in New Mexico. That plan was approved, but first, a significant development in the war was headed to a conclusion. Germany was clearly on the path to defeat, and it was no longer possible to finish the weapon in time to use it on Berlin.

Would the United States use such a device on Japan if Germany was defeated? The sailors on the USS *Hughes* ensured that a suitable base would soon become available for the newly constructed B-29 bombers, which could now reach the Japanese mainland from these captured islands.

But there continued to be the question of what kind of war WWII was. How much did Americans and their Allies hate the

Japanese? What price should the people pay for the misguided policies of their nationalist leaders? What did this new phase of "total war" mean? What price would the people of Japan pay for the wars their leaders had started? It was becoming clear to the scientists and political leaders that atomic destruction would be the ultimate price humanity would have to pay.

On board the USS *Hughes*, so close to actual combat and death at every moment, there was no ambivalence about what the Japanese people deserved. It was black and white, and in their words, "yellow," a dismissive racial stereotype of the times.

"THE CONSTANT HEAT AND TROPICAL RASH ADDED LITTLE TO OUR COMFORT"

"Pollywogs" become "Shellbacks" in a ceremony on the USS Hughes as they cross the Equator. Glen Edmonson collection.

On March 6, 1944, the USS *Hughes* was back in Pearl Harbor for refitting and repairs. Tony Skic recorded, "Received plenty of mail today. Rumors are going around that the whole squadron is going down to the South Pacific to be made into a raider group for that big shithead MacArthur. All we do is hit the Jap ships and bombard Jap bases for MacArthur, and that will be tough and exciting, but who gives a good God damn. I got a new cover for the gun. I think I'll go ashore tomorrow for a few beers. Time to knock off this charity work on the ship after hours." The next day, he went to shore, got drunk, and left a buddy passed out on the dock. "I forgot to bring him back to the ship, but he returned later." But the next day, March 8, he noted, "I worked like a damn fool on the ship." Work and fun were mixed equally when they were in port at Pearl Harbor. On March 10, he wrote, "Went ashore today. Drunker. I got polluted at Richardson and Aiea Naval Barracks. John took a leak in my gear locker."

A few days earlier, while the USS *Hughes* was en route to Pearl Harbor, where Tony Skic would party on the town and work to get the USS *Hughes* ready for her next combat mission, his shipmate Ollie Stine became seriously ill with appendicitis. On February 28, 1944, Ollie noted, "Had an attack of acute appendicitis on the midwatch. Was put in bed." For the next three days, he would receive two pints of plasma daily to keep him alive before getting into port. On Thursday, he noted, "Received two more pints of plasma. The ship is en route to Pearl, where I will be transferred to the hospital." Stine had his operation on March 4, 1944, and was hospitalized until March 18.

Ollie Stine would miss the USS *Hughes* sailing south again on March 15, 1944. He was put on the USS *Russell*, which would escort the *Habbrock,* a transport ship taking soldiers to New Guinea. He would not return to the USS *Hughes* until May 8, 1944, when he wrote, "Left the *Dobbin* at 4:00 PM and proceeded to another anchorage about five miles away to fuel. The USS *Hughes* was alongside the tanker, and I was transferred to her. I am glad to be off the *Russell.*" The USS *Russell* was one of the original members of Destroyer Squadron Two at the beginning of WWII and one of only five that was not sunk during WWII.

Stine would also miss two treasured maritime events on the USS *Hughes.* On March 15, 1944, Tony Skic recorded, "Left Pearl Harbor at 1:00 PM this noon with four death wagons [battleships] and four other destroyers, and we are returning to the South Pacific and our old stomping grounds. We will get initiated this time when we cross the equator."

Sailors who have crossed the equator and been appropriately initiated are known as "shellbacks." New sailors who have not done so are known as "pollywogs." Time and combat permitting, the ancient rite of passage is carried out with vigor. On this occasion, the ceremony went on for days. Seaman Tony Skic was a pollywog. On March 17, 1944, he wrote, "Had a good soaking with a saltwater hose and got the hell beat out of me."

Skic's entry on March 18, 1944, noted:

Fights between pollywogs and shellbacks still going on. I received my summons from King Neptune Rex Larry Jones. The captain read the charges against me; they were as follows:
1) Demoralizing the Navy yard workmen in Hunter Point Navy Yard.
2) Trying to clean house in all the jails in Tijuana.
3) Using gun three as a water pistol to spray all trustworthy shellbacks.

We are having a hell of a time, and all pollywogs like me will get a hell of a pants warming tomorrow.

On March 19, 1944, the ceremony finally concluded. "Initiation was held today, and I really caught it, a good pants warming, a good ducking, all my hair cut off, painted with red, green and black paint then the photographer took my picture." The next day, Skic would write, "My fanny is still sore from the work I got yesterday." But Seaman Tony Skic was now a trusted shellback.

Oliver Jones said, "It was pretty tough. You had to crawl through a long canvas tube, and guys hit you on the butt with all types of things, and you felt it. But afterward, I was pretty proud to get the title of a shellback. I wasn't a pollywog anymore. The Chief dressed up as Neptune and presided over the ceremony at the equator. Everyone enjoyed the heck out of the whole thing."

Chester Bradley and Malcolm Riker fondly remembered their initiations as shellbacks and then as "purple porpoises." After becoming a shellback, only a select few go on to become purple porpoises when they cross the 180-degree meridian at the equator on either the vernal or autumnal equinox, a time, place, and latitude that only exists twice yearly. The benefit of being a shellback is that you're allowed to demand a mug of grog from a pollywog, and a purple porpoise can demand a measure of grog from either. The experience was a great distraction from the war and a hilarious adventure for the officers and the men.

The USS *Hughes* happened to be at that place and time. Sailors have revered this for centuries. Retired Commander Alan Evans, on the *Hughes*, recorded:

Our CVE [aircraft carrier] group left again on 15 March for the strikes at Palau, Yap, and Woleai, which were carried out successfully on 31 March. We were part of the support group for this operation, which carried deep into enemy territory. The force, under Rear Admiral V. H. Ragsdale, had the unusual experience of crossing the intersection of the equator and the 180th meridian on 21 March 1944 when the sun, in its orbit, was directly overhead. For this, we were initiated by Admiral Ragsdale into the Royal Order of Purple Porpoises, whose membership card reads:

"Having entered my most inner sanctuary located at the junction of 00 degrees Latitude and 180 degrees Longitude on the sacred hour of the Vernal Equinox 21 March 1944 AD, be installed as an honored member and respected as such of my Royal Order of Purple Porpoises. By my direction, he shall enjoy the pleasure of frolicking with all mermaids living in or adjacent to the boundaries of my kingdom. He shall also be entitled to and receive from all Short Snorters, Golden Dragons, and Green Turtles one free nogging of grog as a measure of proper respect."

So, Seaman Tony Skic and his shipmates were not only all shellbacks now but also members of the Royal Order of the Purple Porpoises, and, of course, no seaman was ever going to turn down an extra "nogging of grog."

On March 25, 1944, Tony Skic recorded some observations that seemed oddly mixed, but like everyone else, he was changing. "We are at General Quarters. The USS *Taylor* contacted a submarine. About 25 depth charges were dropped. Wrote a letter to Mom and Aunt Vea. The sky is beautiful as the sun sets—a mixture of colors like a rainbow. White fluffy clouds, blue sky, pink, orange, gold, a beautiful array of colors is to be seen, and an amateur cannot describe its beauty as I am. We are spotted by the Japs today. So informed sources say, but who does know."

Throughout early April, the USS *Hughes* was constantly escorting aircraft carriers, making raids on Japanese forces or escorting troops ashore. Some of the missions involved the fleet trying to get the Japanese Imperial Navy into battles so they could further reduce their numbers. But both sides were constantly probing for weaknesses. Like the American Navy, the Japanese had scout planes and submarines in the area. Tony Skic wrote on March 29, 1944, "I slept on the gun last night, and it rained like hell. The USS *Martin* had a submarine contact today, and we had a radar contact on an aircraft last night. It was a Jap patrol plane, but it only came within 10 miles, and we don't know if it spotted us."

Commander Alan Evans noted the changing feelings of the crew on the USS *Hughes,* "On completion of the Palau raid, our force departed for Espiritu Santo. Our amazement at how much the port had changed was nothing to our feelings when we moved on to Guadalcanal on 11 April. There was the same strong scent of flowers and the stillness to the night that had been synonymous with death and destruction two years before. But it was not the same Guadalcanal."

Conditions were deteriorating rapidly on board the ship. Supply lines were stretched thin, and fresh food was gone. It would get worse before it got better. The Americans retook the islands and bases in Western New Guinea and New Hollandia. But the Japanese were not giving up without a fight. On April 10, 1944, the USS *Hughes* entered a dry dock to repair battle damage to her side. Tony Skic wrote, "I got to bed about 2:20 AM and was tired as a dog. The weather is hot. It rained hard last night. The food we are having isn't fit for a God damned dog. Everything is dehydrated and good for shit. The heat is terrific, the food is terrible, and conditions in general are bad."

But Tony Skic's spirits would rise at the first sign of actual combat. "We just got the dope about this operation. We will land on Western New Guinea to take Hollandia, Newak & Madang. The Japs have three airfields on Newak. Our planes will work it over and neutralize it. Our carrier planes are hitting the other places right now. We expect enemy aircraft attacks. We have a large force between us and New Guinea in case the Japs would come to bother us. The battle fleet is ready and raring to go!"

The landings went well, and the expected sea battle and air attack never materialized. Soon enough, Tony Skic was again bored, hungry, and exhausted. "Slept on the gun again all night and got soaked

The sailors on the USS Hughes were growing weary of war and the hot, humid South Pacific. Glen Edmonson collection.

as a rat. The food has been lousy for two weeks. I was writing letters home last night in the armory when the General Quarters buzzer went off. Jap planes were only 14 miles away and closing in, but they didn't hit us." The next day, he recorded, "Still patrolling around New Guinea as usual, nothing new happens, everything is monotonous. This last week of mid-watch has me run ragged."

Half a world away from their homes and after years at sea with no end to the war in sight, the sailors on board the USS *Hughes* were at a low point. The heat and humidity were oppressive, and the conditions became brutal on the ship. The lack of fresh food was a compounding factor. Alan Evans recorded his thoughts about the New Guinea campaign on board the vessel: "While the main forces of the Navy smashed across the Central Pacific, the *Hughes* as a unit of the Seventh Fleet continued the unglamorous New Guinea campaign. This entailed being underway almost constantly. The seizure of another island along the coast would be followed by escorting several echelons of supply LSTs until preparations were made for the next landing. There were no facilities ashore for recreation. We had no mail for three months, few provisions or supplies, and no repair facilities. The constant heat and tropical rash added little to our comfort."

However, the American Navy soon faced a new Japanese weapon of war, the kamikaze, and the Japanese had no idea that American atomic bombs would one day match and counter this weapon. Robert Oppenheimer and Admiral Onishi would soon do battle in the Pacific.

CHAPTER TWENTY-FOUR

"I TRIED LIKE HELL TO UNDERSTAND"

Albert Einstein and Robert Oppenheimer at the Institute for Advanced Study in the 1950s. Public domain AEC photo.

On June 6, 1944, the long-awaited Allied landing in northern France began. Allied nations invaded the beaches in Normandy, starting a campaign to push across German-occupied lands and into Germany. It was clear to everyone that Germany would be defeated, and the Allies were now firmly on the offensive for the first time. But this only highlighted the emerging moral dilemma.

No one would have blamed America and Britain for using atomic bombs to keep Germany or Japan from overrunning the Allies' homelands. But the chances of an invasion on British or American soil were now nil. For the first time, Britain and America had to grapple with using atomic weapons on a foe already on the road to defeat. This would not be a public debate, and few would know about it.

Virtually everyone in England and America was united in the goal of stamping out Japanese and German nationalism. The cost would be measured in the lives of soldiers, airmen, and sailors fighting overseas. Could the atomic bombs lessen those casualties? The Pacific War showed how costly it might be to invade mainland Japan. Estimates of Allied losses were in the millions. Hitler demanded that every man, woman, and child die to defend him. These were chilling realities and weighed heavily on the decision to use atomic weapons. Letters to families of their sons being killed in action were sent by the hundreds each day. The suffering of the sailors on the USS *Hughes* in retaking New Guinea was staggering. How much could they and Americans back home endure? Would the moral cost of using atomic bombs be worth it?

The technical difficulties of the Manhattan Project were also overwhelming. Amassing material for the bombs was coming along very slowly. Design problems for exploding the plutonium bomb were vexing. To make matters worse, Robert Oppenheimer had traveled to see an old love interest named Jean Tatlock in San Francisco. Not only was this a problem for his wife, Kitty Oppenheimer, but he was also under close surveillance by U.S. security agents. Although they might not have cared much about an old love interest, they were deeply concerned that Tatlock was a lifelong communist. They were apprehensive that Oppenheimer was passing secrets to Russia through Tatlock. Oppenheimer was a deeply committed and loyal American of the highest order, but his affair with Tatlock put that reputation in peril.

This came to a head when FBI agents went to General Groves and were on the verge of arresting Oppenheimer and revoking his security clearance. But Groves knew there was no atomic bomb project without Oppenheimer. He was irreplaceable, and Groves knew it. Groves intervened, stopping the security agents and putting his reputation and career on the line. He confronted Oppenheimer and demanded that the relationship stop. Groves knew that Oppenheimer was no Russian spy nor a communist, but this put the entire project in peril. Oppenheimer went to Tatlock in San Francisco one last time and told her he was breaking off the relationship, pushing her into a deep despair.

The risk of this episode ended in early 1944 when Tatlock went into the bathroom of her apartment, filled her bathtub with water, and took a handful of sleeping pills. She had placed pillows around the tub for comfort and began to write letters. The final note, which was never finished, read, "To those who loved and helped me, all the love and courage. I wanted to live and to give, and I got paralyzed somehow. I tried like hell to understand and couldn't. At least I could take away the burden of a paralyzed soul from a fighting world . . ." The letter trailed off as the powerful drugs began to take effect, and she died, her head slipping under the water's surface on that cold winter day. Her body was not found until her father went to her apartment to check on her. Oppenheimer was devastated by the news. He left his office and wandered the hills of the high desert alone in the pine trees, lost in his thoughts and grief.

The Trinity site's development to detonate the first atomic bomb also began that year. Oppenheimer had wistfully picked the name "Trinity" from a sonnet by John Donne:

Batter my heart, three-personed God, for you
As yet but knock, breathe, shine, and seek to mend;
That I may rise, and stand, o'erthrow me, and bend
Your force to break, blow, burn, and make me new.

It also seemed appropriate that early Spanish explorers had named the location the Jornada del Muetro, or Journey of Death. It was isolated, with only a handful of ranches in the area. The ranchers were asked to leave, but they didn't want to and were not told why. Their cattle kept roaming onto the site, so the Army shot them until the ranchers finally left. The cattle had been attracted to the water pumped into tanks by windmills. The Army would disable the windmills during the day, but the ranchers would come in at night and release them to pump water. The Army finally shot the watering tanks full of .45-caliber bullet holes to empty them.

On a larger scale, General Groves had planned to have the bomb operational by early 1945, but in 1944, it was clear that the technical problems were far more significant than initially thought. Scientist George Kistiakowsky was working on the explosives that would detonate the plutonium bomb with an "implosion." The concept was to create a series of exploding lenses that would explode inward to compress the plutonium core, crushing it to release the neutrons and begin the self-sustaining nuclear reaction. This had never been attempted, and the work was arduous. He remembered, "Groves predicted in August of 1944 that we would have implosion by the next spring, and it is becoming clear that we wouldn't. And so I think Oppenheimer began to lose faith in me."

Even worse for Groves, Leo Szilard was agitating with laboratory scientists. Groves called him "a pain in the neck!" He was worried that Szilard was creating a log of information to "make a stink" after the war and embarrass him. Szilard called for a general statement on the project, signed by the scientists, that would be published to the American public detailing its existence and objectives. He got 22 of the top scientists to sign the letter, which described the project, the scale of the new weapon, and how it might affect future international relations. The letter was forwarded to Roosevelt. Groves was furious and mused that he would use the bomb on the scientists in Chicago if they didn't stop this type of talk. Szilard even returned to Einstein and asked him to sign a second letter to Roosevelt. He initially agreed to do so but never did.

In his discussion with Churchill and the Allies, Roosevelt found it clear that Britain would not oppose its use against either enemy, at least as long as Churchill was prime minister. Roosevelt had decided to run for president again in 1944, much to the relief of Churchill. In that election, Roosevelt had chosen a new running mate, Harry Truman, to be vice president. Roosevelt would win the election, but he didn't like Truman and decided not to tell him about the atomic bomb.

However, Groves would not have a deliverable atomic bomb in early 1945. He worried he could not use it on Germany if she were defeated before it was ready. News of German atrocities and the attempted elimination of the Jewish population in Europe were now well-known worldwide. Americans had seen the sprawling concentration camps and extermination centers but did not know what to do with them. They could not imagine bombing prisoner-of-war camps. It seemed far too cruel to imagine. It was a terrible dilemma. Underground efforts in German-occupied countries were desperately trying to get Jews to safety. Some of these survivors told horrific stories that were almost impossible to believe. The Japanese Army was imposing similar atrocities on civilians and American and British prisoners of war.

In Los Alamos, Oppenheimer was chain-smoking, drinking, and eating poorly. He was losing weight rapidly, and even though he was six feet tall, his weight had dropped to 115 pounds. He seemed almost like a ghost at times. Other scientists were beginning to develop a concept of using an atomic bomb to demonstrate its power to the Allies' enemies. They thought this might impress on them what they would face if they did not surrender. Germany and Japan would be invited to such a test so they would see that they were facing utter destruction if they continued fighting.

But Groves thought this nonsense. To begin with, no one knew if the bomb would even work or, if it did, how powerful it might be. A dud would have the opposite effect. Plus, Groves and the Army knew that the American public would someday see that they had spent over two billion dollars to make a bomb to destroy Germany and Japan. They were convinced that Americans would never forgive them for not using it, and they were probably right in 1944. By then, most Americans would have leveled both countries to save a single American soldier, airman, or sailor.

Churchill and Roosevelt were also unaware that Stalin was getting the plans for the bomb from Claus Fuchs, a scientist at Los Alamos. They thought that Stalin did not know about it. They were also deeply worried that Russia might someday build a bomb of its own, which Russian scientists were already working on. At the same time, the sailors of the USS *Hughes* were just about to embark on one of the most hazardous parts of that journey in the Pacific Ocean in the war against Japan.

CHAPTER TWENTY-FIVE

"THEY DO NOT DEPEND UPON MERE LEGENDS AND MYTHS"

Officers of the USS Hughes - Lieutenant Glen Edmonson top left – death and destruction were on the way to Japan. Glen Edmonson collection.

After WWII was over, Emperor Hirohito renounced his divinity and said to the Japanese people, "They do not depend upon mere legends and myths. They are not predicated on the false conception that the Emperor is divine and that the Japanese people are superior to other races." He later mused that his job was much more difficult when he was a god. But in 1944, as the USS *Hughes* fought island by island to retake the Central Pacific from the Japanese, Prime Minister Tojo told them the emperor was a god.

Hirohito didn't create this cult—Tojo did. He used this divinity and religion as a big part of the nationalist regime. Politics and religion were mixed until they were indistinguishable. In Japan, Tojo continued to bolster the myth of the war being divinely ordained. Tojo called for everyone to be willing to die for their god and country.

Among the legends that would perpetuate this myth was the defeat of the 13th-century Mongol army, sunk in a typhoon. This was known in Japanese culture as the "divine wind." In reality, it was just a lucky storm at the right time. The Mongols didn't understand enough about the weather to predict the typhoon seasons. If they had been able to do so, it might have spelled the end of the Japanese Empire many centuries earlier.

However, simple slogans are a primary form of indoctrination, and the more they are used, the more accurate they seem to become. The attachment of "divine wind," or "kamikaze," to the public discourse on the war was not accidental. It had a nice ring to it. It was impossible to argue against without offending the soul of Japan. Propaganda in the news began to shine a bright light on the "heroes" who were signing up to fight in the Special Attack Units. They would become the new divine wind, or kamikaze.

More young Japanese men were writing letters to their homes and families about their coming demise by piloting planes into the decks of American aircraft carriers, their prime targets. There were news stories about the men gloriously joining the units of Admiral

Onishi's new squadrons. The Japanese loved the concept of such bravery in the emperor's name.

Kaname Harada was a highly successful Japanese pilot in WWII. He is thought to have shot down 19 American planes during the battles of Pearl Harbor, Wake Island, Port Darwin, and Guadalcanal. Near the war's end, he was assigned to fly a kamikaze aircraft called a Shushi, a rocket-powered plane designed to intercept and take down American B-29 bombers. He had piloted such an aircraft, which had a failure, and managed to guide it back to the ground and crash-land. His reasoning for fighting for Japan, even in the war's waning days, was simple: "If we survived, we thought we would be treated like slaves by the occupying forces. I would never see my wife and children again, but as a military man, this was my fate."

Volunteers were also required to meet specific standards. They were supposed to be unmarried and childless. They were also expected to come to the program with some flying credentials. In truth, many had families, and as the war dragged on, Onishi accepted almost anyone who wanted to join. A manpower shortage also caused many pilots to be involuntarily assigned to the program.

Some kamikaze pilots were fanatical and genuinely believed in the ideology of the divinity of the emperor and the need to sacrifice themselves for their country. Still, many pilots didn't share these beliefs. Those conscripted into service did not have a choice in their assignment. Additionally, Japan offered rewards and incentives for volunteers, including protection for their families.

Even those who had deep reservations generally flew the missions anyway. The group and societal pressure were immense. One of the most significant motivating factors was the shame of letting down their family, community, country, and emperor. The concept of self-sacrifice was not new in Japan or even the United States. Personal honor was part of the "bushido" code, or what the Japanese called "the way of the warrior," a concept that went back a thousand years. This code emphasized duty, loyalty, and honor above all else.

From some survivors and the letters home from those who perished in their missions, we have learned what they were thinking and feeling. They were far from the fanatical, drug-and-alcohol-fueled madmen they have been portrayed as.

Kamikaze pilot Tadashi Nakajima later recalled Onishi's directions: "The orders from our commander were quite explicit. He told the pilots: 'This is an opportunity that comes once in a thousand years. Put forth everything you have.'"

Soon, a new national slogan was rolled out and posted nationwide for the people to see: "100 Million Ready to Die for the Emperor!" The people were all told to gather bamboo sticks and sharpen the ends into spears to fight the enemy. They were ordered to fight to the death. The Americans and British had never imagined anything like this. The sailors of the USS *Hughes* were seeing it every day now at sea. There were rumors about these new Japanese attacks, but many refused to believe them.

One Japanese pilot who survived the war was Toshimitsu Imaizumi. At the time, he felt so strongly about his commitment to the mission that he was shocked when the war ended. So strong was this commitment that many in his group wanted to continue fighting and fly one last suicide mission to sink American ships. The commander finally had to remove the propellers from the remaining planes to stop them. Imaizumi would see things differently long after the war ended: "War brings pain, suffering, and heartache. Old men start wars; young men fight in them." Asked how he felt about his fellow pilots, he said, "I don't ask that they be glorified, just remembered for their sacrifices."

Defending against Japanese kamikaze attacks was tricky. American destroyers bore the brunt as the first line of defense when planes approached. Their radars sent and received a signal about twice as far as other ships. The sooner an attack could be detected, the sooner the carriers could launch planes to attack the Japanese suicide planes before they arrived.

Navy fliers had, on average, two years of training and at least three hundred hours of flight time, and actual combat pilots had trained them. Although the Japanese Zero fighter was once the undisputed top aircraft in the Pacific, it was soon replaced by far superior American planes like the Grumman FM-2 Wildcat and F6F Hellcat.

Not anticipating a long war, Japan ran out of highly trained, combat-tested pilots. By mid-1944, Japanese pilots who were supposed to have six months of flight training were sent to combat with as little as two months of training. Near the war's end, Japanese fighter pilots had as little as a hundred hours of flight training.

Initially, Onishi recruited kamikaze pilots from the general ranks of naval aviators, but later, he had to recruit them from the general population. Some of these pilots had as little as 50 hours of flight training.

American radar and fire-control computers were in their infancy and sometimes slower than needed to get orders back out to American fliers in the air and deck gunners on the larger ships. Americans had large, long-range guns, but sometimes, they couldn't fire them quickly enough or with sufficient accuracy at the oncoming Japanese planes. As a result, most kamikaze planes were shot down very close to the ships by much smaller 20-mm deck machine guns like the one manned by Oliver Jones on the USS *Hughes*.

These kamikaze attacks would begin on October 25, 1944, and last until July 28, 1945, right before the dropping of the first atomic bomb at Hiroshima. They would be carried out by 2,800 pilots, who would sink 34 American ships and damage 368 others. Some ships were hit by as many as six aircraft, killing or injuring ten thousand American Navy sailors. A staggering 17 percent of all significant American combat ships operating in the Pacific were sunk, and these attacks damaged 64 percent of the rest. If Admiral Onishi had possessed more of these resources, and were it not for the atomic bombs of Robert Oppenheimer and his scientists, he might have prevented the invasion plans of the Allies.

The final ship Admiral Onishi and his Special Attack Units sank was the USS *Callaghan*. Like the USS *Hughes,* a Navy destroyer, the USS *Callaghan* was hit and went down 50 miles southwest of Okinawa on July 28, 1945. This final attack demonstrated how meager the resources were for Onishi. The attacking plane was a wooden Yokosuka K5Y fabric-covered biplane. The proximity fuses of the shells from the *Callaghan* could not detect the wooden aircraft, and it came in low on its second run and hit the ship. One of the bombs on the plane penetrated the aft engine room and exploded. The ship flooded and sank with the loss of 47 of her sailors. This was a far cry from the initial attack by Lieutenant Seki and his group, which hit and damaged or sank four American aircraft carriers on October 25, 1944, at Leyte Gulf, but it resulted in the sinking of an American destroyer.

A young pilot back home in Japan was now preparing to go on his mission to meet the USS *Hughes* at the Battle of Leyte Gulf.

CHAPTER TWENTY-SIX

"THE MACHINE GUNNERS ON THE GROUND RIPPED HIM TO SHREDS"

The crew of the Japanese aircraft carrier Zuikaku salute as the
flag is lowered during the Battle off Cape Engaño, October 25, 1944.
Captured U.S. Navy photo.

The USS *Hughes* was still stuck in the New Guinea campaign. On May 15, 1944, Tony Skic wrote, "We will arrive in Hollandia tomorrow. Seen a school of porpoises today. Jap bombers are overhead now as I write this, and they are bombing the beach."

On May 17, 1944, Skic noted, "Entered Humboldt Bay [New Guinea] this morning and fueled off the tanker. A PT boat tied up alongside and gave us candy captured from the Japs. It was a package with Jap writing on it. The candy was in three colors: red, white, and green, but it all tasted the same. Our cruisers have just returned from bombarding them. The gunnery inspector who visited us for a few days said we had the best-looking guns he's ever seen."

With the seemingly endless missions, oppressive heat, and no time off on shore, tempers were boiling on the USS *Hughes*. Skic captured the sentiment:

At 4:00 AM, we headed back for Humboldt Bay. We had a submarine contact. While tracking it, we had a steering casualty—the executive officer E.B. Simmons, the smart son of a bitch that he is, fouled up the steering gear. The stupid sons of bitches didn't even have enough sense to let the other destroyer take the contact, so we lost it for good. We went to Battle Stations this evening as enemy aircraft were overhead and bombing the beach that we had recently secured. Then, ten minutes later, the gas alarm sounded. Some hysterical bastard pulled the wrong alarm to sound the General Alarm the second time. It rained like a bitch then, and now to take the cake, we anchored right outside the harbor. This ship and its brilliant officers, commonly called 90-day wonders, are so God damned screwed up that it is a crime they even live to run this piece of floating pig iron. They are sad examples of manhood and are worse than a group of hysterical women trying to cover up at the sight of a mouse. What has happened aboard here lately is disgusting and unbelievable.

But after this momentary lapse of composure, Skic went back to fighting the Japanese with his other shipmates. "PT boat ran aground, and we were ordered to destroy it. We hit an ammo dump, which blew up and smoked like hell. We are waiting to intercept some Jap barges tonight."

Frustrations were growing. The men were being pushed to the limit of what they could endure. The cramped, hot, and poorly supplied ship was sometimes almost intolerable. They desperately wanted to be out of these waters and done with this particular mission.

The men's resentment of the Japanese was growing. They were thousands of miles and a world away from their homes. There was no chance to go to shore. The friendly ladies of Australia who liked the Yanks so much now seemed a lifetime ago. The men were out of cigarettes and soap in the oppressive heat of the Central Pacific Ocean. Tony Skic recorded, "All attacking planes were shot down, they look nice when they're smoking and burning, and it makes me happy to see those rotten yellow scum die. I take great pleasure when I can help to exterminate the no-good sons of bitches. I aim to hear their screams and death cries as they squirm and die a painful death." Like other sailors on the USS *Hughes,* Skic was near the end of his rope.

Skic seldom talked about the war when he returned to Chicago at the end of WWII. His uncle Sly never understood why he never wanted to discuss his time in the Pacific fighting against the Japanese. He knew Skic was "Not a Japanese admirer." Men on the USS *Hughes* would carry these images and scars for the rest of their lives. The "Greatest Generation" paid a heavy price for defending democracy and freedom. Few people back home could understand the price they were paying each time they dodged a Japanese bomb or torpedo or killed another Japanese soldier, pilot, or sailor. Killing does not come easy to sane people, no matter the foe.

The fleet would now head to the Philippines, with New Guinea's hostile waters behind them. Anything would be an improvement for the sailors of the USS *Hughes*. But first, they participated in the invasion of the Schouten Islands.

One day, Tony Skic recorded:

We were 500 yards from one island, and we saw a native wave a white flag, so the islands seem to be friendly, but our medium and heavy bombers came in later and knocked the shit out of this place. The USS *Hutchens* was hit by a three-inch shell from a shore battery, knocking down her mast. While I was eating supper in the mess hall, the alarm went off, and then the word was passed that enemy aircraft were overhead. Coming topside, I ran like an ostrich to my battle station, and I saw at least six Jap bombers attacking. The anti-aircraft fire was heavy and accurate. I saw all six bombers crash, each trailing smoke and flames. The day was exciting, and we hope to kill Japs again in a few days!

But then he turned to other thoughts: "Still no mail. It's been two months since we've had any. The postal mail conditions from home are acute." Still, he also records, "While on the lookout this evening, I spotted a whale about 50 yards from the ship and two seals about 20 yards away. I saw an octopus at noon."

On June 2, 1944, Ollie Stine noted:

Arrived off Biak at dawn. I spent a quiet evening, but oh! What an evening. There were three raids. The *Hughes* reported them first, which enabled the Army and Navy to give them a hot reception when they arrived. The first two raids consisted of seventeen Zeros, dropping small bombs and strafing. The *Hughes* was credited with three Zeros shot down. One of the pilots bailed out, but machine gunners on the beach ripped him to shreds before he even got near the ground. The next attack concentrated on the beach. They came over the trees one at a time, and the first of four burst into flames as soon as they cleared the jungle. We left for Hollandia after the attack, but sixteen more planes approached when we were about five miles from the island. We threw up a hot barrage, and they turned away.

The American carriers were in the Central Pacific, so the USS *Hughes* had difficulty getting air cover for missions. Civilian cargo ships also refused to go to Biak in the Schouten Islands, so the USS *Hughes* had to escort smaller naval ships there with supplies. Skic observed, "Rumors say that Admiral Kincade will refuse to send our destroyers to Biak unless the Army gives us some air support." On June 6, 1944, he noted, "The *Mustin* came in today, and she was strafed pretty bad at Biak. Our computer is out of order, and our generators are on the verge of going haywire. Woe to us if they go out during an air attack." But on a more positive note, the next entry states, "I received the Russel Square Community News today!" Mail had finally returned to the USS *Hughes*.

On June 7, 1944, Tony Skic received some of the best news in months: "While lying in my sack last night, the word passed that American and English forces landed on the coast of France."

The operation in New Guinea and the surrounding areas went slowly because the Japanese were learning from their mistakes. They had learned that setting defenses on the beach was a hopeless endeavor as the Americans could kill many, if not most, of their forces with naval bombardment.

Oliver Jones remembers running the USS *Hughes* close to the shore to get Japanese machine gunners in palm trees to shoot at them just to identify where their forces were. Jones would blast at them with his deck gun as the bullets hit all around him, pounding against the metal like the ship was being beaten with so many hammers.

The destroyers were so fast that they were difficult to hit with bigger guns. But these encounters brought in a heavier bombardment from the Americans. The USS *Hughes* could also request air strikes on the Japanese positions when available.

The Japanese devised a new strategy at the Battle of Biak Island. They would leave the beaches empty so the Americans would quickly come ashore. Tony Skic and Ollie Stine noted in their diaries that after intense bombardment from Japanese planes, the landings in this area often met little opposition. The waters were often filled with locals in canoes coming out into the bays to meet the Americans on the ships. On June 4, 1944, Tony Skic wrote, "We got a report of a Jap task force consisting of two battlewagons, three heavy cruisers, one light cruiser, and nine destroyers 50 miles northwest of Biak, Schouten Islands. They are at their base in Halmakera. We patrolled 30 miles from Hollandia while the LSTs were by the beach. It is a nice place with plenty of natives around in canoes. One bag of mail came aboard tonight. The dope is that *Russell* and *Mustin* were strafed while patrolling off Biak."

The Japanese would allow the Americans to land on the beaches largely unopposed, but once in the jungle, the Americans would have to fight for every inch of land. Additionally, American intelligence vastly underestimated the number of Japanese on Biak Island. They had 11,400 troops. The initial resistance on the beaches and attacks against the American naval vessels were designed to get the American soldiers to where the main Japanese forces were waiting.

There were many caves on the island, filled with Japanese soldiers with machine guns, artillery, and mortars to kill approaching Americans. To make matters worse, the Japanese connected the caves with a series of tunnels to move troops without being seen from the air. These fortifications were filled with supplies and ammunition.

The battle to take the airfield on the island went on for days. Even once the Americans took it, the Japanese attacks from the caves kept them from using it. This kept the USS *Hughes* from having desperately needed air cover. The Japanese brought in additional troops and aircraft for the battle and to attack the American ships. Just as the Japanese were about to attempt to land more troops, the Americans invaded the Marianas Islands. This forced the Imperial Japanese Navy to respond to that area and forget the landing on Biak.

In the end, only 1,200 Japanese soldiers landed in the area throughout June 1944, and dozens of their aircraft were lost, many shot down by the USS *Hughes*. The Australians intercepted a radio message indicating that Lieutenant General Takuzo Numata, the chief of staff for the 2nd Area Army, was on the island inspecting troops and had asked to be evacuated. The Japanese Imperial Navy was not able to do so. After additional brutal fighting, Numata burned the regimental flag and committed suicide in front of his men to show them he was not afraid to die fighting for Emperor Hirohito and Japan. Such impressive public displays of loyalty, honor, and courage deeply impacted the remaining troops. The soldiers had only one avenue of escaping death: surrender. Few ever chose that path, which confounded the Americans, who saw suicide charges as nothing short of insanity.

When the situation was reported back to Washington, the top generals and civilian political leaders were astonished at what the sailors on the USS *Hughes* were seeing every day. The war was becoming illogical. No one could grasp an enemy who would fight to the death against hopeless odds. Nothing made sense. War planners were now beginning to calculate American losses for any encounter, landing, or seizing of islands. As the harsh reality set in, so, too, did a deep hatred for the Japanese people for allowing their country to prosecute this war. A limited and moral war was now impossible. America was ready for anything that would bring the war to a close.

Not counting deaths on naval ships, the Americans lost 438 soldiers killed and 2,360 injured in the ground attack. However, the total losses to the Americans included 7,234 non-battle casualties, mostly from scrub typhus. The Japanese lost over 4,700 killed and only 200 captured. Many more Japanese soldiers died on the island from illness due to the terrible jungle conditions.

Biak finally fell to the Allies, but the USS *Hughes* would return there one last time in 1946.

CHAPTER TWENTY-SEVEN

"THIS ONE BASTARD HAD A JAP WRISTWATCH"

Normally friendly and safe, locals visit the USS Hughes in the Pacific —
bringing fresh fruit to the sailors. Glen Edmonson collection.

Retired Commander Alan Evans of the USS *Hughes* summarized the next phase of the war: "Seventh Fleet forces were now ready for the bombardment and occupation of Noemfoor Island. The USS *Hughes* bombarded beach installations before the landing on July 2, 1944, with no resistance. The Japanese were almost gone by the time we got there. However, the Americans weren't taking any chances before landing troops."

Tony Skic noted on July 2:

We went to General Quarters at 8:00 PM last night, ate some sardines and hardtack about midnight. Today, the island took a pasting from our destroyers, cruisers, and bombers. We fired 314 rounds of 5" and 478 rounds of 40 mm. This force laid a terrific barrage on the beach. The airfield was captured by noon, only 800 yards from the beach. The Jap artillery fired at the beachhead and hit one of our tanks and a truck. There was so much smoke from the bombs and shells that we couldn't see the island well. Our first wave only met light machine gun fire and little resistance. I fired 78 rounds today, and we had no casualties.

The USS *Hughes* and other destroyers operating close to shore encountered local villagers in canoes. This was a welcome sight, as they loved trading and getting fresh fruit. But on July 4, 1944, something seemed wrong to the sailors on the USS *Hughes*. Skic wrote:

We went to General Quarters today to investigate five native outriggers. We broke out the rifles and Tommy guns when the native boats came alongside. We searched them carefully and found they had rifles, hand grenades, and ammunition. We took three men off who looked like Japs. They wore helmets, and this bastard had a Japanese wristwatch, dog tag, helmet, and

> khaki uniform. We turned them over to the Naval Intelligence
> in Biak. We will go to General Quarters again at 4:30 AM
> tomorrow before stopping at Noemfoor.

Seaman Stine also remembered the day, which could have been a disaster if the Japanese had gotten onboard the USS *Hughes*. "When nearing Biak, we spotted native canoes and went over to investigate. They were flying the Dutch flag, but we thought we saw some Japs in the cabins. We ordered them to come alongside and took them into custody. There was a lieutenant and two enlisted men. We also found 13 Springfield rifles, several carbines, Tommy guns, two cases of ammunition, and a case of hand grenades."

This was something entirely new. Had the three Japanese soldiers gotten on board the USS *Hughes,* the results could have been disastrous. American destroyers were used to running into locals in canoes. The Japanese had observed this practice and saw an opportunity to attack and possibly seize an American Naval vessel. The watchful eyes of the sailors noticed that something was different with this contact. Encounters with locals would never be as simple again.

Even so, there was a more relaxed pace for the sailors of the USS *Hughes* while preparations were underway for the subsequent invasion. Tony Skic noted about the period from July 9–13, 1944, "Received some mail today and newspapers. I also got the box with the jam and fishing tackle. The box was full of those God damned ants! It rained all day while I wrote some letters home. We went ashore for a while. I drank beer and did some swimming. I had a fair time and got sunburned as hell."

On July 14, 1944, he wrote, "We have an Admiral, a Major General, and his staff on board." The USS *Hughes* was chosen to become Admiral Struble's flagship. Things were changing for the crew of the USS *Hughes.* She became a flagship of the fleet.

Oliver Jones met the admiral about the time he was selected to operate the boat that took people back and forth to shore.

> I was the coxswain on the USS *Hughes* and took the officers off and back onto the ship. So, I got to mess around on the islands a lot. The boat was about 12 or 15 feet long with a motor. The officers were involved in training and manipulating plans, so they had to go ashore a lot. I was the one who took them ashore in New Guinea. When on shore, I could do anything I wanted to until they needed to return to the ship. It was a lot of fun. I visited with the local natives, and they were charming people. They loaded me down with stuff. All kinds of fruit. That was quite a deal.
>
> I talked to the ship's Captain, a real nice guy. He was naturally pleasant, walking around the ship and talking to the sailors sometimes. There was an Admiral once near an island as we were going to battle in the Philippines. I was up on the bow and working on some ratline that got shot up. This guy came and sat down alongside me. We got to talking. Pretty soon, he said something silly, clear out of reason. I looked up, and it was Admiral Struble. I jumped to my feet and saluted, and he told me to sit down and said, "Let's talk." I was so astonished I didn't even remember what else he said or what else I said. He was a nice guy. That was the first time I met him, and then later, I took him back and forth to the shore when they had a get-together as officers plotted the next battle.

In some cases, the Americans left some islands alone and moved on to others. The Japanese, however, didn't think the Americans would skip a single island on the way to Japan.

The Americans knew that without support, the Japanese fortifications would make no difference, and in the words of Alan Evans, they would "die on the vine." So, the USS *Hughes* moved from island to island, sometimes bombarding them, sometimes skipping them. As the Americas moved on, Japanese supply lines were cut, and the Japanese soldiers would usually starve. Although it is impossible to know, the Japanese deaths from disease and starvation probably exceeded combat losses. It was a slow, painful death for the Japanese soldiers, but it saved American lives.

On July 23, 1944, Skic noted, "We got some new boots aboard yesterday. Some old boys have been transferred to new ships and some to school. Our forces landed in Guam yesterday, and that is excellent news." On July 24, 1944, he wrote, "Our troops landed on Tinian today. I was on the beach today and got feeling good on beer. We entered the port at Wadke this morning at 7:00 AM. At 11:00 PM, we will pull out with the rest of the squadron. It's a nice night and a quarter moon; all the stars are out, and the sky is without clouds. The dope is that we will land troops in three places and bombard the landing beach."

The USS *Hughes* would go on to assist in landings on three islands and face intermittent air raids. The on-again, off-again alerts and orders kept everyone on the USS *Hughes* on alert. Tony Skic sometimes slept on the ship's deck for several nights to be ready with his deck gun. On July 28, 1944, in his diary, he wrote:

We were to fire 600 rounds in the bombardment tomorrow morning, but that has been canceled. Air attacks by enemy aircraft are strongly and very much possible. We are ready for anything, and shooting down a few Jap planes will boost our morale. It is a nice night; the moon and the stars are out with no clouds, and the water is like glass, but we do not know what to expect. The word is that a Jap plane we shot down is a Val MK2 Cuchi 99. We still expect an air attack tonight, but no planes have come. This mid-watch is wearing me down.

Americans had landed on Saipan, Tinian, and Guam but skipped other islands. Although island hopping and avoiding Japanese bases and islands was preferable whenever possible, some locations were necessary for the bombardment of mainland Japan. Tinian was a critical part of that plan. Invading the island continued from July 24, 1944, until the first of August. Eight thousand Japanese would be eliminated from Tinian. It would become a base for the 20th Air Force.

Japan had annexed Tinian Island and imported a population of 15,700 Japanese civilians. They also had almost three thousand Korean slaves building war preparations. The Americans began the assault with what was now a familiar pattern, shelling the fortifications with three battleships and 16 destroyers. The Japanese fired back with 150-mm shore batteries and hit the battleship *Colorado*, killing 43 men and wounding another 198. The *Colorado* was shot 22 times. The USS *Norman Scott* was also hit, killing her captain and 18 sailors.

When the Americans landed, they successfully took the beaches at Tinian as the Japanese retreated into caves. The Americans had tested 24 "Satan" mechanized flamethrowers on Saipan and deployed them on Tinian. They were used to devastating effect against the remaining Japanese troops, who were cooked alive in their caves. Marines no longer had to enter caves to root out Japanese defenders. The flamethrowers did that work for them.

By July 30, 1944, the 4th Marine Division had taken the town of Tinian and the airfield. This would soon spell doom for the Empire of Japan. Everything that the USS *Hughes* had been doing up to this moment was accomplished at this location. Far from the warm waters of the Pacific Ocean, President Roosevelt, Prime Minister Churchill, and the scientists at Los Alamos had achieved a strategic objective necessary to drop an atomic bomb on Japan: Tinian Airfield.

Once in American hands, Tinian Airfield would provide the necessary runway length for a B-29 bomber to carry an atomic bomb

The taking of Tinian Island would allow B-29s to drop incendiary bombs on Tokyo, killing Japanese civilians by the tens of thousands. Photo taken by Ishikawa Kōyō around 10 March, 1945. Japanese public domain photo.

into the air and drop it on Japan. Strategic bombers could now hit Japan with conventional and incendiary bombs, something they would begin to do shortly.

An estimated four thousand Japanese civilians had died by suicide on Tinian, which chilled the Americans. This pushed the American policy experts to fear an invasion of Japan even more. Soldiers fighting to the death was one thing, but now they had to consider an entire civilian population willing to do the same.

Once taken, Tinian became the home of 50,000 American troops. Navy Seabees built six seven-thousand-foot runways for the American B-29 Superfortresses.

It was time for the USS *Hughes* to move on. Alan Evans noted:

Our control of New Guinea was established. Protective air patrols were in operation, harrying enemy shipping in the

Dutch East Indies. In the Central Pacific, our forces had completed the bitter Marianas Island campaign, and the way was nearly open for joining forces in the Philippines. However, another stepping stone was needed, and the Island of Mototai was chosen to serve this purpose. This was only twenty miles from the strong Japanese base at Halmahera and within easy striking distance of the Japanese naval bases at Tawi Tawi and Brunei Bay. Preparations were made for its occupation, and Rear Admiral W. M. Fletcher chose the USS *Hughes* as the flagship.

On the way out of the area, Seaman Skic wrote on August 6, 1944:

Worked all day from 8:00 AM to 7:30 PM, and I am exhausted. We leave here at 8:00 PM, which will happen in about 45 minutes. We will go to Aitape and Wewak. The Japs have 45,000 men there, and our forces have them cut off from all possible escape. Squadron Two will do all the bombarding, and we will have a good target, all humans, 45,000 Japs! We expect to kill plenty of the bastards. The only way out for the Japs is by submarine or suicide. Has there been a better opportunity than this in history to have mass murder? We could hear the rumble and concussion of bombs and artillery all day. We have photographers and spotters with walkie-talkies aboard our ship to watch. Some of them will go ashore to the front lines for reports. A General came aboard last night with his staff."

On the 10th, he noted, "We arrived in Aitape early this morning. General Kall and his staff left the ship. An Army spotting party came aboard, and we bombarded all day along the coast. We saw a group of Japs on the beach, and we let them have it. I fired 67 rounds of 5"."

Seaman Ollie Stine remembered, "Arrived at Hollandia at 6:00 AM, but returned to Aitape at 10:00 PM. Left Aitape at 6:30 to bombard Wewok sector. I fired 240 rounds of 5", destroying a bridge, four landing barges and scored hits in enemy barracks and store areas. They also scored hits on three gun emplacements."

The feelings of the crew of the USS *Hughes* about the Japanese soldiers and people grew more bitter each day, just as they did back home in America. America was fully committed to total war. Combat was growing into a routine, but when the sailors had a few days of rest, Seaman Skic noted, "It is the same old routine, and monotony is showing on everyone. The food is still lousy and not worth eating. The blowers are often off, making it very hot below decks in the sleeping quarters. The generator and diesel are on the blink. I fished today but didn't catch anything."

By August 27, 1944, everyone knew that something big was close and that the USS *Hughes* would be at the forefront of this significant mission. Skic wrote, "The dope about this next operation is that we will be in charge of Task Force 77. With the radio gear aboard, we can communicate with the landing force, spotters, all aircraft, ships, and submarines. We will have the Admiral and his staff aboard for about two and a half months. The first operation will take place on the 15th of September. It will be Cahamera and another island."

Ollie Stine recorded, "September 5th, 1944. We left Humboldt Bay at 10:00 PM for Wakde. We have Rear Admiral Fletcher and Major General Persons aboard, plus two Captains, two Colonels, an assortment of commanders, Lt. colonels, Lt. Commanders, and other lesser officers, and about 40 extra enlisted personnel. We now have nine radios installed, which can all reach San Francisco!"

With the addition of Admiral Fletcher, the general, and his staff, 70 more men had boarded the small destroyer, which was already cramped with equipment for the subsequent invasion. To speed things up and protect the top military commanders in the area who were now on their ship, the ship frequently traveled at higher speeds, often at 33 knots. Skic believed they were about the fastest destroyer, or "can," in the Navy, which might have led to her becoming such an important ship in the American fleet. He remembered, "The Admiral and General held a big conference today on the coming operation. Every big shot of the Army, Navy, and even the Australians were on board the *Hughes*."

No matter how war-weary the sailors of the USS *Hughes* seemed at the time, they took great pride in the fact that their ship was one of the most trusted in the fleet. They knew their gunners were legendary, and the ship was the fastest destroyer in the Pacific. As she added battle stars, the USS *Hughes* became one of the most confident in the fleet. Often discouraged and tired, the sailors of the USS *Hughes* were also very aware of how important they were. They were defeating the Japanese and saving American lives. Still, a fearful task lay ahead. "Arrived at Wakde Island and practiced landings," noted Seaman Ollie Stine. "It is our job to go in as close as possible to the enemy beach, drop the hook, and direct the landing operations. We'll be sitting ducks for the enemy planes and shore batteries. We were told it is a great honor to be selected to do this, but I still don't like it."

Along with being the flagship for the fleet, the USS *Hughes* would spend the next three bloody months in the most significant naval battle of WWII: Leyte Gulf.

CHAPTER TWENTY-EIGHT

"I CAN THINK ABOUT NEITHER LIFE NOR DEATH"

USS St. Lo after being attacked by Japanese Special Attack Forces, or Kamikaze, at Leyte Gulf. America was stunned by this new terror. U.S. Navy photo.

The official Japanese kamikaze attacks began in October 1944 against an American ship in Leyte Gulf. Imperial Japanese Naval Ensign Kiyoshi Ogawa wrote a typical letter home to his parents: "I will make a sortie, flying over those calm clouds in a peaceful emotion. I can think about neither life nor death. A man should die once; no day is more honorable than today to dedicate myself to the eternal cause. . . . I will go to the front smiling. On the day of the mission, too, and forever."

On October 25, 1944, 24 volunteer pilots from Japan's 201st Navy Air Group were sent by Admiral Onishi to attack the Americans. One of their leaders, Japanese Captain Motoharu Okamura, stated, "I firmly believe that the only way to swing the war in our favor is to resort to crash-dive attacks with our plane. . . . There will be more than enough volunteers for this chance to save our country."

The attacks would lead to staggering losses for both sides. The objective of the Japanese was to inflict terror, emotional distress, and fear on the Americans back home, and they succeeded. "I simply didn't believe it when I first heard from other sailors about the kamikaze attacks," wrote Seaman Oliver Jones. "It did not make sense that anyone would kill themselves by running their plane into a ship. I thought it was a mistake and that the pilots were either dead or had parachuted out before the plane hit a ship. But first one and then another. Finally, I saw one for myself, and then I knew it was true. I don't understand it to this day."

Even now, Jones has difficulty understanding the brainwashing of the nationalist Japanese leaders that led to Japanese men doing this act. As much as he hated them back then, he now suspects that they were probably not all that different from the young sailors of the USS *Hughes*, with all of the hopes and dreams of any young man. But these pilots never expected to return home, which is still difficult for Jones to grasp. Even now, he is at a loss for words to express what he saw and could never fully understand.

The USS *St. Lo* was the first American carrier sunk by a kami-kaze. All carriers in her group, except the USS *Fanshaw Bay*, were hit that day. The Mitsubishi A6M2 Zero flown by Yukio Seki crashed into the flight deck at 10:51 AM. Seki aimed for the USS *White Plains*, but after his plane was damaged by anti-aircraft fire, he changed course and dove into the USS *St. Lo*. His bomb penetrated the flight deck and exploded on the hanger deck, where aircraft were being refueled. The USS *St. Lo* was engulfed in flames and sank in 30 minutes. One hundred thirteen Americans were killed, and 30 others died later of their wounds. Japanese pilots of the Special Attack Units would sink 34 ships in Leyte Gulf alone.

This Japanese tactic staggered the imaginations of the American military and civilian leaders back in Washington, D.C. Admiral Halsey, who at least publicly feared nothing, remarked that the concept of Japanese suicide attacks against the ships terrified him and that it was almost impossible to defend against them. At first, the Japanese seemed to have discovered a tactic that might work against the growing American fleet in the Pacific.

The Japanese also perfected their techniques as the Americans began to find ways to shoot down the kamikazes. The initial defense was to identify the range of the attacking planes and shoot them with everything a ship had when they got close enough. So, the Japanese circled in the sky, just outside the range of the Americans' guns, and carefully made their plans. Admiral Onishi told his pilots not to hurry but to take time to identify their target and then make their attack. The Japanese also learned that a direct attack would lead to planes being shot down if on a steady course. They modified their attack, diving to sea level at high speed and then quickly turning up and arcing down at the last moment to strike the ship. This led to only a few seconds being available to shoot the plane down. The pilots were also told to die with their eyes open, so they stayed on course until the last moment. This made them even more difficult to defend against.

The Japanese dropped propaganda on the Americans that their wives and girlfriends were having sex with handsome men back home while soldiers, sailors, and airmen were dying in the Pacific. Chester Bradley collection.

Time after time, the USS *Hughes* would encounter kamikaze aircraft attacking her or the ships nearby. The sailors of the USS *Hughes* were fully aware of the dangers of the new Japanese attacks against them in Leyte Gulf. Often, the only things that saved the USS *Hughes* were her speed and small size. The Japanese wanted to sink the largest ships, particularly aircraft carriers, troop ships, and battleships. The USS *Hughes's* speed and agility made her a problematic target. The larger ships were slower and could not turn anywhere near as quickly as the *Sims*-class destroyers.

Admiral Halsey would say, "It was the only weapon I ever feared in war." But the Americans would soon have a comparably terrifying weapon of their own. Robert Oppenheimer and Admiral Onishi would soon fight each other in the Pacific. It would be a race to see who was terrified the most by the other's weapon and who would blink first at the prospect of total war.

WWII was no longer about one army defeating the other in battle. It would be won in the Pacific by the side that could invent and deploy the most incredible instrument of terror. This marked a new standard in human conflict that would change the world forever. But it also held a question for humanity that many scientists at Los Alamos had already foreseen: could such a weapon, as terrible as it might prove to be, also be so terrible that it could one day make war between nations unthinkable? That concept would be tested in the coming months in the fight against Japan and later in the following peace and what would become known as the Cold War.

WWII changed human conflict forever, but on the day the USS *St Lo* was sunk, the USS *Hughes* sailors watched from their ship's deck at Leyte Gulf as the "divine wind" kamikaze attacks opened the door to a new age. Robert Oppenheimer and his scientists would soon have the American response to Admiral Onishi and his Special Attack Units.

CHAPTER TWENTY-NINE

"IGNITION OF THE ATMOSPHERE WITH NUCLEAR BOMBS"

Although most scientists dismissed Edward Teller as crazy and irrational, he found a friend and beliver in Ronald Reagan. Official U.S. government photo - National Archives.

The first atomic bomb test in New Mexico would ignite the atmosphere and turn the Earth into a star. That was Edward Teller's warning just as the project under Robert Oppenheimer was progressing towards the first test at the Trinity Test Site. Teller, generally called the father of the hydrogen bomb, was in some ways brilliant, but he was also vain and arguably insane. In the years to come, he would never forgive Oppenheimer for building the atomic bomb instead of moving on to building and using a hydrogen bomb, thousands of times more powerful. Instead of tens of thousands of deaths, Teller wanted a single hydrogen bomb that could kill millions at a time. Teller felt Americans should do it quickly and skip the simple atomic bomb. He thought such a bomb, like the ones used on Hiroshima and Nagasaki, was a waste of time.

Always needing attention and adoration, Teller openly said that the hydrogen in the atmosphere and water vapor could be fused into helium, and the ignition could vaporize the planet when the Trinity test device was detonated. The earth would become a small star. Most of the scientists working on the project thought he was nuts, and for good reason. But Roosevelt and his advisors, along with General Groves, were concerned. As wacky as they deemed Teller, they quickly went to work to see if he was right.

A report was issued confirming what most scientists already believed. It concluded: "It is shown that, whatever the temperature to which a section of the atmosphere may be heated, no self-propagating chain of nuclear reactions is likely to be started. The energy losses to radiation always overcompensates the gains due to the reactions." Edward Teller was wrong.

Teller was far from done with outrageous and irrational ideas and sentiments. Long after the war, he stalked the halls of American politics, trying to find politicians who would listen to him and his crazy ideas. He was pushy and persuasive. One day, he met Ronald Reagan, and Reagan became a believer. Reagan bought into his fantastical vision of the Strategic Space Initiative, usually called "Star Wars." America spent billions of dollars on Teller's ideas. One part of the plan was to circle the Earth with hundreds of warheads and simultaneously detonate them, which would possibly eliminate the planet's polarity. This was a portion of a larger idea he called "Brilliant Pebbles." Once complete, it was possible no electrical device would ever work again on Earth, and the people who survived, if any, would go back to the stone age. The idea was insane and eventually abandoned. Few scientists back at Los Alamos in 1944, or anywhere else, paid much attention to him, and most felt the project in 1944 would have been better off without him. Oppenheimer chose to keep him around but would regret that decision in the coming years.

Groves was still concerned that Teller might be right about igniting the atmosphere with the Trinity test. Still, Oppenheimer reminded him that the whole thing was theoretical. Nothing was ever 100 percent when it was only a theory. In any event, if Teller were correct, no one would be around to be blamed anyway. Groves saw the logic in this argument but always found that moment troubling.

The fall of 1944 brought another significant development. On Friday, October 12, 1944, Allied forces liberated Athens, Greece, from German occupation. A substantial battle on another front resulted in the Germans being defeated in Finland, from which they were now retreating. Even though Germany was now launching their V-1s and V-2s, or "vengeance" weapons, against England, it was clear that Germany was losing the war in Europe.

One of the technical problems was how much U-235 was necessary to make a bomb work. A bomb could only be delivered once this was known. Scientist Otto Frisch was assigned to run the Critical Assemblies Team at a secret location called "Omega." By far the most dangerous part of the project to date, it was called "tickling the dragon's tail." The scientists would drop a slug of U-235 through a ring of almost critical U-235 slugs, and for a moment, there would be a nuclear explosion generating 20 million watts of electricity. They hoped to keep the reaction under control, but many of the scientists had concerns. Some would leave the area as the concept progressed, just in case.

Fermi's group was working close by and became nervous about the test. One person who seemed drawn to the test was Oppenheimer, who would come by and sit while the scientists carried out testing. Although later tests at this lab resulted in the radiation deaths of two scientists from using a plutonium sphere called "the Demon Core," the test for the Trinity device was a success, and the scientists learned the quantity of U-235 necessary for the first bomb, called "Little Boy."

Another significant development for Oppenheimer and the other scientists at Los Alamos was the liberation of Niels Bohr from German-occupied territories. Bohr was one of the most respected nuclear psychists in the world. The Allies wanted to get him to the West to help with the bomb. He contributed to the understanding of atomic structure and quantum theory, for which he received the Nobel Prize in Physics in 1922. Bohr founded the Institute of Theoretical Physics at the University of Copenhagen, now known as the Niels Bohr Institute, which opened in 1920. But Denmark had been under Nazi control since 1940. To keep the Nazis from capturing some of the gold Nobel Prize medals from other scientists, Bohr melted them down and hid the gold, later returning it to the Nobel Commission, who re-poured and cast the medals back into their original form. The Nazi occupation of Denmark, like in all occupied countries, was horrific. They hunted people of Jewish descent without mercy and sent them to death camps for extermination. The meeting with Heisenberg over the possibility of an atomic bomb alarmed the Allies. The Allies wanted Bohr out of Nazi-occupied lands.

In September of 1943, Bohr and his brother discovered that the Nazis considered him and his family Jewish since their mother was

Jewish, marking them for death. The Danish resistance mobilized to get the world-famous physicist and his wife out of Denmark and into Sweden. Bohr met with the king of Sweden the day after his rescue and compelled him to offer asylum to Jewish refugees from Denmark. Due to these efforts, over seven thousand of Bohr's countrymen were rescued and saved from German extermination. Once again, the sheer ignorance of Hitler and the radical German Nationalists blinded them from seeing how Bohr might have helped their war efforts. Bohr was brilliant, but the Nazis could only think about putting him and his family to death for being Jewish.

The Allies learned of Bohr's escape and wanted him to come to England and America. In October, he was put on board an aircraft that could fly at such high altitudes and speeds that the Germans could not find or shoot it down. Bohr was given a parachute, flying suit, and oxygen mask. He spent the several-hour flight lying on a mattress in the aircraft's bomb bay. During the flight, Bohr did not wear his flying helmet, as it was too small, and he did not hear the pilot's intercom instruction to turn on his oxygen supply when the aircraft climbed to a high altitude over Norway. He passed out from oxygen starvation and was only revived when the plane descended to a lower altitude over the North Sea.

Bohr met with British government officials and scientists and then went to Washington, D.C., where he met with General Groves. At Los Alamos, Bohr caught up with Oppenheimer, but his thoughts were on two other matters. Bohr was surprised at how far the Manhattan Project had progressed in separating U-235 to build a nuclear bomb. He knew it would be difficult, but the Americans were far ahead of his expectations. But Bohr was more concerned about post-war control of nuclear arms. He also believed that the Russians should be informed about the bomb.

Oppenheimer wanted Bohr to work on the bomb, and to some degree, Bohr did, but he also became one of the most vocal scientists about its post-war use. He met with President Roosevelt in 1944 and urged him to consider the possibility of a nuclear arms race in which countries with such weapons gained the power to destroy one another. He began to advocate for an international commission to control nuclear weapons. In 1944, Roosevelt was already working on his plan for the United Nations after WWII, so there would be a structure to consider such ideas. Bohr also met with British Prime Minister Churchill to advocate informing the rest of the world, especially the Russians, about the weapon, but Churchill strongly disagreed. Churchill believed that Bohr ought to be confined or made to see that he was near the edge of mortal crimes for his thoughts. For now, Churchill and Roosevelt agreed to keep the bomb a secret, and Bohr was not arrested.

Bohr did not stay at Los Alamos but made extended visits there over the next two years. He downplayed his contributions to the project in later years, saying, "They didn't need my help in making the atom bomb." But Oppenheimer disagreed and declared that Bohr was very helpful, especially to the younger scientists, who revered him. Oppenheimer credited Bohr with discovering and creating the initiators that would ignite the bomb in its core. "This device remained a stubborn puzzle," Oppenheimer noted, "but in early February 1945, Niels Bohr clarified what had to be done." Bohr continued to have deep moral concerns about nuclear bombs.

After WWII, Bohr's ideas were taken to the United Nations, and decades later, international arms control agreements were made between some of the major nuclear powers. But this would not occur until America alone had produced over 70,000 atomic bombs. For now, there was a race to build and drop the bomb on somebody before WWII was over.

"THIS PLACE IS LOADED WITH SHIPS, AND MORE COME IN EVERY DAY"

Moratai Sept 1944. The USS Hughes and her destroyer screen off the port side of a transport ship. U.S. Navy photo.

The USS *Hughes* was headed for the Philippines and Leyte Gulf. Before the main invasion, the Islands of Dinigat and Homonhon would have to be taken. The USS *Hughes* was sent to do the job. The commander for this temporary operation was Rear Admiral Struble, and he made the USS *Hughes* his flagship. An admiral was on the USS *Hughes* once again. Alan Evans proudly recalled, "For the invasion of Leyte to be successful, the islands of Dinigat and Homonhon, guarding the entrance of Leyte Gulf, must be seized before the arrival of the main landing force. A small group of Rangers was detailed for this job, and the operation was under the command of Rear Admiral Struble. He chose the *Hughes* as his flagship, and on 12 October, our tiny force set out."

Seaman Skic remembered this top naval officer joining them again: "October 11, 1944. The Admiral's staff is already aboard. We will leave here tomorrow at noon." But the task force was small. "We left Humboldt Bay at 3:30 PM. We have five APOs: fast transports loaded with Rangers and one tug that rammed us on our port quarter and put a hole in our side. One gunboat, a minelayer, three minesweepers, and two destroyers."

They were counting on speed and secrecy to carry out this mission. The main invasion would depend on their success. If any sizable Japanese fleet discovered them, they would have little chance of survival. They would rely on their skill and the speed of the group members to make the mission successful. The hole on the side of the USS *Hughes* was quickly repaired and did not impact the mission.

The admirals and generals repeatedly picked the USS *Hughes* as their flagship. Other ships often requested her as their escort, and she won many praises and awards from the top brass. Times might have been tough, and the sailors often complained. Still, they were a team, held together by immense pride in their professionalism and skill in shooting down Japanese planes and shelling Japanese shore installations at close range. Everyone on the ship knew his job by now, and no one needed any prodding to stay alert. They were especially aware of how the lives of everyone onboard depended on every man doing his duty at all times.

There was little time for rest. During any pause in the action, the men worked feverishly on chipping, painting, and maintaining the guns. They took great pride that no other Navy ship could outshoot them when they participated in training exercises. The reality of kamikaze attacks made that preparation all the more critical. Seaman Tony Skic often had a single entry in his diary: "Worked like a dog today" or "Worked hard all day, and the heat has been terrible for the last week," The men were in a life-and-death struggle each moment at sea, and they knew it.

The weather turned bad on their way to the mission. This kept the Japanese from discovering them, but it was a nightmare on board the destroyer, not to mention that aircover could not fly and keep their eyes on the mission. The initial plan was to have hundreds of aircraft covering the mission. This was no longer possible. On October 15, 1944, Tony Skic noted:

> The success of the whole operation depends on us. We will be the first man of war in the Philippines. We have already been spotted by the Japs. The weather is pretty rough, with plenty of rain and spray, and right now we are 36 hours from the Philippines. We will go to General Quarters tomorrow and stay in that condition until the 21st. The sea is rough, and we are tossed around like a cork. Visibility is abysmal; it is raining like hell, and there is plenty of lightning. We will follow the minesweepers right in.

The next day, the battle began. Skic wrote:

> At 4:00 AM, we went to battle stations. The weather was terrible; we had terrific rainfall, heavy seas, and a 61-knot wind! At 5:00 AM, a Jap aircraft dropped a flare on us and lit us up like Broadway. The minesweepers swept the channel, and we went right in and shot up the beach. There were few Japs there. They killed some of our Rangers. Heavy seas wrecked 14 of our 16

landing craft. Our ships repelled Jap fighters who strafed us. We secured the island, left General Quarters at 4:30 PM, and patrolled further out to sea a few miles.

By now, surviving a risky attack on Japanese-held installations and landing Army Rangers to take the beach was routine. In the days before the landings on this mission, Seaman Ollie Stine made fatalistic notes in his diary:

Friday, October 13th, 1944. We are going to land in the Philippines! D-Day is the 20th, but we are going in ahead of the main force and land our Rangers on the 17th. We are the first Americans to land in the Philippines, but it is a doubtful honor. We expect to have our hands full until the main force arrives. Our force is so small that we hope the Japs will think this is just a diversionary raid and will expect the main landings elsewhere. We naturally suppose the Japs will try to get us, but we hope everything will come out okay.

The heavy weather ended up being a godsend to the sailors on the USS *Hughes*. Stine noted on October 16, 1944, "Rough as hell and getting rougher. Visibility is poor as hell, and the heavy winds and rough seas are probably why we have not been attacked yet." Then, on October 17, 1944, he wrote, "Fighting a typhoon all night and this morning. We arrived in Leyte Gulf at dawn."

On October 18, 1944, after the Rangers took the island, Stine noted, "Came into the gulf and anchored near the beach that our Rangers are on. This place is very mountainous, so we cannot pick up planes on the radar. We were surprised twice by a strafing twin-engine bomber and once by a Val dive bomber, but neither did any damage to us." They contacted the local people: "Came in at first light again. These Filipinos are happy to see us. They came out and saluted us and appeared overjoyed to see Americans again. In the afternoon, we were attacked by two dive bombers. One of their bombs fell about fifty yards from our fantail, but that was the best the Japs could do. Later, two minesweepers were attacked by three Val dive bombers but suffered only a little damage. They started for us, but we opened up with our five-inch, which caused them to change their minds."

The USS *Hughes* led the invasion and re-taking of Dinigat Island, leaving only Panaon Island before the main attack of the Philippines. She was still the flagship of the admiral in charge of the operations. The main landing force came up to assist in the next attack, but by then, the Japanese were pulling back and reinforcing their positions on the mainland. They knew they could not defeat or even slow down the Americans on unfavorable ground. Additionally, 45,000 Filipinos were ready to assist the American invasion.

The USS *Hughes*, now familiar with these waters, would lead the task force to the beach on Panaon Island. Alan Evans remembered, "On the night of the 19th of October, the main landing force approached, and in the early morning of the 20th, the USS *Hughes* met a group of transports in the entrance to Leyte Gulf and led them through the channel to Panaon Island. The USS *Hughes* was again the flagship for the landing on the 20th. This landing was carried out without resistance. The chief difficulty was the overwhelming reception by the natives, who swarmed out in canoes to welcome us to such an extent that normal operations could not be carried out."

October 20, 1944, Ollie Stine recorded:

The main force arrived this morning, so we have lots of support this time. We went 35 miles north of the main force and landed 15,000 troops there. Hundreds of people came out in boats bringing us gifts of chickens, eggs, bananas, etc., which we refused as they were destitute. The Japs burned their villages and made off with everything they could carry. We gave them clothes, and they were grateful! I've never seen anything like this before! Some of their gals are very cute. Just like little dolls! Three Jap planes attacked us at dusk but could not hit us, nor us them, and they stayed plenty high.

By now, the Japanese planes could quickly identify ships with gunners who could hit them at long range. After watching the fire from the ships, they would determine the risk, and if the gunners were too good, they would move on to other vessels that were less deadly targets. They were, by now, intimately familiar with the range at which the shells would explode.

The USS *Hughes* was a challenging target. Tony Skic recorded the same attack: "We were attacked by a Jap plane, and we laid a terrific and murderous barrage. We are surprised how he escaped it. A lieutenant and two Filipino guerillas came aboard in an outrigger. They have fought here for five years against the Japs. He said the people were glad to see us back. The women here sure look good! We got some souvenir money from them." The young fighting sailors of the USS *Hughes*, even if for only an hour or so, had a chance to think back over their happy visits to brothels and bars in San Francisco and Australia when they saw the beautiful women of the Philippine Islands.

While the Allies and the USS *Hughes* were getting ready for the assault and re-taking of the Philippines, the Americans were just completing the new airfields on the islands that the destroyer had helped reclaim in the Pacific. This would allow Roosevelt to use the new B-29s to drop bombs on Japan and return without refueling. They were just waiting for Oppenheimer and his scientists to prepare the atomic bombs. B-29s began attacking aircraft factories in Japan with mixed conventional and incendiary bombs. The Japanese still had enough airplanes to shoot some of them down. The B-29s were also vulnerable to antiaircraft fire.

A decision was made to bomb Japanese cities with incendiary bombs. Still controversial, planes loaded with these bombs would soon decimate significant population centers. The wooden and paper houses of the Japanese civilians burned, and fires spread in the hurricane-force winds created by the conflagrations. No price was too high for victory, even if it meant the destruction of Japan.

CHAPTER THIRTY-ONE

"THE GREAT NAVAL BATTLE HAS BEGUN"

Crewmembers of the USS Hughes were about to enter the fateful battle of Leyte Gulf, from which some would never return after being attacked by multiple Japanese Kamikaze aircraft. Glen Edmonson collection.

The greatest battle of WWII in the Pacific was now underway. Japan's fear was coming true. There was no hope left that they could win the war. Their only objective was to keep their home islands from being occupied by Americans. Okinawa was at their doorstep, and before that, the Philippines. The island hopping across the Pacific would stop, and the Americans would invade and retake the Philippine Islands. The Japanese would dig in on Okinawa and attempt to use the kamikazes and surface fleet to deliver a devastating defeat to American naval ships at Leyte Gulf.

Ollie Stine recorded the beginning of attacks by suicide bombers: "Expect to arrive at Leyte Gulf in the morning. We received word that a suicide dive bomber crashed into our sister ship, the USS *Anderson*, killing her skipper. That makes two captains the *Anderson* has lost this year." The USS *Anderson* would survive the war, even after being hit by a kamikaze attack.

Alan Evans wrote about the first significant suicide attacks against the USS *Hughes*:

On November 5, 1944, the *Hughes* left with a supply echelon for Leyte. Our arrival on the 12th coincided with the first clear weather in two days, and the Japanese poured suicide plane raids throughout the day. By 1:00 PM, four raids were completed when we went alongside a tanker in San Pedro Bay to fuel. Another raid came in, and one of the planes circled the USS *Hughes* and the Tanker *Caribou* as targets. As he dove on us, there seemed little chance of stopping him in time, even though we were pumping a stream of shells into him. At 500 feet, we braced for the crash. He suddenly rolled over and splashed harmlessly alongside. We had cut our lines to the tanker during the fight to get away. We began to steam at 20 knots through the crowded channel. We went alongside the *Achilles*, which had been hit by a suicide plane, and took onboard her casualties.

We gave them medical care before delivering them to a hospital ship. Another raid of eight planes came in as we stood out to the bay, and we knocked down one, making our score two for the day.

The Japanese were having success. Ollie Stine recorded, "There is a shortage of escorts as the Japs have been making suicide dives into our destroyers at Leyte. The Office of Naval Intelligence has informed us that 800 Jap dive bombers have pledged their lives to the Emperor and have the annoying habit of crashing their planes into our ships!" It now seemed possible to the Americans that Admiral Onishi could win this war of terror and attrition.

Tony Skic noted, "The dope is that the Jap dive bombers crashed into our ships, so now we are getting ready." Just about the time it seemed things could not get much worse, they did. On November 12, 1944, he wrote in his diary:

> The third attack of the day came when we were tied up along-side a tanker refueling. Three planes came over us. One dived directly on us. The tanker had her decks full of high octane in drums. Our searchlight was turned on, and our 20 mm guns opened up. We hit him and also blinded him with the light. He crashed on the side of the tanker. I saw his two bombs in their racks and braced myself for the explosion and flame. I was also looking right into the barrels of his guns. The red circles on his wings were very bright. We think we killed him with our 20 mm guns. Several ships were hit. The Japs come out of nowhere and get in a dive and crash on a ship just like that. The tanker gave us credit for saving her with our effective fire.

He later noted a message from the fleet commander: "We received a message of thanks and congratulations from the captain of the tanker for saving his ship and one from the commander of this force for our excellent shooting and screening. We got an honorary membership in his flotilla. He also wants us on all his trips up into Leyte Gulf."

The same day, Ollie Stine recorded the attacks:

As we were proceeding to our area, a Jap plane burst into flames 500 feet over the convoy and crashed into the water, narrowly missing several ships. We received word that 60-70 Jap planes were headed our way. Four suicide planes attacked, and two of them crashed into ships. When the suicide planes came in, two crashed into a Liberty ship and an LST, and the other dove for us. We opened fire with our forward five-inch gun and 20 mm guns. Our 36-inch spotlight was also on him, and this combination either proved too much for him or else our 20 mm's killed the pilot as he did a wing over and crashed into the sea 500 feet from us. The good lord was certainly with us, for if he had crashed into us or into the tanker, whose topside was covered with drums of 100 octane gas, very few of us would have been left alive. What a day this has been, and I hope I never see another like it!

Tony Skic wrote in his diary, "Went to battle stations three times today as three large groups of Jap planes were looking for us. They missed us but attacked the *O'Bannon* and an LSO behind us. We were attacked by 12 Bettys, some Vals, and Zekes. One Zeke was shot down." But this was quickly followed two days later by, "Just a routine dull life here."

Few, if any, people back home in Montana, Kansas, Missouri, or Chicago would have considered what the sailors on the USS *Hughes* were experiencing now to be a "routine, dull life."

So far, nothing in the war had been as terrifying as Onishi's kamikaze attacks. Onishi believed he could sink American ships faster than the Americans could build them. This was now being put to the test. For a time, it was true. He believed the sailors could not sustain such terror each day. But he was wrong.

The sailors of the USS *Hughes* were on a leading ship in the invasion of the Philippines. They endured suicide attack after suicide attack and kept on fighting. The journals of the sailors and officers showed that they could not only take these attacks but were becoming used to them and bored when they were not occurring. Admiral Onishi had seriously miscalculated his enemies and the depth of the spirit of the American sailors on the USS *Hughes*. America was in this to the finish. Had the Japanese realized this at the end of November 1944, the war could have been shortened, and millions of lives saved. But this was not to be.

The Japanese soon faced a horror of their own when B-29 bombers bombed Japanese cities, killing tens of thousands of civilians with firestorm-inducing incendiary bombs. The American pilots could smell the burning flesh of the Japanese on the ground as they dropped their loads from only five hundred feet at night.

As the battle raged on at sea, the USS *Hughes* was once again the flagship of Admiral Struble and now Major General Bruce, who was in charge of the invasion. Allen Evans noted in his writings:

> Our foothold in the Philippines was not so secure as was planned. Heavy rains bogged down our ground forces and delayed the building of additional airfields. We could not accommodate enough planes for air cover for the fleet. The sky was filled with Japanese planes from the surrounding islands. The Japanese also brought strong reinforcement to their positions. Our timetable was being delayed, and we could only move on to Luzon once we had control of Leyte. We decided to attack Ormoc Bay and cut off the Japanese from their supply lines. Running

the gauntlet of enemy-held islands without effective air cover would be necessary to get to Ormoc Bay. For this hazardous and critical mission, the 77th Division under Major General Bruce was named with Admiral Struble in command of the Naval Forces, and Admiral Struble named the USS *Hughes* as his flagship for the attack. On the 6th of December, our force of destroyers, ADPs, and LSTs left San Pedro Bay.

CHAPTER THIRTY-TWO

"EVERYONE GAVE THANKS WHEN DARKNESS FELL"

An aerial view of the USS Hughes in October of 1944 at Panaon Island in the Central Pacific campaign against the Empire of Japan. U.S. Navy photo.

"Thursday, December 7, 1944, the third anniversary of the war," wrote Seaman Ollie Stine. He continued:

> We arrived in Ormoc Bay and made our landings. Shortly after 10:00 AM, nine Vals came over, and our P-38s shot down six of them. The destroyer, USS *Mahan*, got two, but they were suicide planes, and one dropped a bomb on the *Mahan* and then dived into her. Three more dove at the *Ward*, but only one hit her. The fires got out of control, and the USS *O'Brien* had to come alongside and sink her with shell fire. The *Hamman* also had to be sunk. A twin-engine Jap plane made a bombing run on the *Lamson* but missed and was shot down. Then a suicide plane came at her and crashed into the *Lamson's* bridge. One dove on us, and we hit him early in his dive, and he went right over us and crashed into the water. Everyone gave thanks when darkness fell, and we passed a peaceful night.

Although Stine survived the attacks of the next few days, this was the second-to-last journal entry he would ever make aboard the USS *Hughes*.

The USS *Hughes* had just seen two of her fellow destroyers sunk by the kamikaze attacks. Seaman Tony Skic noted the actions of that bloody day in the stifling tropical heat:

> We had about ten air attacks, and two American ships sunk. Thirty-four planes were shot down by P-38s and eight more by our ships. We lost quite a few good men on these ships today. We got some shrapnel in our ship from the attacks, and three correspondents from *Time Life* and *Look* magazines were on board. It was an exhilarating day! A Jap plane dived on us and almost hit us, but our gun bursts knocked him off his suicide dive course, which saved us. Today, I've seen planes bursting

into flames and crash-diving into the sea. The wounded were put aboard the hospital ship Mercy. The dead were taken to the beach to be buried.

The American objective of landing troops at the rear of the Japanese forces and cutting them off from their supply lines was successful. This would be a turning point in the conflict, but the Americans paid a heavy price in Ormoc Bay. Alan Evans recorded:

> Beginning at 9:30 AM, the most continuous and vicious suicide attacks in our experience were directed at the force throughout the day. The USS *Ward* and USS *Mahan* were badly damaged by suicide planes and were sunk by our forces. The USS *Liddle* had all officers killed by another suicide plane, and we sent over our doctor, pharmacist mate, and signalman to assist them. Many ships were hit. Our air cover shot down 43 planes, and our ships shot down another 14, two by the USS *Hughes*. Over 100 suicide planes attacked our forces in Ormoc Bay.

As distressing as it was, sinking their own ships was necessary when there was no hope of saving them. It's an image that Seaman Oliver Jones can still see as if it happened yesterday. "We were sad to see these ships slip below the waves and know our friends had died in combat. I lost friends on those ships." Generally upbeat and verbose, Jones becomes sullen and quiet when remembering that day in Ormoc Bay. "They went down so fast."

The USS *Hughes* would fight one last battle at Leyte Gulf only two days later as the battle raged for control of this critical area. The Japanese knew that if they lost, resupply would be impossible for the troops on land, and they would be left to die of starvation or face even worse from the locals. They had treated the indigenous peoples with such brutality that they knew they could expect no mercy in return. Death would be far preferable to capture, especially by the local Filipinos.

The USS *Hoel* was to face her fateful battle against the far superior Japanese fleet and go down in history for her gallant defense of the troop ships destined to land in the Philippines. Admiral Onishi would unleash his aircraft in devastating raids on American ships in ever-increasing measure, and his reign of terror would continue for months. Admiral Halsey was tricked into chasing what he thought was an aircraft carrier fleet that only carried a few planes, opening the way for the Japanese Imperial Navy to sail against the American surface fleet intent on landing troops for the invasion. At no other time was the fog of war as thick as it was at the Battles of Guadalcanal or Leyte Gulf. The Battle of Surigao Strait was the final significant battle fought between surface ships with their guns. It was the end of the battleship era.

The losses to the Japanese were devastating. More importantly, Japan had run out of fuel. They lost the fleet carrier *Zuikaku*, along with three light aircraft carriers. This was also the end of three Japanese battleships: the *Musashi*, the *Yamashiro*, and the *Fuso*. They lost a fourth battleship, the *Kongo*, when it tried to escape back to Japan. They also lost six heavy cruisers, four light cruisers, and 11 destroyers, dwarfing American losses. The Japanese could no longer refuel their ships in this area of the Pacific and had to try to make it back to Singapore or Japan. Many of them never made it. Those who wanted to get to Manila Bay were sunk or severely damaged as the Americans moved to the Philippine capital. Many who made it to Japan and were awaiting repairs were sunk in Japanese waters. The ever-increasing American presence was due to the new bases throughout the Pacific that the USS *Hughes* had helped liberate for American planes.

The Battle of Leyte Gulf would establish a beachhead for the 6th Army to begin the grueling task of re-taking the Philippines. But brutal fighting lay ahead. The USS *Hughes* and others were tasked with attacking re-supply ships for the embattled Japanese troops.

This effectively ended the Imperial Japanese Navy as a fighting force. Failing to stop the Americans at Ormoc Bay was the beginning of the end. It would stop oil and gas shipments and most of the Japanese offensive operations. Surface ships would never leave port again. An American aircraft carrier would soon sink the Imperial Japanese Navy battleship *Yamato*. When Admiral Ozawa was questioned on the battle after the war, he replied, "After this battle, the surface forces became strictly auxiliary, so that we relied on land forces, special [*Kamikaze*] attack, and air power. . . . There was no further use assigned to surface vessels, except for some special ships." Admiral Mitsumasa Yoni, navy minister of the Koiso Cabinet, said he realized that the defeat at Leyte "was tantamount to the loss of the Philippines." As for the significance of the battle, he said, "I felt that it was the end.'"

However, some of the most brutal fighting for the American Navy still lay ahead. Now began the darkest days of the Pacific campaign as the kamikaze forces under Admiral Onishi took center stage. With no naval battles possible for Japan, she would rely on destroying the American fleet and fighting spirit with suicide attacks by single aircraft, one at a time. They would be relentless.

The battle to save Japan had changed. The admirals of the Imperial Japanese Navy would take a back seat to Admiral Onishi and his kamikaze forces. Meanwhile, American leaders were putting their faith in Robert Oppenheimer and his scientists at Los Alamos to provide them with an atomic bomb that would counter that Japanese terror with an American terror of far greater magnitude.

A sullen quietness spread over the USS *Hughes*. Gone were the days of bravado and talk of seeing Japanese pilots screaming while burning to death in crashing planes. Something had changed. The hatred of "yellow Jap bastards" was as strong as ever, but there was a new respect for their fighting spirit, as complicated as it was. The danger was now ever-present, and no one could make a mistake. Watchful eyes replaced the idle talk on deck. There was no more time for fishing. The sailors knew they were facing the greatest peril of the war, and it was getting worse by the day. Americans didn't even know where the Japanese planes were coming from. The aircraft could appear from the small airstrips in the jungles of any of a hundred islands. Admiral Onishi and his attack forces were tough to defend against. In this new phase, it seemed to the sailors of the USS *Hughes* that the war might go on forever. Home seemed little more than a distant memory, and most now seriously questioned if they would ever see home again. Many on the USS *Hughes* would not.

"STILL TAKING OUT THE DEAD"

USS Hughes crewmembers in the Philippines not long before being hit by a Kamikaze aircraft in Leyte Gulf. Glen Edmonson collection.

On December 10, 1944, a young Japanese man woke up for the last time in his life and went to work. His office was a single-engine aircraft loaded with fuel and a single bomb. He was given a map with alternate landing sites and was taught to take off and land his aircraft in case he could not find a suitable target.

The sailors of the USS *Hughes* would soon recover the map he took with him. It would be critical to the war effort to detect and neutralize the dispersed landing fields that Onishi and his attack forces used. The young man placed it in his coat pocket. He wore the traditional samurai head scarf of the fliers in his unit, with slogans and the red rising sun of Japan. His actions on this day would be calm and deliberate, even in the face of death and withering fire from the deck guns of the USS *Hughes*. He had been told that he would become immortal when his life ended, but only the dead themselves would ever know what he would become, if anything, after he died. He did not expect to return or see his family again.

Tony Skic noted a fateful decision on December 10, 1944: "The Admiral and his staff had left for the USS *Nashville*." The general and his staff had left the ship two days earlier. Had both the admiral and general stayed on board, this Japanese kamikaze pilot might have killed them in the next few hours.

The crewmembers of the USS *Hughes* who were not on watch woke up to one of an endless number of hot, tropical, and humid days with only the promise of more attacks by enemy aircraft to look forward to. At dawn, the water temperature was 84 degrees, and the air was 78 degrees, but it would also climb to a stifling 84 degrees as the day wore on in the hot, humid air. The generator had gone out, and no air moved below deck. The men were covered with salty, baked-on filth from days of almost constant combat. It was hard to come to terms with the losses on their sister ships that had unfolded before their eyes. They had not been able to re-provision with fresh fruit and meat. Rations were unappetizing and, at times, unpleasant.

The morning mess was unusually quiet. The sailors had received more bad news. They all knew what it meant, but no one wanted to discuss it. Kamikaze attacks were now well known, and the best defense was air cover by P-38s. But today, they had been told there would be no P-38s. They were to patrol alone for the first time in days. They needed a typhoon or some bad weather, but the day began with clear skies, a 15,000-foot ceiling, and visibility of eight miles. This was depressing news. Seaman Norris Brooks sat down to eat, not knowing that this would be his last sunrise and meal on the USS *Hughes*. Like the Japanese pilot on his way to meet the USS *Hughes* in battle, he would not survive the day. Many on the ship would be dead or wounded before the day was over.

Retired Commander Alan Evans noted, "We were to patrol independently, without air cover, and within easy reach of Japanese airfields. By 4:45 PM, we were under attack by ten planes. They split into two groups and attacked from all sides. We successfully avoided five bombs, but one plane peeled off from the others and began a suicide dive on our ship. We hit him many times, but we could not stop him. He crashed into the port side of the USS *Hughes*."

Tony Skic's December 10, 1944, journal entry was short: "Dive bombers hit us. They straddled us with bombs. One hit between the forward engine room and after fire room, and the suicide plane dived and crashed into us. My best buddy was killed in the engine room. All power was out. Ten planes were overhead, at least four dived on us, and one hit." The next day, he only wrote, "We are taking out the dead." The following day, he wrote, "We are still taking out the dead. The Jap pilot looked like hamburger meat." Two days after that, his only entry was: "The *Nashville* came in today with 125 dead and 150 injured. A buddy of mine was hurt there, too." His friend would also die of his injuries in the coming days. It was a very dark and confusing time.

One of the sailors on the USS *Hughes* that day was Seaman Louis Swan from Texas. Louis joined the Navy as soon as he was barely old enough and after his parents signed the paperwork, but by that time, his four older brothers were already in the service: Ray, Clifford, and Lloyd in the Navy and Julius in the Air Corps. Louis Swan penned a remarkable story of the fateful event at Leyte Gulf on December 10, 1944. He called it "Those Damned Kamikazes." Although not written contemporaneously with the event, it closely follows other reports and the official deck log from the USS *Hughes* from that day. The story states:

Seaman Louis Swan was on the USS Hughes on December 10, 1944, when it was hit by a Kamikaze plane and almost lost.

Even though the date was December 10, 1944, the weather was hot and humid. It was always hot in the Philippines, and my ship was the first to return since the Japs had taken over a few years earlier. We had just finished the Ormoc landing and were in Leyte Gulf. We had been the flagship of Rear Admiral Struble, and we spent the day taking on provisions and ammunition. However, as in any hot war, a day of rest has to end, and it ended for us at 2:00 PM when we were sent to depart for picket duty. The ships on picket duty were to cruise around the area and try to pick up enemy planes on radar that could not be detected by land-based radar due to the mountainous terrain.

The account continues:

We were supposed to relieve another picket-duty destroyer. However, we never saw the other ship. We were then told that our radar might not be too effective due to the mountains jutting out of the sea in the area. Just as the skipper passed the word on the P.A. system, another voice was heard in the background informing him that a flight of ten bogies (enemy aircraft) had been picked up on radar. No sooner had the word come over the loudspeaker; the General Quarters' alarm sounded.

I was working the mid-shift in the radio room that week and decided to sleep through chow. I lay in the sack listening to the voices coming through the speaker, and when I heard the alarm, I jumped up. I was fully clothed except for my shoes. I slipped them on, not bothering to tie them. My bunk was forward of the mess and galley area near the bow of the ship, and my battle station was on the twin-mount 40 mm guns just aft of midships. I rushed through the mess hall and up the ladder to the main deck leading aft. I was the third loader for my gun position."

All hell was breaking loose. The 5" 38-caliber guns were firing simultaneously, and the 20-mm and 40-mm guns chattered like a cage of excited monkeys.

The enemy planes were circling just outside the range of our weapons, probably deciding who would be the first to die for his glorious Emperor. Suddenly, one of the planes broke in formation and was approaching the USS *Hughes* from our starboard side, where he intended to crash into us. However, the hail of fire was so great that he swung in a circular motion around the stern of the ship and was coming in on our port side now.

All guns were trained on this lone challenger, and tracers could be seen flying all around him. At last, we could see that his engine was on fire. We had scored a hit!

Everyone was excited and thought the plane would explode or crash into the water. But no, although the plane was burning fiercely, the plane was still heading in a death dive for our ship. We tried evasive action but to no avail.

The plane crashed into our port side midships, gouging a huge hole in the side and main deck. The plane's engine continued into the engine room, where a tremendous explosion shook the destroyer.

Mass confusion seemed to reign for a few moments. Everyone was running around and shouting orders. Using a megaphone, the skipper instructed all hands, not manning guns, to move aft of the ship and await further orders. The damage control party started putting out the fires still enveloping the ship. Pumps were set up in the engine room to pump water out of the ship. I lost both shoes but kept going. I could feel something sticky on my feet. When I reached the stern, my feet were soaked in blood. Shrapnel had found its way to our gun mount, and several crewmembers were bleeding badly.

Then water continued to pour into our side. Flying debris had started fires around the ship. It seemed that the USS *Hughes* was doomed. Badly listing from all the water pouring into her bowels, it must have appeared to the remaining Jap planes that they would not be needed to finish us off.

All power was knocked out when the boilers in the engine room exploded. Using his megaphone, the skipper informed all hands that we were not to fire any guns at the remaining planes so they would think we were finished. However, at the precise moment that he was giving the order, one of the crewmen on the 5" gun, due to the excitement, kicked out a round at the circling planes (although we had no power, the guns could still be fired manually). It was pitifully short of the target and only seemed to infuriate the enemy planes into further action.

A second plane peeled off from the formation and headed for our ship. Everyone was waiting tensely by their guns for the plane to come into range. They knew they would have only one chance to knock him out of the skies before he would be on us. When we thought it would all be over, a flight of the most beautiful P-38s came to our rescue. One of the men on duty in the radio room had found and manned a battery-operated radio that had been left aboard from the Ormoc Bay landing and had sent out a distress call. The P-38s had picked it up and came to our rescue.

As soon as the Jap plane spotted the P-38s bearing down on him, he turned and fled into his formation, and they left the area. With the P-38s still in hot pursuit, the enemy planes disappeared into the mountains and were not seen by us again. Later, it was reported that some of them crashed into other ships. The weather changed, and soon, we were in drizzling rain and fog, which had closed in on us. Those who survived were all wet and miserable but glad to be alive. One thing was certain—we would not make it to Leyte Gulf alone. We received word that help was coming but had to stay afloat until it arrived.

Seaman Oliver Jones remembers things only slightly differently. When the attack began, he was manning a 20-mm gun on the ship's starboard side.

We were cruising that day, off Leyte Gulf, just over the horizon's edge. We were on guard duty reporting planes we saw. We saw Jap planes coming in over the tops of the ships in our area. A fleet of Jap planes came in over us. Maybe a dozen planes or so. We shot down planes. One gunner claimed he shot down five planes, but I am unsure. They made a big splash when they crashed into the ocean, but we were unhappy because so many more planes were coming in. That day, they came in droves against us. There were eight or ten of them in each group. We could see and hear them. I used binoculars, and we fired every gun at the Jap planes. I shot at them with the 20 mm gun, but everyone else was firing simultaneously, so we never knew who shot down any particular plane. We tried to be careful not to shoot at American planes. But when the Jap planes got close, we could see the orange spot on the wings.

Some planes circled us multiple times, checking us out on the USS *Hughes*. After circling us, one plane peeled off and came toward us. It felt terrific when we hit the Jap plane because I knew that Jap was finished. But he kept coming at us, so we were distraught when he kept coming. I don't know how he kept flying at us because the plane was burning. I remember that day well. I was on the other side of the ship when it hit us. It went right down to the keel of the ship. I ran to get the bilge pumps. It was a tremendous crash. It shuddered just like a rooster shaking water off himself. Then the bomb went off right after. When I went down to get the water out of the ship, all the sailors from the engine and fire control rooms were dead. They were bled entirely out. It was terrible to see. I saw a terrific mess. Their blood was all over us. I stayed with the water pumping to keep the ship from sinking. A lot of guys were killed there. The whole side of the ship was blown open. Then the ship went lower in the water.

I went down and saw where the Japanese plane was and saw the pilot. He looked just like meatballs. You could tell it was a person, but he was shot to pieces. The plane was pretty much blown up by the bomb it was carrying. You could see the pilot because the blood and guts lay there. Most of the killed crew were floating on the water's surface. It was an awful scene. I'll never forget it. Trying to man the pumps was tough when I saw the dead sailors floating on the water right by me. They were my friends and shipmates. Some were good friends. The water was coming in, and we sent out a mayday for help, and a destroyer picked it up, and so did a tugboat. The U.S. planes also got the mayday, and they came to save us from another Jap plane attack. The destroyer was the first to come to our aid, and they tied up to the side of us, keeping us from sinking. If they had not done that, we would have gone to the bottom of the ocean. The water was up to my chin. We were sinking. Fortunately, the US planes ran the other Jap planes away from us.

A lot of guys were injured above the deck. The medics were running around trying to help people. I was sad to see an excellent buddy of mine was dead. He was from Utah. Some guys were buried at sea right away. Some guys had to be dumped over the side because so many things were happening, and we thought the ship was sinking. We just put some weight in a sack, put the dead in, and put them over the side. We just waved at them and said "goodbye." It was sad. Yep. That's pretty much what we did. Not all the dead guys were found immediately; it was a warm day in the tropics, so it was awful later when we returned to a dock with dead guys still inside.

When Jones said the sailors were "bled out," he was referring to what a body looks like after a massive steam explosion on a ship. It was an eerily terrifying sight. Jones remembers it well today, and it still haunts his thoughts.

Soon, the rescuing destroyer chained herself to the USS *Hughes* to keep her from going under. That was one of Oliver Jones's last memories of that event. This would be his final battle at sea. He would survive his injuries from that day and return to his home in Montana many months later. Still, more than 50 years would pass before he would tell his family about what he had seen and done in the war so far from the hills of Montana. About a year after he returned, he wrote down some of his stories, but they were only recently shared. He would go on to marry and have a family, but they knew little of his time as a sailor on the USS *Hughes*.

Jones's burden is still a heavy one. Many of his shipmates never returned from this battle. Some lie on the bottom of the sea at Leyte Gulf, and some are buried on the beaches of the Philippines. Upon reading this manuscript, he said, "Thank you for writing this book. People need to know the story, but I don't believe I deserve the honor. I can't tell you how much it means to me now."

Alan Evans noted the crew's spirits that day: "Although she was without power and flooding rapidly, her men did everything possible to save her. In the end, we won. The fires were put out, and the flooding stopped. That day, every man on the ship was a hero, and outstanding acts were commonplace. Eighteen were dead, and many more were wounded seriously." Many men suffered injuries. Damage to hearing was commonplace. Others were hurt in the rescue efforts or while tending to injured shipmates. "The USS *Quapaw* began emergency repairs to get us underway," wrote Evans, "but it had cost us heavily. One engine room was demolished. There was a great gaping hole on our port side. Our personnel losses were heavy. But our efforts paid off, and the USS *Hughes* returned to life eight days later, but still in bad shape."

Evans further noted, "During this time, many messages came to us expressing sincere regrets over our damage, for the USS *Hughes*, in its many months of operations in the Pacific, had made numerous friends. A message came in from a hospital ship nearby: 'Many of the men on duty here are from the *Liscome Bay* [the first ship sunk by a kamikaze attack]. We are very sorry you had to get it.'"

The commander of the USS *Hughes* that day was E. B. Rittenhouse. The navigator was D. E. Skinner, lieutenant junior grade. Alan S. Evans, lieutenant, USNR, entered and signed the deck log. That log, from December 10, 1944, contains the following note:

4:38 PM. Commenced patrol of Surigao Straight. 4:45 PM sighted eight planes on the starboard quarter. General Quarters. Changed speed to 25 knots and commenced radical maneuvers. 4:48 PM twin-engine bomber identified as a Nell approached on the starboard quarter, then retired as guns were brought to bear. 4:49 PM two single-engine planes came out of the clouds ahead and dropped bombs fifty yards on port beam. 4:50 PM two near misses on starboard side and one astern. 4:52 PM four planes sighted on port quarter. 4:53 PM one plane, identified as a Val, peeled off from the group on the port quarter and commenced suicide dive on the ship. Commenced firing. 4:55 PM suicide plane hit many times but continued approach and crashed into main deck on the port side at frame #105 and bomb exploded. A large fire started in area of torpedo shack. Floater net raft port side afire. Towing hawser and reel blown by the explosion from main deck to frames 103 and 109. Bulkhead between the forward engine room and after fire room shattered. Both main generators demolished, and the ship lost all power. The repair party immediately began fighting the fires. 5:00 PM enemy planes circled overhead and then retired to the north. Ship smoking badly and dead in the water. Ceased fire. 5:05 PM rigged the emergency battery radio and called for air cover and assistance of a tug. Fire on the bridge is out.

The log notes that Henry Fiddler and William Line were buried at sea. Many other of the dead were kept on board the ship.

The deck log also says, "5:15 PM friendly aircraft appeared in the area as air cover. Surface assistance was reported on the way. 5:30 PM Repair parties proceeding below decks to fight the fires. 5:35 PM all fires out. 6:00 PM forward engine room flooded to the floor plates. The after-fire room is flooding. Attempted to get steam up in forward fire room and after engine room. Unsuccessful because of inability to keep up pressure. The ship is dead in the water, drifting slowly towards Panaon Island."

Rear Admiral Julian Becton, the commanding officer of the USS *Laffey* at the time, noted disturbing casualties onboard the USS *Hughes*. He remarked how great the gunners were on the USS *Hughes*, famous throughout the fleet, but they could not shoot down this one plane that was diving on them. He described how the plane hit the ship's middle, how the engine and boiler rooms were torn apart, and how vast pieces of metal flew through the air after the impact and explosion. Flaming gasoline enveloped the ship, igniting the men's clothes, and many suffered dreadful steam burns. Although they had seen many ships and sailors killed and witnessed horrible injuries, Becton and his men said they had never seen anything like what they found below decks on the USS *Hughes*. Those who assisted on the USS *Hughes* rescue would be haunted by what they saw among the living and the dead.

Chester Bradley recalled:

On December 10, 1944, I was not on radar that day, but I assisted Herb VanDerBeek in retrieving the battery-operated radio we used to call for help. This was one of the radio sets left behind on the ship from the landings at Leyte Gulf by the Army officers. We were so lucky it had been left onboard the ship, and without it, we would have very likely sunk. Once it worked, we could reach multiple Navy planes about fifty-eight miles away with this radio. They arrived to stop the Japanese second attack on the USS *Hughes*. The American planes immediately moved in to attack the remaining Japanese planes, and they took off and left us. That bought time for our ships to come in and save us.

Bradley was from Trinidad, Texas, a tiny town with less than a thousand people.

The day the USS *Hughes* was hit, my cousin Milburn Johnston was 300 miles away on the *Boise*. The *Boise* came to give aid to the *Hughes*. Milburn had the signalman send a message asking if Chester Bradley was alive. The USS *Hughes* radioed back, and he received a signal in return saying, "Yes, Chester Bradley is alive." He had a signalman send a message asking permission to board the ship. The USS *Hughes* radioed back a message that permission was denied because the USS *Hughes* was under quarantine due to the damage and casualties. It was amazing that two cousins from such a small town in Texas were joined by this fateful event so far from home.

Another radarman, Joseph Prociak, was on duty in the radar room.

I was on duty in the radar shack. I noticed a large number of blips off in the distance. I pushed the IFF button to determine if they were friends or foes. The response was no ID, which meant they were approaching unfriendly aircraft. I notified the officer on duty of the enemy aircraft. He looked at the blips and said that there were too many to be aircraft. He was wrong! As it was close to my shift changing, I showed the blips to Bob Chambers, who was coming on duty and went to my bunk for some sleep. Not more than five minutes later, they went to General Quarters. When not in the radar shack, I reported to my five-inch gun, which was my assignment. There were twelve Jap planes circling overhead. We shot down two of them, but much to our dismay, one was headed right for us and hit the USS *Hughes* mid-ship. I was blown off my five-inch gun. We ran to put out the fires and rescue our injured shipmates. We were taking on water, and I was ordered below to help with the aftermath. I could see several of my shipmates' bodies floating but did not know who they were then. I saw the remains of the Kamikaze pilot, and someone removed his headband from his head. We wrapped his body parts in a sheet and gave them to the ship's officer. I'm not sure how they disposed of the body. There was never panic. The USS *Hughes* was one of the finest in the Navy. My shipmates were the best that ever manned a destroyer. I was only 17 years old then, and that day will remain with me always.

Soon, the USS *Phoenix* and USS *Boise* assisted the USS *Hughes*, and the *Laffey* tied up alongside her to keep her from sinking as rescue efforts were underway. All of this was done in heavy weather, making the task all that more difficult as the storm increased. The USS *Hughes* began to transfer her dead and wounded to the *Laffey*. The Navy tug *Quapaw* arrived at 10:30 PM and took the USS *Hughes* under tow. The forward engine room remained flooded to 11 feet three inches. It took two more days to get into the forward engine room, where rescuers discovered four more dead sailors. They again lowered their flag on the ship to half-mast when these men were transferred off the USS *Hughes*. It was a stifling 85 degrees, with high humidity and little air movement below decks. The work inside the ship was slow and gruesome. The tropical heat was overwhelming. The smell of death was everywhere.

On December 16, 1944, Tony Skic, in a brief journal entry, noted, "We had a church service today for our shipmates who died."

The ship underwent repairs for the next nine days. On December 19, 1944, Seaman Skic recorded, "Left Leyte Gulf at 3:30 PM and are going to Humboldt Bay. There are twelve of us destroyers." The next day, he was happy to report, "Still making 14 knots, but all we have is salt water showers. I got a message from Admiral Struble: 'Good luck and smooth sailing on a well and hard-earned rest.' We have been getting reports of Jap planes."

Alan Evans wrote, "A convoy of crippled ships was gathering, and on the 19th of December, we left for Humboldt Bay, steaming on

Seventeen-year-old Seaman John Poehl, a signalman on the USS Hughes on December 10, 1944. USS Hughes Reuinion Group photo.

one propeller and with our emergency diesel generator as the only power source. We arrived successfully at Humboldt Bay on the 23rd of December."

Tony Skic and the remaining sailors on the USS *Hughes* were to spend this Christmas on their badly damaged and barely floating ship in Humboldt Bay, New Guinea, far from his home in Chicago, Illinois. "December 25, 1944. Had a pretty fair Christmas dinner today. We only had two meals as all power was out on the ship."

On January 13, 1945, they left for Pearl Harbor, but their problems were far from over. The kamikaze attack had left a massive hole in the ship, and the damage below the waterline was significant. The temporary decking was not ready for heavy seas. Alan Evens recorded:

As the trip progressed, the heavy seas we encountered proved too much for the temporary plating on our port side. On the 18[th,] a six-foot crack developed in the main deck, and there were fears that the ship might break apart. By steaming in the wake of the Australian ship *Canberra,* and with continuous patching and welding of the crack, we could keep going and finally arrived in Pearl Harbor on the 23rd of January.

Finally, after so many months at sea and almost constant battles against the Japanese, Tony Skic returned to one of the places he loved best, aside from his hometown in Illinois: Pearl Harbor. On January 27, he noted, "Went ashore again today! Got feeling good!"

Soon, the USS *Hughes* was on the way back to San Francisco, but just as the coast of California was in sight, and their long and stressful journey seemed at an end, disaster struck. Alan Evans stated, "As we approached San Francisco, our troubles seemed over, and we streamed our homeward-bound flag. We were almost premature, however, for our jury-rigged generator supply on the main deck gave out as we neared the Golden Gate Bridge. Our steering control was lost, and we nearly collided with the bridge before we could control it again. We finally arrived at Hunters Point Naval Drydocks on the 2nd of February, and an extensive overhaul began."

Seaman Tony Skic, who, on October 26, 1943, first stepped on board the USS *Hughes* looking for adventure and combat, wrote his final log entry in his diary, "Arrived in Frisco this noon. Here is where I will stop this log until I leave." Tony would never forgive the Japanese for what he had seen in the Pacific. He seldom talked about what he had written in this journal, and it has mainly been a secret until the writing of this book. Later, his daughter would go back and transcribe the document. It is remarkable and extensive. The story of the USS *Hughes* was far from over, but it would go on without Tony Skic.

Seaman Ollie Stine also stopped writing in his journal on December 9, 1944, one day before the kamikaze attack on the USS *Hughes*. He survived the attack, but we will never know what he thought about it in the following days except as memories he shared with his immediate family. His daughter, Laurie Finger, said that he had no lingering resentment about the Japanese after the war. "My dad didn't have any hard feelings against the Japanese after the war. He always said the people were not to blame as their society held that the Emperor was a God, so they were honor-bound to do what he said."

Seaman Oliver Jones would also survive the battle and return to San Francisco. He would spend months in the hospital before returning to Montana. He is one of only two surviving crew members of the USS *Hughes* as of the writing of this book in the fall of 2023.

> I was injured that day and don't remember much of what happened later, but I remember we almost hit the Golden Gate Bridge on the way back because the steering went out. We only missed it by a hair. We were having a hard time. I've thought many times how bad it would have been to have hit the bridge and sunk after all we had been through. We got by the bridge and got into the dock. The ship got fixed back up and returned to battle at sea. I was put into a hospital. I don't remember what all happened.

When asked if he was injured, Jones said, "Yeah." When asked how he was injured, he replied, "I have no idea. But anyhow, I was in the hospital for quite a while, and then they discharged me with a medical. I don't recall how long I was in the hospital, but I know I was there for quite a while. My back was injured, and many of us got thrown around when the ship was hit. I also lost a lot of my hearing. That's why I've got hearing aids. I hope that helps your story."

Asked several times how he was injured and why he spent so long in the hospital, he would only say, "I don't remember." He did recall being able to get around some on the ship on the return trip to America, but not much else. His injuries and scars were profound. Back then, people didn't talk about such things.

For the years that the USS *Hughes* was in WWII, only four deck logs are missing from Naval Archives. One of them happens to be the log for January of 1945. What happened to this deck log has been lost to memory and time. One can only surmise that the surviving sailors of the USS *Hughes* had a lot to celebrate but also much to grieve and lost friends to mourn. This was true of the officers as well as the enlisted men. The reputation of the USS *Hughes* as a fighting ship proceeded her, and everyone in Pearl Harbor was aware of what she had been through and the losses she had suffered. Oliver Jones and some of the other sailors on our journey in this book were hospitalized. Many would never sail again. Others would return to battle.

In Japan today stands the Tokkō Kannondō temple. It is dedicated to the "Special Attack Goddess of Mercy." The image enshrined within is a six-foot replica of the Yumechigai Kannon, a national treasure at Hōryū-ji. The name of the kamikaze pilot who crash-dived his plane into the USS *Hughes* on December 10, 1944, is written on a pice of paper within her womb.

CHAPTER THIRTY-FOUR

"THE GREATEST AND MOST HORRIBLE CRIME"

Concentration camps and extermination centers were everywhere throughout Germany and occupied Europe. Fence at Flossenbürg concentration camp. U.S. Army photo.

In the early months of 1945, the USS *Hughes* would be repaired and returned to combat under Vice Admiral Frank Fletcher, who had commanded the task force under which the USS *Hughes* had fought at Guadalcanal.

The spring of 1945 also saw staggering events that shocked the world. The first occurred on April 12, 1945, at Warm Springs, Arkansas. British Prime Minister Winston Churchill couldn't believe the news. President Franklin Roosevelt had died. Churchill was devastated by the loss of his friend and ally.

> I admired him as a statesman, a man of affairs, and a war leader. I felt the utmost confidence in his upright, inspiring character and outlook, and my personal regard and affection for him is beyond my power to express today. His love of his own country, his respect for its constitution, and his power of gaging the tides and currents of moving public opinion were always evident, but added to these were the beatings of that generous heart which was always stirred in anger to action by spectacles of aggression and oppression by the strong against the weak. It is a bitter loss to humanity that those heartbeats are stilled forever.

That same day, American General Eisenhower visited the Nazi concentration camp of Buchenwald. What he found there was almost impossible to believe. He was so horrified at what he saw that Martin Gilbert wrote, "He at once telephoned Churchill to describe what he had seen, and then sent photographs of the dead prisoners to Churchill, who circulated them to each member of his cabinet." Churchill reported, "There is no doubt that this is probably the greatest and most horrible crime ever committed in the whole history of the world, and it has been done by scientific machinery by nominally civilized men in the name of a great State and one of the leading races of Europe."

Also, that same day, Edward R. Murrow of CBS walked through the death camp at Buchenwald and reported back to America and the world: "There were two rows of bodies stacked up like cordwood. They were thin and white. Some of the bodies were bruised, though there seemed to be little flesh to bruise. Some had been shot through the head, but they bled little. If I've offended you by this rather mild account of Buchenwald, I'm not the least sorry."

Similar reports were coming daily about Japanese atrocities against civilians and Allied soldiers in the Philippines. Japanese officers ate the livers of some executed American airmen shot down at Chichi Jima. Prisoners were being executed and worked to death by the thousands. If there had ever been any doubt about what the world would look like if Japan and Germany won the war, they were far in the past. There seemed to be no end to the horrors committed by the nationalist regimes. Before it was all over, 60 million people would be dead. Unconditional surrender was the only acceptable term for Germany and Japan.

Robert Oppenheimer and his scientists at Los Alamos received shipments of U-235 and plutonium in sufficient quantities to make three atomic bombs. Just as they were getting ready to test the bomb at Trinity, two events occurred.

First, Germany was defeated and surrendered on Monday, May 7, 1945, at Supreme Headquarters in northeastern France. Hitler was defeated, and the Jewish scientists at Los Alamos saw the threat against their friends and family members who were still alive diminish. However small, there was now light at the end of the tunnel for finding the remaining European Jews. Although Japan was still a significant problem for the Allies and the scientists, it had no such Jewish concentration camp issues.

Second, America had a new president, Harry Truman, who had never been told about the atomic bomb by Roosevelt. They had seldom talked, and Roosevelt had shared little with Truman of consequence. Truman was as surprised as everyone else to wake up one day and find himself president of the United States during WWII. He was even more surprised when he was briefed about the existence of the soon-to-be-tested atomic bomb that Roosevelt had planned to drop on Germany and Japan.

Roosevelt had created the atomic bomb project before America entered WWII. He had wanted to ensure that Hitler didn't beat America to an atomic bomb and use it on the Allies. Churchill was more than willing to drop bombs on Germany until Hitler was defeated or no Germans were left to drop them on. Roosevelt had ordered the Navy to clear the islands of the Pacific so that American B-29s could bomb Japan. Very little, if any, of this had been discussed with now-President Harry Truman. Yet Harry Truman would now have to finish all these policies and end WWII.

That stage was now set. Incendiary bombs were killing tens of thousands of Japanese civilians, but Japan showed no sign of surrendering anytime soon. All who knew about the bomb knew it was a weapon of such devastating power that it would be almost impossible to comprehend. If it worked, Truman had been handed the keys to a device that could end the war with Japan. Only he could make the decision to use it. It was a baptism by fire. Oppenheimer was summoned to Washington, D.C.

Meanwhile, a number of the scientists on the Manhattan Project were now directly asking for a say in using the bomb. Some wanted to tell the Japanese about it and see what they would do. Some called for a test where the Japanese would come and watch it go off. Some thought Japan would soon be defeated, and the Allies didn't need to use it. Others felt that America needed to drop the bombs on Japan and finish the war as quickly as possible. General Groves was furious. He believed this to be a political decision and that the scientists had nothing to do with it.

The military assessed American losses if it had to invade Japan, and the numbers were staggering. Soon after taking the Philippines, America invaded Okinawa. Admiral Onishi doubled down and unleashed a horrific attack of kamikaze suicide attacks against the American fleet in that battle.

Okinawa would prove to be a bloodbath for both soldiers and civilians alike. In this conflict, the Navy suffered the highest number of servicemen killed in action. This was primarily due to the kamikaze attacks from Admiral Onishi's unit. The Americans suffered over 4,400 causalities in this one encounter.

On top of that, over 15,000 were injured by non-battle incidents, including ones brought on by psychiatric events. Japanese losses were estimated to be around 110,000. Only 7,401 Japanese were taken prisoner. Most were killed in combat.

An American aircraft carrier sank the super battleship *Yamato*, one of the only significant fighting vessels left in the Japanese Imperial Fleet, further underscoring that the era of the battleship was over. Sixteen additional Japanese ships were also sunk at Okinawa. The once almost invincible Japanese Imperial Navy would never fight the Americans again. The fate of Japan's fortunes for the rest of the war would now rest with the suicide pilots, ground troops, and civilians, who were expected to fight to the death with sharpened bamboo spears.

The civilians on Okinawa were told that the Americans were barbarians who would rape and kill them. They were urged to commit suicide, which they did in mass numbers. Some locals killed their families and then themselves to keep from being captured. What the Americans on Okinawa witnessed was insanity. The number of soldiers breaking down from emotional distress was growing. This was like no war anyone had ever imagined. There is famous movie footage by the American troops showing civilians throwing their family members and themselves over the cliffs to their deaths on the rocks below.

What happened was not entirely insanity but a carefully calculated and scripted message to America. It was similar to the

Child soldiers In Okinawa where Japan pressed children
into military service of the Emperor and enlisted them to
kill Allied soldiers. U.S. Army photo.

kamikaze suicide attacks, designed to instill fear of what would happen if America attempted to invade mainland Japan and go after the emperor. If Harry Truman had ever had any doubts about using the atomic bomb in Japan, they were erased when he saw the reports from Okinawa. General Groves used this event to convince others that the American losses in an invasion of mainland Japan would exceed a million soldiers, possibly more.

From April 6 through June 22, 1945, Admiral Onishi sent out 1,465 kamikaze aircraft in huge, carefully designed sorties against the American fleet. The Americans had vastly underestimated the number of Japanese aircraft in the area. The Japanese were adept at disguising their aircraft and, in some cases, disassembling them in dispersed regions to keep them from detection. Hiding aircraft for use in kamikaze attacks became a significant part of the operation.

The impacts of the kamikaze attacks continued to be devastating. Like the sailors of the USS *Hughes*, other naval sailors couldn't believe what they were seeing and, more importantly, had a challenging time defending against them. Vice Admiral C. R. Brown said, "There was a hypnotic fascination to the sight so alien to our Western philosophy. We watched each plunging kamikaze with the detached horror of one witnessing a terrible spectacle rather than as the intended victim." The fleet seemed to have sailed into an alternate reality without sanity or reason.

On shore, things were no better. The rain covered the ground in mud to the soldiers' knees. The smell of rotting flesh was so overpowering that it was difficult to breathe in the hot and humid climate. Dead Japanese and locals were everywhere. Even worse, children were pressed into service to fight the Americans. The soldiers could not tell the Japanese from the locals, as the Japanese troops usually hid with the locals in villages. Americans had to kill everyone in places where combat was intense. This had a devastating effect on the troops. In the end, almost a quarter of a million people perished from the campaign and the Japanese occupation, far more than most American servicemen serving there could bear.

The threat of a hundred million Japanese dying to save their country from American occupation was vastly overinflated, as only 72 million Japanese were in Japan during WWII. However, even facing 72 million Japanese with sharpened bamboo sticks seemed daunting. The battle at Okinawa virtually assured that Japan would be the target of American atomic bombs.

CHAPTER THIRTY-FIVE

"WE CONSENT TO OFFER SOME POWS AS FORCED LABOR"

Soviet Prime Minister Josef Stalin, President Harry S. Truman, and British Prime Minister Winston Churchill pose for photos at Postsdam - NARA - 198797. UK public domain photo.

Neither Churchill nor Truman trusted Joseph Stalin. That relationship got worse in the coming years. But for now, America, Britain, and Russia were allies. With the defeat of Germany, it was time to decide what post-war Europe would look like and who would be in charge of rebuilding Germany.

The "Big Three," Churchill, Truman, and Stalin, met at Potsdam from July 17, 1944, to August 2, 1944. They aimed to decide on a post-war strategy to stabilize the world and avoid the next war. The plan would ultimately fail, as Stalin planned on taking as much of Eastern Europe as he could get his hands on. Still, there were two significant issues yet to be resolved. Truman and Churchill hadn't told Stalin about the atomic bomb, and Oppenheimer still hadn't set one off.

Japan had, at the same time, been reaching out to Russia to help reach an end to the war that left Japan largely intact. That was their last hope. However, they also feared that Russia might change its mind and attack them to gain the territories they held. This would happen very soon.

Truman and Churchill met for the first time, and the meeting went well. Churchill still missed Franklin Roosevelt deeply, but Truman seemed a man he could deal with. The Potsdam Conference was a success in that Russia would soon declare war on Japan, and Stalin was told of the atomic bomb test, as the Trinity test occurred during the conference. But in truth, Stalin had been informed on every step of the bomb by his spies at Los Alamos and was already working on an atomic bomb of his own. Stalin knew a lot more about the bomb than Truman did.

But then, when Churchill returned to England, the unthinkable happened in the election on July 25. Churchill woke up early that morning and right away had a profound feeling that something bad had transpired and that the worst possible thing had happened in the recent election. His hunch was correct. The British voters had fired him. With the death of Roosevelt, the two men who had guided the world through much of the war against Hitler were off the main stage. Churchill couldn't believe it, but Labour leader Clement Attlee had beaten him in the general election.

Truman talked a lot about the utter destruction of the Japanese, but this wasn't very American when it came down to it. It was also contrary to the conventions of war. Although some wanted the Japanese wiped off the face of the Earth, most people just wanted the war to end. Now, most Japanese people didn't support the war and certainly didn't by the summer of 1945. Anti-war and anti-nationalist sentiment in Japan was growing by the day. The Japanese people were sick of the simple-minded nationalists.

Emperor Hirohito had a deeply divided cabinet. Three of the six ministers wanted to sue for peace. Three wanted to fight to the death. Ministers Konoe and Saki drafted a plan to have Japanese soldiers remain on foreign soil as slave laborers to keep the emperor in power. This was part of the negotiations with the Russians on a peace plan. It included a provision that said, "We shall demobilize the military overseas in the places they are stationed and endeavor to repatriate them. If that is impossible, we shall consent to leaving some of them where they are for a while. We consent to offer some POWs at forced labor for the Soviet economy."

If offering Japanese soldiers, sailors, and airmen as slave labor would keep the Americans out of Japan and the emperor in power, so be it, but the hardliners on the council wanted them all to fight to the death. In the end, the Russians didn't need to make a deal. They could gain Japanese territories on their own and put the Japanese soldiers in forced labor camps anyway. This is precisely what they did when the war was over.

Even in the dark times of the Battle of Okinawa, Truman and the American military leaders hadn't completely given up on getting Japan to surrender without using the atomic bombs. The USS *Hughes*, once again, was sent on an extraordinary mission to help end the war. Americans were sure that the Japanese mainly existed on rice and fish. They conjectured that if the Japanese ran out of fish, they would starve in such numbers that they might consider surrendering. The primary Japanese fish source was the Kurile Islands north of Japan. Most of the canneries were located there.

By May 1945, the USS *Hughes* was back in service after being repaired from the damage of the kamikaze attack at Leyte Gulf. Alan Evans remembered this new mission to hasten the war's end:

> One of the main staples of the Japanese people is fish, and the main fishing grounds and canneries were in the Kuriles. By striking these, our blockade of Japan would be more effective. On June 4th, we departed for Adak in the Aleutian Islands. Following an intensive training program, a sweep was made of the Kurile chain. The main enemy base at Paramushiro was heavily bombarded on the 22nd of July, where we destroyed numerous canneries there. While searching for enemy shipping, we entered the Okhotsk Sea and searched far toward the Japanese Empire. Our ship was once more operating properly, and a third sweep of the Kurile chain was made, and the enemy base as Matsuwa was bombarded.

The USS *Hughes* was blowing up fish and fish canneries, a last-ditch effort to end the war without using the atomic bomb by starving the Japanese people into surrender.

Events in New Mexico would soon alter this mission.

CHAPTER THIRTY-SIX

"NOW WE'RE ALL SONS OF BITCHES"

Trinity "Gadget" - for the first atomic explosion on Earth. AEC photo.

A storm filled the night sky at the Trinity Test Site in New Mexico. Everyone was waiting in anticipation on July 16, 1945, for the first test of a plutonium bomb. At 4:00 AM, the rain stopped. The weather was reported: "Winds aloft very light and variable to forty thousand feet, surface calm. Conditions are holding for the next two hours. Sky now broken, becoming scattered."

Oppenheimer ordered the test to go on at 5:30 A.M.

"It is now zero minus twenty minutes," said the voice over the loudspeaker at 5:10 AM. Many scientists and government officials were over 20 miles away at Compania Hill, a location deemed a safe distance from the blast site. They were given welder's glasses to view the explosion to keep from losing their eyesight. Edward Teller, always seeking attention, covered his face with a thick coat of sunscreen. He also thought it would protect him from ultraviolet radiation, but this unnerved others, his primary intent.

Oppenheimer and several other scientists were much closer to the blast in a bunker. He was nervous and walked in and out of the bunker in anticipation. Joe McKibben was in control of a cutoff switch should the test need to be aborted at the last moment, and he noted Oppenheimer's tense state. To lighten the mood, he said, "What's likely to happen, Oppie, is that, at minus five seconds, I'll panic and say, 'Gentleman, this can't go on,' and then pull the switch." Oppenheimer was not amused. "Are you alright?' he asked coldly.

The countdown continued over the loudspeakers, and as it did, a Voice of America radio broadcast interfered with the system and began to broadcast Tchaikovsky's "Serenade for Strings." It was surreal: classical music mixed with the countdown for the first nuclear blast on Earth. Samuel Allison, the man doing the countdown, ran out of the bunker to see the explosion in person as he counted: "Ten . . . nine . . . eight . . . seven . . . six . . . five . . ." but then he thought that lightning from the blast might kill him. He dropped the microphone and said, "ZERO."

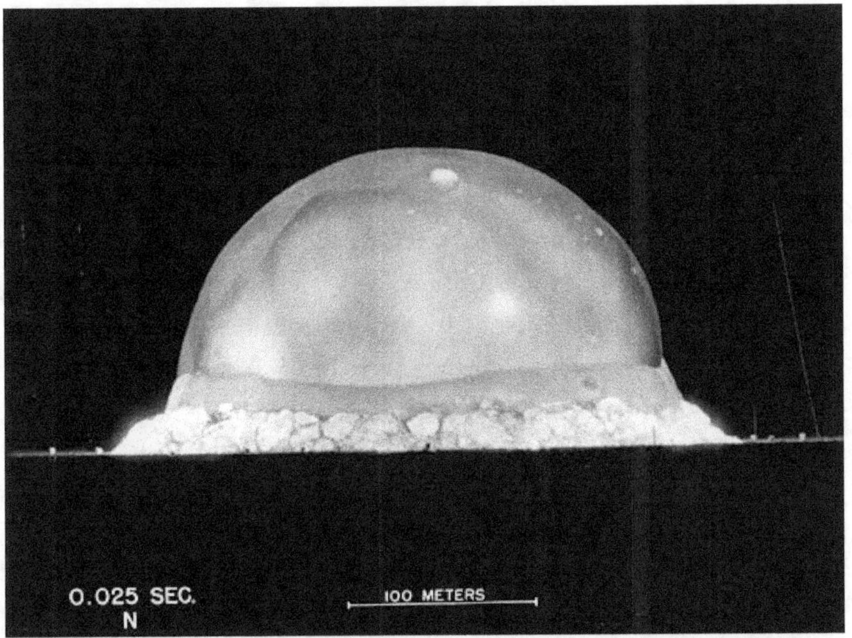

Trinity Test Fireball 25 milliseconds after explosion July 16, 1945.
AEC photo.

Scientist Otto Frisch recorded, "And then, without a sound, the sun shone, or so it looked. The sand hills at the edge of the desert were shimmering in a very bright light, almost colorless and shapeless. It was an awesome spectacle. The bang came minutes later, quite loud though I had plugged my ears, followed by a long rumble like heavy traffic very far away."

It was a success. General Groves and Robert Oppenheimer had won.

Phill Morrison recalled, "You felt the morning had come, although it was still night because your face felt the glow of this daylight—this desert sun during the night."

Oppenheimer later said, "A few people laughed, a few people cried, and most people were silent. A line from the Bhagavad Gita floated through my mind in which Krishna is trying to persuade the Prince that he should do his duty: 'I am become death, the shattered of worlds.'"

Immediately after the test, Ken Bainbridge walked up to Oppenheimer and said, "Oppie, now we're all sons of bitches."

Enrico Fermi had invented a test at the base camp, miles away. At the time of the blast, he dropped tiny pieces of paper and measured how far they were pushed by the blast right as the shock waves hit. Using this test and how far the pieces of paper were displaced, he calculated that the explosion was equivalent to 20,000 tons of TNT, a remarkably close assessment. The actual yield was 17 kilotons, equal to the blast of 17,000 tons of TNT being exploded. Oppenheimer had expected it to be only three kilotons. Edward Teller was wrong. It did not ignite the atmosphere and vaporize the Earth into a miniature sun.

Isidor Rabi remembered the blast: "The experience was hard to describe. I haven't gotten over it yet. It was awful, ominous, and personally threatening. I can't tell you why."

Oppenheimer's scientists had already built two more bombs, Little Boy and Fat Man. They had been shipped to Tinian Island, one of the Pacific islands the USS *Hughes* had liberated from the Japanese. Some of Oppenheimer's team left to prepare for the bombs' delivery to Japan.

Truman saw a chance to end the war before Russia could attack the Japanese. He felt he had done his duty to Stalin at Potsdam when he told him, "We have a new weapon of unusual destructive force." Stalin had barely responded at all, a strange and ominous reaction.

Chester Bradley, on the USS *Hughes* in the waters north of Japan, remembered receiving odd orders the day before the first bomb was dropped on Hiroshima: "The day before the giant atomic bomb was dropped, the USS *Hughes* was instructed to move 100 miles offshore. All our shipmates were told to bathe and wear clean uniforms.

Later, we found out why. The scientists and military leaders were not sure of the repercussions of the atomic blast at the time. They feared the atomic bomb might cause a tidal wave across the oceans and capsize the ships near any shore."

On August 6, 1945, the *Enola Gay*, a B-29 bomber, left Tinian Island for Japan and dropped the first atomic bomb. Just after 7:00 AM, air raid sirens sounded over Hiroshima. This was the third alarm in only two hours. A single aircraft seemed inconsequential to the Japanese, who essentially went about their business. It was morning rush hour, and people were busy. After the American weather plane left, the *Enola Gay* arrived with her atomic load. At 9:14 AM, Major Thomas Ferebee threw the switch and dropped the bomb. Pilot Paul Tibbets put the plane into a steep banking dive to avoid the blast. Several minutes later, a brilliant flash lit up the entire interior of the *Enola Gay*, and a massive shock wave hit the plane.

The fireball rose to 30,000 feet. The Americans couldn't fully understand what they had unleashed on the people below. They sent a mundane report back via their radio: "Clear-cut results, exceeding TR test in visible effects, and in all respects successful. Normal conditions continued in aircraft after delivery was accomplished."

On the ground, it was a different story. Some survivors recalled:

"I thought it might have been something which had nothing to do with the war—the collapse of the Earth, which it was said would take place at the end of the world and which I had read about as a child."

"Everything seemed dark, dark all over. Then I thought, the world is ending."

"A blinding flash cut sharply across the sky. I threw myself on the ground in a reflex movement. At the same moment as the flash, the skin all over my body felt a burning heat, then silence. A huge boom came probably a few seconds later, like the rumbling of distant thunder."

Hiroshima was destroyed in an instant by the American atomic
bomb in 1945. U.S. Navy Public Affairs.

"There were dead bodies everywhere. There was practically no
place to put my feet on the floor. At the time, I could not understand
why all these people were suffering or what illness had struck them
down."

Others felt they had entered hell or what they thought hell might
look like. Although the death toll would rise for months, many people evaporated instantly, leaving shadows on the ground where they
had once stood. Others died from blast injuries. Still others would
die slowly from radiation poisoning. There is no agreement on the
number of dead from the blast. The United States put the death
toll at 78,000 at the time. The City of Hiroshima lists the dead as
exceeding 200,000. What is not in dispute is that this single bomb
destroyed 60,000 buildings. This blast was equal to 68,000 five-hun-
dred-pound bombs being ignited simultaneously.

Hirohito and his cabinet could not believe what they had heard. They sent a team to investigate and report back. That same day, Truman told the Japanese that they must unconditionally surrender or "expect a rain of ruin from the air, the like of which has never been seen on this earth." More bad news came the next day: Russia declared war on Japan. All hope of a negotiated settlement through Russia was gone. Soviet troops attacked the Japanese in Manchuria the following day.

"A MOST CRUEL BOMB"

B-29 Enola Gay with crew members. Captain Paul Tibbets
in center. U.S. Army photo.

The emperor and his cabinet didn't know what to do. The militarists told him that America could have only one such bomb. But on August 9, 1945, a second B-29 left Tinian for Kokura, Japan. Only inclement weather kept this city from the destruction seen in Hiroshima. The secondary target was Nagasaki. One hundred thousand people were killed almost instantly at Nagasaki. Twelve hours later, the city was still engulfed in flames.

In the meantime, the Americans dropped leaflets informing the Japanese people directly of their future. The note said, "The Japanese are facing a critical autumn. Our three-country alliance presented your military leaders with thirteen articles for surrender to end this unprofitable war. Your army leaders ignored this proposal. The United States has developed an atomic bomb, which had not been done by any nation before. It has been determined to employ this frightening bomb. One atom bomb has the destructive power of 2000 B-29s." It was deeply concerning to the emperor that the people were receiving these messages directly.

The rational ministers had had enough of the militarists. Japanese Premier Suzuki asked the emperor to accept the offer of unconditional surrender but with one caveat. The emperor would be spared, and his dynasty would be preserved, at least in some form. Hirohito was increasingly aware that the people were fed up with the empire and the war. He believed that a popular uprising was close. Suzuki remembered, "I thought by then that it was impossible to continue the war. How could Tokyo be defended under such conditions? How was a battle possible? I saw no way."

The Americans promised an ever-increasing number of Japanese cities destroyed by atomic bombs every few days. In truth, this was a bluff. America was out of nuclear bombs. It would be months before new ones would be ready. The Japanese didn't know that. Japan offered to surrender if Hirohito could remain in power.

The United States accepted the unconditional surrender but said that the fate of the emperor would be in the hands of the supreme military commander, Douglass MacArthur. Secretary of State Byrnes responded to the Japanese: "The authority of the Emperor and the Japanese Government to rule the state has passed into the hands of the Supreme Commander of the Allied Powers." The Emperor was to order all Japanese military authorities at home and abroad to "Cease active operations and to surrender their arms."

The Japanese agreed, and on the morning of August 15, 1945, the radio stations in Japan asked the people to listen to the emperor give a speech at noon. Never before had they heard his voice. But Hirohito knew that the Japanese people needed a good reason to commit to surrender, something they were told they could never do with honor. He blamed it on a more dishonorable device and military action: the atomic bomb. For if the bomb was shameful enough, then surrender couldn't be all that bad in comparison. He told the Japanese people:

> TO OUR GOOD AND LOYAL SUBJECTS,
>
> After pondering deeply the general trends of the world and the actual conditions obtaining in our empire today, we have decided to effect a settlement of the present situation by resorting to an extraordinary measure.
>
> We have ordered our government to communicate to the governments of the United States, Great Britain, China and the Soviet Union that our empire accepts the provisions of their joint declaration.
>
> To strive for the common prosperity and happiness of all nations as well as the security and well-being of our subjects is the solemn obligation which has been handed down by our imperial ancestors and which lies close to our heart.
>
> Indeed, we declared war on America and Britain out of our sincere desire to ensure Japan's self-preservation and the stabilization of East Asia, it being far from our thought either to infringe upon the sovereignty of other nations or to embark upon territorial aggrandizement.
>
> But now the war has lasted for nearly four years. Despite the best that everyone has done—the gallant fighting of the

military and naval forces, the diligence and assiduity of our servants of the state, and the devoted service of our one hundred million people—the war situation has developed not necessarily to Japan's advantage, while the general trends of the world have all turned against her interest.

Moreover, the enemy has begun to employ a new and most cruel bomb, the power of which to do damage is, indeed, incalculable, taking the toll of many innocent lives. Should we continue to fight, not only would it result in an ultimate collapse and obliteration of the Japanese nation, but also it would lead to the total extinction of human civilization.

Such being the case, how are we to save the millions of our subjects, or to atone ourselves before the hallowed spirits of our imperial ancestors? This is the reason why we have ordered the acceptance of the provisions of the joint declaration of the powers.

We cannot but express the deepest sense of regret to our allied nations of East Asia, who have consistently cooperated with the Empire towards the emancipation of East Asia.

The thought of those officers and men as well as others who have fallen in the fields of battle, those who died at their posts of duty, or those who met with untimely death and all their bereaved families, pains our heart night and day.

The welfare of the wounded and the war-sufferers, and of those who have lost their homes and livelihood, are the objects of our profound solicitude.

The hardships and sufferings to which our nation is to be subjected hereafter will be certainly great. We are keenly aware of the inmost feelings of all of you, our subjects. However, it is according to the dictates of time and fate that We have resolved to pave the way for a grand peace for all the generations to come by enduring the unendurable and suffering what is insufferable.

Having been able to safeguard and maintain the Kokutai, we are always with you, our good and loyal subjects, relying upon your sincerity and integrity.

Beware most strictly of any outbursts of emotion which may engender needless complications, or any fraternal contention and strife which may create confusion, lead you astray and cause you to lose the confidence of the world.

Let the entire nation continue as one family from generation to generation, ever firm in its faith in the imperishability of its sacred land, and mindful of its heavy burden of responsibility, and of the long road before it.

Unite your total strength, to be devoted to construction for the future. Cultivate the ways of rectitude, foster nobility of spirit, and work with resolution—so that you may enhance the innate glory of the imperial state and keep pace with the progress of the world.

In essence, the emperor's speech said that everything they had done had been for the common good, but they might have made some mistakes along the way, and the "cruel bomb" was so dishonorable that surrender would be all right. It was a stunning speech, but the effect was immediate. People wanted the war to end anyway, so this was the chance to do it and blame it on the militarists and nationalists, but not Emperor Hirohito himself.

While the men on the USS *Hughes* were destroying the food supply of fish for the Japanese people, the atomic bombs were dropped. They learned the war would end soon when they returned to Adak Island, and the ship was quickly sent out on another critical mission connected with Japan's surrender.

But first, Admiral Onishi had to come to grips with the defeat of his Special Attack Units by Robert Oppenheimer and the scientists at Los Alamos and their atomic bombs. The news of the successful

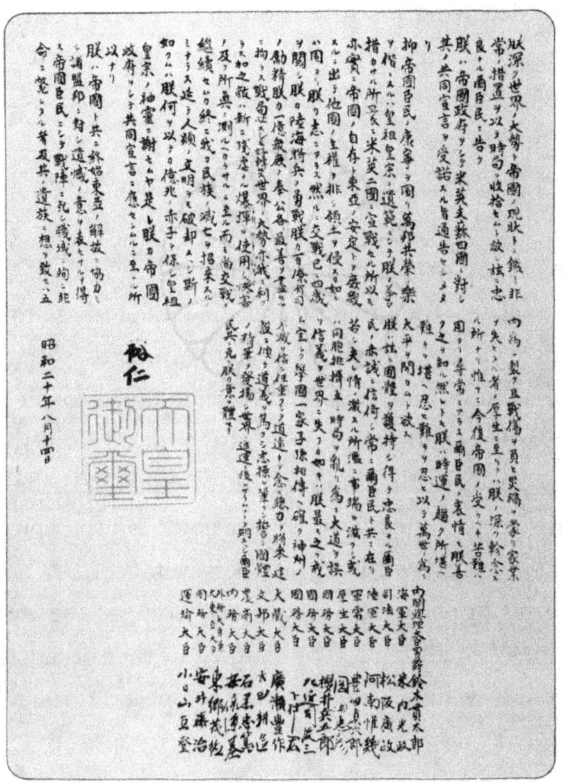

Japanese Imperial Surrender Rescript on ending the war against America and her Allies. National Archives.

bombings in Japan was met with joy at the labs at Los Alamos. The entire laboratory staff gathered together in the auditorium with shouts and praises when Oppenheimer entered the room and spoke. One of the attendees noted, "He entered that meeting like a prize fighter. As he walked through the hall, there were cheers, shouts, and applause all around, and he acknowledged them with the fighters' salute—clasping his hands together above his head as he came down to the podium."

Admiral Onishi received no such welcome when he returned to his office. On August 16, 1945, following Emperor Hirohito's radio address declaring his intention to surrender, Onishi committed ritual suicide in his office. His suicide notes, written the night before, expressed his apology for sending the Special Attack pilots to their deaths and urged the people of Japan to follow the lead of the emperor for a peaceful occupation by the Americans:

> I wish to express my deep appreciation to the souls of the brave special attackers. They fought and died valiantly with faith in our ultimate victory. In death I wish to atone for my part in the failure to achieve that victory and I apologize to the souls of those dead fliers and their bereaved families. I wish the young people of Japan to find a moral in my death. To be reckless is only to aid the enemy. You must abide by the spirit of the Emperor's decision with utmost perseverance. Do not forget your rightful pride in being Japanese. You are the treasure of the nation. With all the fervor of spirit of the special attackers, strive for the welfare of Japan and for peace throughout the world.

In the tradition of the samurai of old, Onishi committed ritual suicide by thrusting his sword into his abdomen and slicing it open. Onishi's death was not immediate. That was the point of ritual suicide. It wasn't supposed to be fast. True samurai were expected to linger in pain and contemplate their death calmly. When others found him and offered to assist in hastening his death, he declined their assistance. It was not uncommon for a mortally wounded samurai to be helped when he had inflicted a mortal wound, usually by cutting off his head. But Onishi took the path of a purist. He chose to die slowly. "Do not try to help me," he said, choosing to suffer 15 hours of pain to repay the debt of sending off so many Special Attack pilots to their deaths. By the standards of ancient Japan, his was an honorable death.

The sword with which Onishi committed suicide is kept at the Yushukan Museum in Yasukuni Shrine in Tokyo. Onishi's ashes were divided between two graves: one at the Zen temple of Soji-ii in Tsurmi, Yokohama, and one in a public cemetery in the former Ashida Village in Hyōgo Prefecture.

Hideki Tojo also faced the consequences of his actions. He chose a death that was not an honorable one by samurai standards. When American Army soldiers went to this house to arrest him, he shot himself in the chest but missed his heart. As a result, the Army had medical personnel present during the later arrests of other Japanese war criminals.

Tojo told Japanese reporters: "I am very sorry it is taking me so long to die. The Greater East Asia War was justified and righteous. I am very sorry for the nation and all the races of the Greater Asiatic powers. I wait for the righteous judgment of history. I wished to commit suicide, but sometimes that fails." Later, at his trial, Tojo accepted full responsibility for his actions during the war and made this speech:

It is natural that I should bear the entire responsibility for the war in general, and, needless to say, I am prepared to do so. Consequently, now that the war has been lost, it is presumably necessary that I be judged so that the circumstances of the time can be clarified and the future peace of the world be assured. Therefore, with respect to my trial, it is my intention to speak frankly, according to my recollection, even though when the vanquished stands before the victor, who has over him the power of life and death, he may be apt to toady and flatter. I mean to pay considerable attention to this in my actions and say to the end that what is true is true and what is false is false. To shade one's words in flattery to the point of untruthfulness would falsify the trial and do

incalculable harm to the nation, and great care must be taken
to avoid this.

Tojo was sentenced to death on November 12, 1948, and he was executed by hanging, which happened 41 days later, on December 23,
1948. Before his execution, he gave his military ribbons to one of his
guards; they are now on display at the National Aviation Museum
in Florida.

Emperor Hirohito was never charged with any crimes related to
his participation in the war. General Douglass MacArthur used his
assistance to rebuild Japan as a democracy without a god figure as its
leader. Hirohito renounced his divinity in public but became revered
as the father figure of Japan. His popularity only increased over the
years. The monarchy survives but with no real power in government
affairs.

CHAPTER THIRTY-EIGHT

"THE FINAL CAPITULATION OF THE ENEMY"

Seaman Chester Bradley detained a train and these operators so the sailors of the USS Hughes could search the occupants for weapons in occupied Japan. Chester Bradley collection.

There were still fanatical loyalists in Japan. The official surrender by the Japanese dignitaries was a long and drawn-out process. There was more than one signing ceremony in more than one location. There were thousands of details yet to be worked out. The country had to be de-militarized.

Americans flew reconnaissance missions over Japan to see what was happening. They wanted to find out if everyone would abide by the cease-fire. Some were worried that the Japanese would attack the Americans when they came to enforce the terms of the surrender. When B-32s flew over, the Japanese tracked them. On August 18, 1945, Japanese fighters attacked four B-32s. At first, the Americans wanted to find out if these were authorized by any official, which they were not. Then they were concerned that the Japanese might oppose the Americans until the actual surrender documents were signed, which presented the problem of the officials being shot at when coming to the signing events.

Commanders were profoundly concerned and sent additional flights to test the will of the Japanese. The next day, two more American B-32s were attacked by Japanese pilots. An American was killed, two others were wounded, and another plane was damaged. The Japanese assured the Americans they were not to blame and that these pilots had acted without authority. The Americans demanded that all propellers be removed from remaining Japanese planes, and the Japanese government promised to do this. The surrender was off to a bad start. The main surrender document would not be signed until September 1945, and others would be executed in the coming months throughout the Pacific.

Alan Evans noted that they were far from done in Japan and wouldn't be headed back anytime soon: "On August 31, 1945, the USS *Hughes* left Adak with the Northern Occupation Force under Vice Admiral Fletcher. We were to proceed to the Ominato Area of northern Honshu, Japan, to enforce the terms of the surrender."

USS Hughes sailors on shore in northern Japan at the
war's end. Chester Bradley collection.

Japan began signing surrender documents throughout the Pacific after the signing in Tokyo Bay. Commanders in Japanese-occupied lands needed to understand and follow the dictates of their government. More than 5,400,000 Japanese soldiers were taken prisoner during the war. Imperial Japanese Navy prisoners numbered over 1,800,000. Feeding and repatriating them would be a significant task because the Japanese economy was destroyed. Making matters worse, some isolated Japanese soldiers never agreed to surrender and fought in remote Asian jungles until 1990.

The USS *Hughes* played a significant part in picking up Japanese dignitaries and secretly transporting them to and from the USS *Pan-amint*, where official negotiations on the final terms of occupation were hammered out. During these high-level talks, the USS *Hughes* and USS *Anderson* were tasked with covering the USS *Panamint*. Alan Evans was proud of this final secret mission, "After all the months and years which the USS *Hughes* spent fighting the Japanese under all conditions and in all parts of the Pacific, it was fitting that she be present at the final capitulation of the enemy." Many of these meetings and transports were detailed in the ship's log. They were classified at the highest level at the time and were extremely sensitive. The last thing the Americans wanted was for the war with Japan to re-ignite.

The USS *Hughes* was also ordered to disarm the Japanese soldiers on land. But no one on the USS *Hughes* spoke Japanese. Chester Bradley remembered:

After the atomic blast, my shipmates and I were told to go ashore and take the guns away from the Japanese soldiers. We wondered if the Japanese soldiers even knew the war was over. After removing their guns, I was approached by a man who said he was a doctor and wanted to invite me to dinner at his home. I thought that would be nice and boarded his rickshaw. As the man began taking me far away from the others, I wondered, as it began to get dark, if they were taking me away to be killed. Surprisingly, we arrived at the doctor's home, where I enjoyed a good home-cooked Japanese meal. They were very nice and gave me several gifts I have always cherished. I asked for their Japanese flag, but they were unwilling to part with it.

Chester Bradley and his shipmates even stopped trains, detained the conductors, and searched the people for military weapons. They did not understand that the people of Japan were fed up with the army and nationalists who had destroyed their country and economy.

Japanese shame was the fault of their nationalist leaders, not the Americans.

Some USS *Hughes* sailors took a dim view of the Japanese. Bradley recalled liberty parties fueled by beer. At times, the crew committed what Bradley called "high-handed vandalism." Personal property was destroyed, and people were roughed up. Liberty was canceled until more rules could be implemented. "I didn't trust the Japanese at first," said Bradley. "Smiles and bows. We were invited for tea and food, but many were wary." He felt that the poor treatment by some crew members would lead the Japanese not to accept democracy. When invited into a home, they sat at a table, were offered tea

Seaman Monroe from the USS Hughes in Japan at the end of the war during the occupation. Chester Bradley collection.

and food, and talked in sign language. Bradley took photos, made sketches, and wandered around the local towns, but he was careful going down dark alleys at night. The more he learned about Japanese people, the safer he felt over time. Once the war ended, Chester Bradley was not hostile toward the Japanese. "They were serving their country just like the Americans were."

The men continued these tasks until October 20, 1945, when Destroyer Squadron Two, or what was left of it, set sail for Midway Island and then on to Pearl Harbor. In the end, it was a lonely voyage home. Only four of their fabled squadron were left afloat, sailing the peaceful waters of the vast Pacific Ocean: the destroyers *Hughes*, *Mustin*, *Anderson*, and *Wainwright*. They felt lonely and hollow on the return trip. Their war experience was impossible to explain to those back home.

When the USS *Hughes* arrived at San Diego in mid-November, she received orders to proceed to an East Coast port for decommissioning. However, she soon received new orders. On December 27, 1945, she was to return to the Central Pacific for a new mission at Bikini Atoll. Alan Evans noted, "For the war period, it must be said that the USS *Hughes* fought long and hard on many fronts. She inflicted great damage on the enemy. All sailors of the USS *Hughes* are justly proud of this tradition." But none of them would be proud of the final mission.

CHAPTER THIRTY-NINE

"A WITCHES BREW"

Bikini Atoll tests Able, and Baker tests two atomic bombs on U.S. Navy and enemy-captured ships. The USS Hughes was one of the targets. AEC photo.

America was now building more atomic bombs. They needed to do something with them. America had done a great job of gearing up for war but didn't know what to do with the newly won peace and decided to bomb islands in the Pacific to test their atomic weapons. In truth, these tests were unnecessary.

It would take a lifetime to fully assess the damage and ongoing biological injuries to the Japanese in the two cities subjected to atomic bombs. However, military leaders decided to test more bombs in 1946. There would be a rivalry between the different branches of the military to see who would have atomic bombs in their arsenal. Senator Brien McMahon of Connecticut called the newly minted nuclear bombs "the most important thing in history since the birth of Jesus Christ." He said, "The resulting explosion should prove to us just how effective the atomic bomb is when used against the giant naval ships."

By October 1945, Rear Admiral Edward Cochrane called for "broad-scale experiments with the atomic bomb to clear up its major influence on naval warfare." He wanted to see what atomic bombs would do to different types of naval ships, and he proposed detonating three Fat Man-type plutonium bombs near warships. The Joint Chiefs of Staff glowingly approved this idea.

Not everyone agreed. The scientists and many military men at Los Alamos thought this idea was crazy and that the risks were unwarranted and unnecessary. Major General Thomas Farrell, the deputy commander at Los Alamos, wrote to his boss, General Leslie Groves, and said that the underwater explosions "would contain so many major hazards that it should be ruled out at this time." The scientists argued that the entire area would be contaminated by radioactive materials that would travel on ocean currents and into commercial shipping lanes. Henry Newson, one of the leaders of a technical group at Los Alamos, said that the area would become a "witches brew with enough plutonium near the surface to poison the combined armed forces of the United States at their highest wartime strength." He warned the ships would be indefinitely dangerous to anyone boarding them.

The scientists also pointed out that this could be safely calculated with the current data already on hand. They warned that humans should never be allowed to reboard the ships after such a test. However, most of the naval leaders felt that they needed to test naval vessels with atomic detonations to see how they would survive. They ignored how hard it was to hit a ship with a bomb, something they were well aware of from WWII battles. Admiral Halsey said, "Ships are not particularly profitable targets for atomic bombs. Their ability to move makes them almost impossible targets for super rockets. In short, they are hard to hit."

Robert Oppenheimer was opposed. He reiterated that the test results would be worthless. What was the point of testing a bomb to see if it would survive with an utterly dead crew? He wrote to President Truman about his objections and said he would not attend such tests. By this time, Truman was tired of Oppenheimer and took little notice of the letter.

Rear Admiral William Blandy was assigned to run the task force to bomb naval ships, and the tests would go on. But these tests would not be happening in Boston or Los Angeles. Once more, the peaceful islanders in the Pacific would become the victims of colonial powers.

Bikini Island in the Central Pacific was chosen. The islanders would have to be removed. On January 15, 1945, President Truman declared the United States was the sole trustee of all Pacific Islands held by Japan before and during WWII. Therefore, they had the right to remove the local inhabitants for bomb tests.

A Navy ship blasted a channel into the harbor at Bikini Lagoon without telling the local islanders why it was doing so. On February 10, 1945, Navy Commodore Ben Wyatt arrived and told the local islanders biblical stories similar to what they had heard from missionaries. He told them they had to leave their homes and that the Navy would lead them to the promised land, just like the Israelites in the Old Testament.

A month later, he attempted to film a reenactment with the villagers participating in their removal. This film was to show the world that they were willing to go. The chief of the people was repeatedly told his lines to say for the camera, but despite such promptings and seven re-takes, he would only say, "We are willing to go. Everything is in God's hands." He refused to give the speech about following the Navy into the promised land from the Bible and would not recite the rest of the script. To this day, the area remains unpopulated.

The public was told about the upcoming atomic tests, called Operation Crossroads, but people wanted to move on from the war. The tests were not popular. Letters poured in from Americans protesting the need to detonate more atomic bombs. Sailors who had sailed on the ships wrote to their congressmen to stop American ships from being destroyed by atomic blasts.

There was something deeply unsettling about the whole thing to the seamen who sailed on these majestic ships of war. A ship sunk in battle, and now on the bottom of the ocean, was a graveyard, sacred ground forever. That was okay. A properly de-commissioned ship with full military honors was also understandable and accepted as a fitting end to a fighting ship. But to blow them up and irradiate them with an atomic blast was deeply distasteful. To a man, the sailors of the USS *Hughes* felt that this was offensive and disrespectful to the dead. There would be no honor in it. The dead would not rest in peace.

Oliver Jones, at his home in Arizona, said, "That was a darn shame. They shouldn't have done it. She was a great ship, and she didn't deserve that. I thought at the time it was wrong, and I still do today. There was no reason for it." To Oliver and his shipmates, the souls of those who died on the ship are not at peace with this end.

In November of 1945, General Dwight Eisenhower proposed getting rid of the Navy to save 25 percent of the military budget. This completely ignored the fact that it was the Navy and the USS *Hughes* that had cleared the way to drop the atomic bombs on Japan, and it was the Navy that had kept the United States from being bombed by Japan or Germany throughout WWII.

Halsey was incensed and kept up the battle to defend the Navy. As bombastic as ever, he was loved by the American public. He felt the Crossroads test was a mistake and would yield nothing of value that was not already known. He also wanted the American people to consider a future without a Navy. "Nothing has happened since V-J Day to shorten the eight thousand miles of water between us and the enemy." Even before nuclear missiles could be launched from warships, Halsey could see future conflicts between nations as naval encounters. The country with the best fleet would rule the seas. But it was all too little too late. Crossroads would proceed, and a part of the American fleet that fought bravely in WWII would be dishonorably destroyed.

As the plans came together, there were obstacles. It would take 42,000 personnel, most of them Navy sailors, to conduct the tests. Although many wanted to go home after the war, people willing to spend one more year in the service were offered the chance to watch the atomic blasts in person for re-enlisting. Fuel and oil were loaded onto the ships to see what would happen during the explosions. The coral reefs would never fully recover. The waters that the sailors of the USS *Hughes* fished during WWII would be destroyed.

As opposition mounted, William Blandy continued to defend the tests. When it became clear that the objective of testing ships against atom bombs was pointless, he decided to add almost six thousand live animals to the tests to see how they would die. But this concept only increased opposition. Americans were tired of death and thinking about how people could die from atomic bombs.

People also did not want to think of the Japanese still suffering and dying from the first two bombs.

In June of 1946, America had nine Fat Man implosion bombs, but only seven were operational due to the lack of initiators. Almost half would be expended in the Crossroads tests when the Cold War with the Soviet Empire was heating up. This didn't matter to Blandy, who wanted the grand public spectacle to go as planned.

CHAPTER FORTY

"WHERE'S YOUR BOSS?"

Officers of the USS Hughes - Lieutenant Glen Edmonson on the left and Commander Alan Evans on the right. Glen Edmonson collection.

Retired Captain David Bill of the USS *Hughes* was on board the ship on December 27, 1945, when he and the crew received their new orders. Describing that day, Captain Bill said:

> We arrived back at Pearl on the 2nd of January. We offloaded the ammunition, finished offloading all our records, and stripped the ship. We had drained all the freshwater; the only fuel left on board was one emergency generator. The ship was towed over to some mud flats south of Pearl City. The ship was ready to be put into mothballs. The day the Admiral came over to haul down the flag for the decommissioning ceremony, we got an emergency message: "Get underway ASAP! Proceed to the shipyard and prepare for the Bikini tests!"

According to Captain Bill, he ordered the chief water tender to go below and immediately light the fires. "But Captain," the chief water tender said, "there isn't any water in it."

"Fill it with seawater and light her off," Captain Bill replied. However, this was risky to the ship and crew. Without fresh water, there was a risk of damage from salt.

Captain Bill continued:

> So he locked the crew in there. They lit her off, and there was no flare back, thank God! They had top and bottom blow going continuously, and we soon made some steam with the salt water. We ran that into the auxiliary generator and its condenser. We filled the #3 boiler, and soon she was full, and we lit her off.
>
> But by that time, we had no records, no nothing on the ship. We went over to Base Supply to get some food. Now, by this time, the Navy had gone to packaged meats. The top grade was #1, and that junk on the bottom wasn't fit to eat—well, maybe it made stew. But I ordered nothing but #1 packages of

beef and pork and everything else we thought we needed to go
to Bikini.

But the clerk said, "I'm sorry, you can't have this. You've got to take
the normal spread."

Captain Bill told him, "I've got no permission number, no allot-
ment or anything else, but we're going to eat. I don't even know who
this will be charged to, but this is what I'm ordering."

"But sir," the clerk replied, "you can't do that."

"Where's your boss?" Captain Bill demanded.

"Just a second," the clerk said.

Soon enough, the commander came out and told the clerk,
"Charge the food to Operation Crossroads, and that is the end of
the debate." Still, the commander asked Captain Bill to return to
his office, saying, "I've got stuff here that is so expensive that even
the submariners can't afford it, and you know submarines—they eat
high off the hog. If you take this off my hands, we will charge it to
Operation Crossroads, and you can have all you want."

Captain Bill remembered, "We ate top sirloin—filets and the
best pork. And caviar! I tell you, the caviar we ate to the point where
I set a bowl of it down on the mess table, and we would come back,
and the whole thing was still there because we had eaten so much of
it. When I think of what that would be worth today!"

However, the USS *Hughes* faced new problems on this unplanned
voyage. Even though the men would eat like kings, the ship's engine
steamed on salt water with a very inexperienced crew. Captain Bill
said of the situation:

About that time, we got 30 recruits and two or three young officers right out of boot camp. I turned to the old timers and said,
"Look, we've got a real problem. We've got to steam this ship
with less than half of the people we should have. We'll get there,

but it will be harder with so many green recruits. Everyone will have to be alert for mistakes."

Soon enough, we were trying to steam out of the channel, and one of the new kids shut the wrong valve and killed the engine, and we were drifting without power. Well, we didn't run aground, so that was good." It looked like it would be a long, arduous trip to Bikini. To make matters worse, they only had one operating propeller shaft.

CHAPTER FORTY-ONE

"AND THEY MISSED!"

The first atomic bomb blast at Operation Crossroads
at Bikini Atoll - Test Able. AEC photo.

The USS *Hughes* finally made it to Bikini. Captain Bill reported on the mission:

By that time, we had inherited the Inner Target Division of destroyers, which I think contained the remaining Sims Class Destroyers and a couple of other ships, maybe seven or nine of them. They gave us all the instruments to put on the ship, and everything was in place for the test. Some of the scientists on board said, "Well, Captain, you won't have to worry about it. You won't have any post-damage reports to make because your ship will be disintegrated." After a few months of sitting and eating caviar and filets, we were put on a transport, maybe twelve miles away outside the lagoon, and the Air Force came over and dropped the first bomb. And they missed!

On July 1, 1946, at 9:00 AM, a B-29 Superfortress dropped the Fat Man-style atomic bomb on the ships at Bikini Lagoon. It had a yield of 23 kilotons, or 23 thousand tons of TNT. Five ships were sunk, but the bomb was dropped a half-mile off target, sparing most vessels and the USS *Hughes* from a direct blast but not the radiation. Because the press was so far away, the explosion didn't seem as big as expected, and everyone running the tests was disappointed.

Secretary of the Navy James Forrestal went on defense and said that it was hard to sink Navy vessels without underwater damage. The director of the tests, Admiral Blandy, was furious. An investigation ensued, and the bomb site on the plane was tested. Pumpkins were dropped by other aircraft, and they seemed to work fine. Had the bomb dropped on the target, many more ships would have been sunk.

"As a matter of fact," Captain Bill said, "the bomb went off right over the *Anderson*. The *Anderson* was about halfway out, and it went off right over her, and she went down. I had expected her to disintegrate, being told this would happen. But a diver went down, and she was intact. She had just sunk. So, we returned to the lagoon on the third or fourth day after the test. The radioactivity was negligible, and we moved back on board." This was a terrible idea for the crew of the USS *Hughes*.

The entire area was radioactive. It was not safe to return to the ship. The sailors had badges to show how much radiation they were receiving, but these badges often malfunctioned, reporting their exposure *after* they were irradiated. The badges prevented nothing. Moreover, they could not measure internal plutonium, which the sailors inhaled, the most dangerous substance they were exposed to.

Nevertheless, the ship returned to normal, and they fired her up and steamed her to another location in the lagoon. Below the test site, the ships received ten thousand rems of initial nuclear radiation. Even people serving below deck, who were shielded from 90 percent of the blast, would have received a lethal radiation dose. A report by the *Bulletin of Atomic Scientists* states, "A large ship, about a mile away from the explosion, would escape sinking, but the crew would be killed, and only a ghost ship would remain, floating unattended in the vast waters of the ocean." No one would sail or fight on a Navy ship near a nuclear explosion. It would be a floating coffin, just as Oppenheimer and the scientists already knew.

But things on the ship did not look bad to the sailors of the USS *Hughes* when they returned. Captain Bill described the scene:

We went down and looked over the ship. There had been an apple sitting on the Ward Room table, and when we came back, the apple was still sitting there. We entered the fire control rooms, and the walls were all laid back. We needed to repair them and a few other things. So again, we closed the fire rooms, got her underway, moved her alongside the tender, and began getting ready for the second test.

They moved us around a bit, and we were the closest destroyer to the next bomb. The water was quite deep, so we married the two anchor chains together and had about 130 fathoms out to the anchor. . . .

Once again, we took off outside the lagoon. This time, I had a guarantee that the USS *Hughes* would no longer exist because the scientist knew exactly where the bomb would go off.

CHAPTER FORTY-TWO

"THE BOMB WENT OFF, AND IT WAS QUITE A SIGHT!"

The next bomb was detonated underwater and had disastrous impacts.
Crossroads Test Baker explosion. AEC photo.

On July 25, 1946, test Baker would be detonated in 90 feet of water, only four hundred feet from the USS *Hughes*. Anyone in the area was stunned by what they saw. The test led to the most iconic picture of any atomic blast ever detonated. The pressure from being set off under the ocean caused a massive explosion that mixed ground and sea materials. The contamination was beyond what anyone had expected, except for the scientists at Los Alamos, who had warned against such a blast in the first place.

Scientists had no words to explain what they saw. It almost needed a new language. Two months after the blast, a scientific study group was assembled to create the terms to explain what had happened in accurate ways that others could understand.

The expanding gas bubble created a supersonic hydraulic shock wave as it breached the surface that crushed most of the hulls of the ships nearby. It traveled faster than the speed of sound in water, over five times the speed of sound in air at the surface. A very dark ring of water and a powerful shock wave spread out from the center of the blast. This was later named the "slick," followed by a white slick called the "crack."

As the expanding gas bubble reached the floor of the ocean and the surface, it dug a hole in the bottom and breached the surface in a spectacular geyser of water that went up into the atmosphere. This all happened in four-millionths of a second. One second after the detonation, the water and seafloor rose above the Earth at 2,500 feet per second. This initial column of water, coral, and seafloor was three hundred feet wide and over a mile high and was called the "column." This was attended by a supersonic atmospheric shock wave almost impossible to describe. For a moment, the explosion was enveloped in a dense fog called the "Wilson cloud," but this quickly passed to reveal the upward-climbing mushroom cloud. The top looked like a cauliflower, and this material began to spread out and descend back to Earth, bringing deadly radiation.

USS Hughes covered with white decontamination foam at
Bikini Lagoon in 1946. Sailors would reboard her and she would
go back to the West Coast of America. AEC photo.

The blast was infinitely more potent because it was detonated
underwater, and the radiation was also substantially worse. Captain Bill noted, "The bomb went off and was quite a sight! The tugs
returned in three or four days and washed the ships down. The USS
Hughes was afloat but was sinking slowly. They washed her down
with cornmeal. It didn't improve the radioactivity much, but at least
it washed off the dust and loose stuff."

But they were wrong. The USS *Hughes* was severely contaminated. Although 18,880 film-badge dosimeters were issued to about
10–15 percent of the workforce, they did not measure plutonium.
When sailors returned on board, the silent killer was the dust they
inhaled. When badge radiation levels got too high, the sailors' sleeping quarters were moved closer to the center of the vessels. Of the
total amount of radioactive particles created by the Baker explosion,

over 85 percent was unfissioned plutonium not detected by the film badges. Even Geiger counters could not measure it. The blast had produced over five billion doses.

Regarding the blast's effect on the USS *Hughes*, Captain Bill said:

Finally, they beached the USS *Hughes*. In a week or so, we came in, and they said we could take part of the crew every other day for two or three hours. We were told not to eat, smoke, or even breathe!

On the water burst, not a single soul on board could have survived. Their skulls would have been fractured and their legs broken because they hit the overhead on the initial impact and then down on the next. It would have wiped them all out. By the time we returned, most of the ship was flooded. One scientist showed me a picture of the blast. Up about 300 or 400 feet, there is a black patch of water. That was the *Hughes*. The Hughes did go up in that column of water, and she was flopped end for end and then dropped, so you had two fantastic events. The *Hughes* was not hurt on the outside all that bad, but the inside damage was beyond belief.

The sailors were only supposed to spend minimal time on the USS *Hughes*, but her deck logs showed they spent many hours each day on the ship. The crew patched the holes, got her floating again, and towed her off the beach. The USS *Hughes* was back at sea once more.

Scientists began to give dire warnings about the level of radioactivity the sailors had been exposed to. At first, Admiral Blandy refused to believe it. Finally, they pulled a fish from the lagoon and laid it on a piece of film, creating an X-ray image of it. This was irrefutable evidence that even Blandy couldn't argue against. He ordered all de-contamination operations to stop. It would be years before they fully understood what they had done at Bikini Lagoon.

CHAPTER FORTY-THREE

"I DON'T KNOW WHERE THE HELL HE GOT ONE"

The last photo of the USS Hughes was taken as she was bombed, torpedoed, and finally sunk. U.S. Navy photo.

Retired Captain Del Cummins was the executive officer during Operation Crossroads. He succeeded David Bill as commander of the USS Hughes for her final days. At a reunion many years later, he said of the USS Hughes:

> The ship was unique. Of all the ships I served on, I never heard the expression, "This is such and such a yard-built ship," but they say that about the USS Hughes. "This is a Bath-built ship," and it is said with pride.
>
> It was an interesting experience to go back and live abroad for three weeks after that first test bomb. The Baker test was on July 25, and after a couple of days, Dave Bill would take a group aboard for an hour or so and carry out decontamination procedures. The next day, I'd take a different group aboard. We worried more than a little about radioactivity. We never did get around to decommissioning the *Hughes*. I don't know how long after the second test before they towed the *Hughes* to Bremerton. No one wanted to work aboard her because they feared the radioactivity.

First Lieutenant Harley Nygren served on the USS *Hughes* and was in Seattle.

> Sometime in the late spring or early summer of 1947, I was lounging on the beach in Seattle when the USS *Hughes* came down the Sound on a towline. There was no mistaking the rake in her mast. I knew it right away. I took the journey over to Bremerton, and there she was, behind a chain link fence with a red log boom around her. As I approached, I was accosted by some excited Marine guards who warned me about "dangerous radiation." I showed them my Joint Task Force #1 ID card from the USS *Hughes*, which convinced them it was too late for me.

They knew that the JTF #1 card was only carried by people who had been at Operation Crossroads.

The end of the USS *Hughes* was close at hand. Here is the Associated Press dispatch from October 14, 1948: "A dozen of the 76 ships used in the 1946 Bikini Atom Bomb Tests are still afloat. Three are still dangerously hot with radioactivity. The Navy said that the Heavy Cruiser *Pensacola* and the Destroyer *Hughes* will be sunk in the forthcoming naval maneuvers because it would cost more to decontaminate them than could be realized from their sale as scrap metal."

The end of the USS *Hughes* was recounted from St. Louis at a USS *Hughes* reunion in June 1980. This is the tape-recorded account of Joseph Zuccaro, who was a signalman second class on the USS *Hughes* from 1943 to 1946:

When I saw her go down, I cried.

I was on the USS *Henderson*, DD-785, Desron 51. We were assigned to rendezvous with a ship that would be a target for aircraft. It was Saturday, 16 October 1948.

We didn't know who it was. All we knew was that we were supposed to rendezvous with the target and her tug south and west of the Farallon Islands off San Francisco beyond the hundred-fathom curve. We were out of San Diego, and the target was towed out of Hunters Point.

The flagship was the USS *Rowan*, and the USS *Henderson*, the USS *Sutherland*, and the USS *Gurke* were units of Desron 51. We rendezvoused, and when I saw that single stack sticking up there, I said, "OH, NO!"

I told the skipper that I was on that ship during World War II, and he said, "Well, I'm sorry to tell you this, but we have one squadron of Naval Reserve Aviators out of Los Alamitos Naval Air Station that are going to be using it for target practice."

I said, "Well, I'd rather not watch it."

The skipper, Captain Cunningham, said I was the senior man on the bridge and he would need me as one of the observers, along with the executive officer. I was working in navigation at the time.

The USS *Henderson* was assigned some air controllers, and they guided the planes in. The first wave came over about 10:00 a.m. and dropped about 14 bombs. I saw three hits, and the others were near and far misses. They made four runs on her, and she was still there. She took about eight hits, all told.

After a while, they took off and went back to base, and I thought that was it because the guys started to come back. The commanders waved the tugs off and sent another wave of Marine pilots from El Toro who happened to be in the area. Their bombing targets were obscured by fog, and we were a target of opportunity.

They got permission to use the USS *Hughes* for their target. I think there were eight aircraft making high-level bombing runs. They dropped their loads, and I didn't see anything because I couldn't bear to look. The report I got from my third-class quartermaster was, "She got hit four times and was still there. They will *never* sink her! They are going to have to do better than sending an aircraft."

The commodore had a contingency plan that two destroyers would make torpedo runs on what remained of the target. Fortunately, the USS *Henderson* wasn't one of them.

The USS *Sutherland* made a run on the starboard side. They fired four fish, and two hit her. She took two torpedoes, one forward and one aft, but she was still there.

Then the USS *Gurke* got word to go ahead and make her torpedo run on the port side. Four fish, three went by, but one got her midships.

You would see her roll over. I have seen a couple of ships sink, and usually, they go up—show their bow or stern—and then go down. The old lady rolled over and said, "To hell with you—I'm going down flat."

I think I got to the old man on the USS *Henderson*, Commander Cunningham. He gave me a handkerchief, and I don't know where the hell he got one.

And that's how she went down, without any fanfare.

CHAPTER FORTY-FOUR

GHOSTS

Gunnery lieutenant on the USS *Hughes*, Glen Edmonson, didn't say much about what he had seen during the war. He had been climbing the ladder from the deck to the bridge when the kamikaze plane hit on December 10, 1944. Glen didn't even talk much about the war to many of his relatives. Glen's son Bruce Edmonson recalled:

He gave me the impression that heroism should be private. He didn't have any use for VFW activities, for example. My brother and I occasionally heard war stories from another dad, but our dad's reaction was to shrug. He wouldn't directly criticize a vet for telling a war story. Most wartime "heroes" don't consider themselves heroic. Usually, they consider themselves "doing their job," living up to a patriotic or religious ideal, looking after their buddies, or simply being lucky to survive. To elevate oneself above fellow warriors was just repugnant to my dad. As he got older, into his 80s, he would occasionally choke up if the conversation turned to WWII. He had seen death up close (and narrowly escaped it himself). The sadness was still there, and it got harder for him to keep it bottled up. Most of the time, though, he kept the hatches battened down.

When Glen Edmonson left to return home, he was given the samurai sword of a Japanese naval officer as a souvenir because he was an American naval officer. He took it back to Seattle with him, along with a Japanese rifle.

Oppenheimer and the scientists were correct about pure science. Anything that can be discovered can and will be found. But during the insanity and ravages of WWII, they also warned that the moral consequences of such discoveries have no scientific basis. Humans alone possess such thoughts and responsibilities for using what nature has provided. After the war, a new principle emerged with the discovery and creation of atomic and hydrogen bombs: the concept of mutually assured destruction, referred to as MAD. Weapons of war are now so powerful that even a tiny fraction of them can eliminate all life on Earth. So far, that fear has kept humanity from nuclear destruction.

The atmospheric atomic bomb tests at Operation Crossroads were the first of many between 1946 and 1958. The largest was on March 1, 1954, when a hydrogen bomb called Castle Bravo had a yield three times larger than expected. Contamination immediately reached over a hundred miles away, irradiating 15 islands in the area, and the vast fireball could be seen from over 250 miles away.

In 1963, such tests were banned forever, and no one has violated that ban so far. The bomb created at Los Alamos all those years ago, helping to end WWII, is still a weapon of unspeakable destructive power. After the war, Robert Oppenheimer tried to warn the world about its dangers and was vilified for his efforts; he even lost his security clearance and was called a traitor by those who felt that America could, and should, use the bomb against its enemies without concern. Time has judged Oppenheimer a hero and loyal American, but he died of cancer and in disgrace in 1967, deeply saddened by his treatment after WWII.

Also in the ash heap of history are Worth Ishmuel Capps's six journals. They were only read by his wife, who left no record of what they contained after burning them.

The world moved on. Franklin Roosevelt, Winston Churchill, and the leaders of Japan and Germany are all gone, and history has rendered its verdict on the causes that gave rise to WWII. Radical nationalism, fueled by racism and colonial ambitions, is a disease of the human soul. Once thought dead, it is rising in the world again today.

Oliver Jones is the only remaining sailor from the USS *Hughes* left alive to tell her story in April of 2024. The samurai sword of Admiral Onishi, with which the admiral took his life, now rests in a museum in Japan. Lieutenant Glen Edmonson's samurai sword, given to him at the war's end, is hidden inside a wall in a house in Seattle, Washington, where he placed it many decades ago to hide the memories of Leyte Gulf on December 10, 1944. Glen is buried in a cemetery in Port Angeles, Washington, and the location of the samurai sword was buried with him. The USS *Hughes*, still covered with scars from radioactive bombs, sits at the bottom of the Pacific Ocean in her secret place. All are now relics of a distant war. The ghosts of that war still haunt our collective human soul.

GENERAL BIBLIOGRAPHY

Bohr, Niels. *Atomic Theory & The Description of Nature*, Guildford, England, Cambridge University Press, 1934.

Ball, Howard. *Justice Downwind – America's Atomic Testing Program in the 1950s*, New York, Oxford Press, 1986.

Bix, Herbert. *Hirohito And The Making of Modern Japan*, New York, Harper Collins, 2000.

Broad, William. *Teller's War*, New York, Simon & Schuster, 1992.

Cork, James. *Radioactivity and Nuclear Physics*, New York, D. Van Nostrand Company, 1947.

Dubois, Markey. *Collected letters, notes, papers, documents, and photos of the USS Hughes Reunion Group and from the personal collection of Chester Bradly and Malcolm Riker*, all unpublished, were donated to this project in 2023.

Einstein, Albert. *Relativity – The Special And The General Theory*, New York, Crown Publishers, 1961.

Evans, Alan. *Manuscript - Experiences on the USS Hughes*, Unpublished – Donated to USS Hughes Reunion Group, donated by USS Hughes Reunion Group to this project in 2023, original presentation in 1985.

Feynman, Richard. *Six Easy Pieces*, New York, Addison-Wesley Publishing, 1995.

Surely, You're Joking, Mr. Feynman, New York, Bantam Books, 1985.

Finger, Laurie. *Collected letters, notes, papers, documents, and photos of Ollie Stine*, unpublished, donated to this project in 2023.

Friedman, Norman. *U.S. Destroyers*, Annapolis, MD, Naval Institute Press, 2004.

Glines, Carroll. *The Doolittle Raid*, Atglen, PA, Schiffer Publishing, 1991.

Glines, Carroll. *Attack On Yamamoto*, Atglen, PA, Schiffer Publishing, 1993.

Goodchild, Peter. *J. Robert Oppenheimer – Shatterer Of Worlds*, New York, Houghton Mifflin, 1985.

Harris, Michael. *The Atomic Times – My H-Bomb Year at the Pacific Proving Grounds*, New York, Random House, 2005.

Hornfischer, James. *The Fleet At Flood Tide – America At Total War*, New York, Random House, 2016.

The Last Stand OF The Tin Can Sailors, New York, Random House, 2004.

Neptune's Inferno – The U.S. Navy At Guadalcanal, New York, Random House, 2011.

Ship Of Ghosts, New York, Random House, 2006.

Who Can Hold The Sea, New York, Random House, 2022.

Hoyt, Edwin. *Japan's War – The Great Pacific Conflict*, Westport, CT, McGraw-Hill, 1986.

The Last Kamikaze – Matome Ugaki, Westport, CT, Prager Publishers, 1993.

Warlord – Tojo Against The World, Lanham, MD, Scarborough House, 1993.

Hunter, Jon. *Inventing Los Alamos*. Oklahoma, University of Oklahoma Press, 2017.

Jones, Oliver. *Personal Interviews With Author*, Unpublished, 2023.

King, Dan. *The Last Zero Fighter*, Rockwall, TX, Pacific Press, 2012.

Kleiner, Sam. *The Flying Tigers*, New York, Random House, 2018.

Lamont, Lansing. *Day of Trinity*, 1985, Fairfield Pennsylvania, Anteneum Press., 1985.

Lanouette, William. *Genius In The Shadows – Leo Szilard – Man Behind The Bomb*, New York, Macmillan Publishing, 1992.

Larson, Erik. *The Splendid and the Vile*, New York, Random House, 2020.

Layton, Edwin. *And I Was There – Pearl Harbor and Midway – Breaking the Secrets*, Saybrook, CT, Konecky & Konecky, 1985.

Meacham, Jon. *Franklin & Winston*, New York, Random House, 2003.

Morton, Scott. *Japan – It's History & Culture*, New York, McGraw-Hill, 1970.

Oppenheimer, J. Robert. *Atom And Void*, New Jersey, Princeton University Press, 1989.

Rhodes, Richard. *Dark Sun – The Making Of The Hydrogen Bomb*, New York, Simon. & Schuster, 1995.

The Making of the Atomic Bomb, New York, Simon & Schuster, 1986.

Skic, Rose. *Collective letters, notes, papers, documents, and photos of Tony Skic*, unpublished, donated to this project in 2023.

Sanger, S.L. *Hanford And The Bomb*, Seattle, Living History Press, 1989.

Shirer, William. *The Rise And Fall Of The Third Reich*, New York, Simon ^& Schuster, 1960.

Skic, Anthony, Personal Diary, donated by family, unpublished, 1945.

Stine, Ollie. *Personal Diary*, donated by family, unpublished, 1945.

Swan, Louis. *Those Damn Kamikazes*, unpublished, original written date unknown, but presented to the USS *Hughes* reunion group in 2018.

Szasz, Ferenc Morton. *The Day The Sun Rose Twice*, Albuquerque, NM, University of New Mexico Press, 1984.

United States Navy. *Official Deck Logs USS Hughes DD 410*, U.S. National Archives,

Weinberg, Steven. *The Discovery Of Subatomic Particles*, New York, W. H. Freeman & Company, 1983.

Wyden, Peter. *Day One – Before Hiroshima And After*, New York, Simon & Schuster, 1984.

ABOUT THE AUTHOR

Author Christopher Hurst is a native of Washington State. His grandfather served on the Battleship *New York*, his father was in the USNR after WWII, his uncle Glen Edmonson was the Gunnery Lieutenant on the USS *Hughes* in WWII, and his son served in the 173rd Airborne, U.S. Army in Iraq and Afghanistan.

Christopher is an FAA-certified Airline Transport Pilot with a college degree in Aviation. Christopher served 25 years as a commissioned law enforcement Detective and retired as the Commander of a 15-city Homicide and Violent Crimes Task Force in 2006. He was elected and served in the Washington State House of Representatives for 14 years. He was Chairman of the Public Safety, Commerce and Gaming, and Select Committee on Community Security.

Christopher and his wife, April, love adventure. They have spent a lifetime together hiking and climbing mountains (including twice climbing Kilimanjaro), traveling, SCUBA diving in Hawaii, the Florida Keys, and Grand Cayman, and fishing the waters of Northern Vancouver Island in Canada.

Also, By Author Christopher Hurst – Both are available on Amazon today!

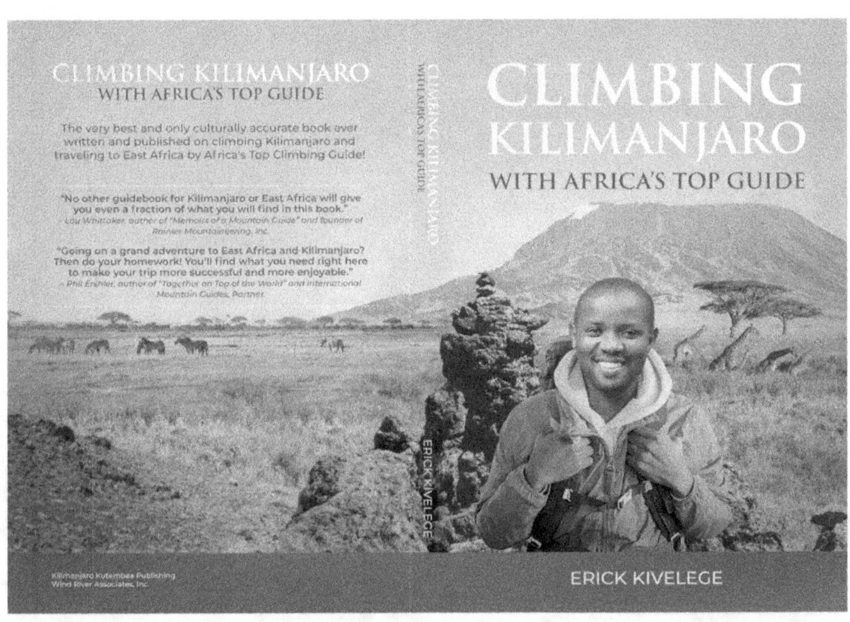

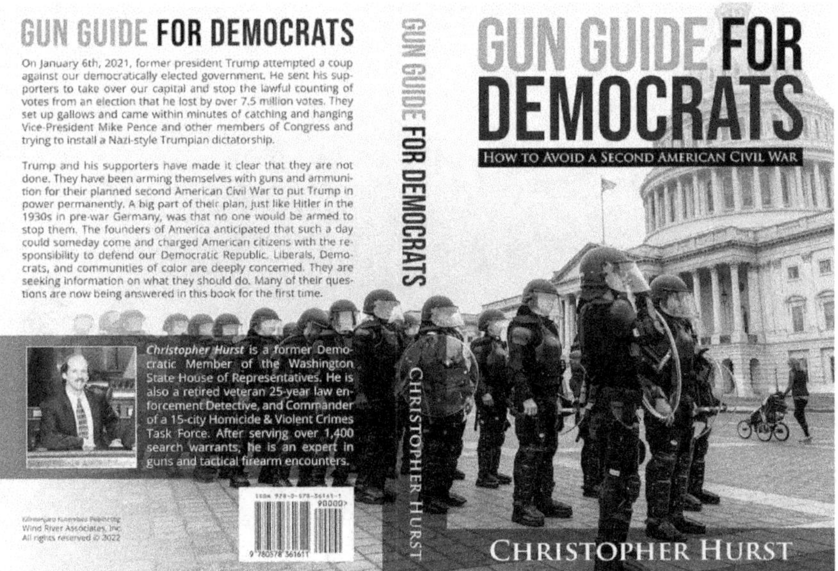